CHAINED TO HISTORY

CHAINED TO HISTORY

SLAVERY AND US FOREIGN RELATIONS TO 1865

STEVEN J. BRADY

CORNELL UNIVERSITY PRESS
Ithaca and London

First published 2022 by Cornell University Press

Library of Congress Cataloging-in-Publication Data

Names: Brady, Steven, 1967– author.
Title: Chained to history: slavery and US foreign relations to 1865 / Steven J. Brady.
Description: Ithaca, NY: Cornell University Press, 2022. | Includes bibliographical references and index.
Identifiers: LCCN 2021011500 (print) | LCCN 2021011501 (ebook) | ISBN 9781501761058 (hardcover) | ISBN 9781501761607 (pdf) | ISBN 9781501761591 (epub)
Subjects: LCSH: Slavery—Political aspects—United States—History. | Slavery—Government policy—United States—History. | United States—Foreign relations—1783–1865. | United States—Politics and government—1783–1865.
Classification: LCC E183.7.B6925 2022 (print) | LCC E183.7 (ebook) | DDC 306.3/620973—dc23
LC record available at https://lccn.loc.gov/2021011500
LC ebook record available at https://lccn.loc.gov/2021011501

For Monica

CONTENTS

Introduction

Speaking of Slavery

The president had a vision. He had support from some of the most significant political leaders of the nation. He certainly had skill. Indeed, he was one of the most gifted diplomats that the young American republic had yet produced—and that was saying something. The one significant thing he did not have, however, was success. Try as he might to take a singular opportunity to advance his policies for America's role in its hemisphere, the president found only frustration. His failure to achieve one of his important foreign relations objectives came as the result of a number of causes. One of the key factors was slavery.

John Quincy Adams's vision was that the United States would take on the role of leader in the constellation of independent nations of the Western Hemisphere—which, like Adams's own country, had emerged from the age of Atlantic revolutions. So when the Latin American liberator Simón Bolívar called for a congress of nations in the hemisphere, Adams and Secretary of State Henry Clay pricked up their ears. Despite Bolívar's reluctance to propose US participation in the Congress of Panama, an invitation was extended to Washington, DC, in April 1825. Adams and Clay responded with alacrity. Such a meeting of American neighbors would present "a perhaps unique opportunity to spread the American diplomatic, political, and commercial model throughout the New World."[1] Additionally, unity among the republics in the hemisphere would go a long way toward precluding renewed European intervention in the

Americas. In fact, in the words of Adams biographer James Traub, "the Pan-American Congress was shaping up to be the most popular initiative of Adams' young presidency."[2] The upcoming congress held forth the prospect of strengthening the Monroe Doctrine without requiring a "police role" for the United States and of forestalling "Latin American commercial exclusivity." US participation in the meeting would also, in Adams's words, serve as a "token of respect to the southern Republics."[3] Panama appeared to hold out nothing but promise—so much so that Clay ranked the diplomatic mission to the congress behind only those to Paris in 1783 and Ghent in 1814—which brought an end, respectively, to the American Revolutionary War and the War of 1812—in its significance for the nation.[4] Who could oppose an opportunity such as that?

The answer, in the atmosphere of mid-1820s America, was that a great many could do so. The Congress of Panama in fact "became a political lightening rod, drawing increasingly bitter attacks from the followers of presidential aspirants" like Vice President John C. Calhoun, Treasury Secretary William Crawford, and, most notably, Adams's nemesis, Senator Andrew Jackson. Opponents of US participation raised red flags concerning the hallowed policy of freedom from entangling alliances, as well as the threat of economic competition from Latin nations.[5] Perhaps domestic politics and foreign policy concerns alone would have been enough to scuttle Adams and Clay's visionary policy.

But there was another—and to southerners more ominous—threat posed by US involvement in a move toward such hemispheric cooperation. This was none other than the possibility that this early attempt at Pan-Americanism could undermine slavery. Southerners, including Adams's own vice president, emerged as some of the most virulent opponents of Adams's hemispheric plan. For these foes of the president's policy, the "underlying issue" was slavery.[6] The danger seemed to loom that the Congress of Panama would "seek to abolish slavery." In addition, southerners expressed horror that diplomats from the United States might find themselves working alongside those from Haiti, a nation that was founded by revolutionary slaves who had liberated themselves and, in the process, killed large numbers of their former masters. The prospect that Washington might even recognize the government of Haiti was especially galling.[7] Then, too, there was the certainty that the upcoming congress would take up the issue of the slave trade, and "who knew where this could lead?" Although the dispatch of American representatives to Panama was finally approved by the US Congress, the delay, along with the death of one of the emissaries on the way to Panama, had prevented serious US participation in the conference.[8]

Most likely, American recalcitrance—or even "unjust and deliberate sabotage"—was not the primary reason that the so-called Amphictyonic Congress of 1826 failed to achieve Bolívar's objectives; that result was primarily a consequence of divisions among the Latin American nations themselves.[9] The fact nevertheless remains that the Adams-Clay Latin American policy—which Samuel Flagg Bemis has called "a noble experiment"—had brought no concrete results.[10] The administration found itself hamstrung in its attempt to participate in an international assembly that had seemed to offer significant prospects for advancing its "noble" agenda. This had happened due to domestic opposition to the initiative, and a major motivation for that obstructionism was fear for the security of the institution of slavery. Thus slavery, and more precisely the desire to preserve and protect it, had exerted a significant impact upon an issue that, at first blush, would appear to be unconnected to the subject of bonded labor in the United States. Even such skillful statesmen as Adams and Clay found themselves thwarted when they ran afoul of slavery's American advocates.

Nor was slavery's impact on US foreign relations manifested only in the frustration of policies that did not redound to the institution's benefit. The fact was that the new republic found itself drawn into the wider Atlantic world in significant—sometimes distressing, frequently unwanted—ways as a result of what would come to be called the South's peculiar institution. Despite, for instance, a strong desire to limit entanglements with the empires of Europe, Washington found itself pulled deeply into diplomacy, even conflict, with just these powers. Nor was the nation able to consistently assert its unilateralist proclivities in policy toward the world outside the Western Hemisphere. Slavery drew the nation into relations with the broader Atlantic world in ways that prevented this unilateralism. And, as in the case of the Congress of Panama, slavery sometimes prevented the consummation of Washington's preferred policies. In time, even the sacrosanct proscription against British search of American-flagged vessels in peacetime fell victim to the demands of conducting foreign relations for a nation riven by slavery.

Additionally, an international history approach to these matters also helps to explain the motivations of the slaveholders who played an outsize role in shaping American foreign policy. Matthew Karp has impressively demonstrated their confidence.[11] An international history, showing the limits of their ability to shape international relations in the Atlantic world, also demonstrates another element: fear. Fear for the preservation of slavery in the United States itself served to influence American policy during a period of profound developments in the Atlantic world.

The inconsistencies—the sheer messiness—in policymaking present yet another highly significant leitmotif of American foreign relations in this book. Because, try as they might, US policymakers could not impose their will regarding the foreign policy of slavery on a recalcitrant world. American policy would have to accommodate itself, and thus its priorities and goals, to the policies, priorities, and power of other nations, as well as the realities of the environment—figurative and literal—in which these polices were implemented. The decision to seek to colonize freed Blacks abroad provides one of the clearest illustrations of this problem. The realities of the international system—and indeed of the physical world—prevented the United States from developing anything like a consistent and effective policy toward one of the issues that policymakers deemed vital for the well-being of the nation as a white-ruled republic.

An international history of these events thus serves significantly to illustrate the reasons for the inability of the slaveholders who so frequently directed America's foreign relations to implement some of their cherished policies, and to impose their will on the world beyond America's borders. It helps as well to explain why a nation that would have preferred to keep its relations with the eastern littoral of the Atlantic world largely limited to commerce found and felt itself compelled to conduct an active diplomacy with the Old World, even to the point of establishing—albeit with great reluctance—transatlantic connections with sub-Saharan Africa. Oddly enough, the foreign relations of slavery even brought Washington into contact with the Eurasian world, as Russia was lured on two occasions into intervention in US relations with European nations far to the west of St. Petersburg.

This proclivity of slavery to enmesh the nation with the wider world in unwanted ways was manifested again and again throughout the time period up to 1865. From vainly seeking the return of escaped slaves under President George Washington to the failed attempts of President Abraham Lincoln to settle their freed brethren somewhere—anywhere—else, one sees the real limits placed on the nation's ability to shape and implement a consistent foreign policy. One sees as well that the foreign relations of slavery exerted an impact not only on the policies of slaveholders and their northern allies but on the Lincoln administration itself, an administration whose central foreign policy goal was precisely to limit the extent in which foreign relations were even relevant to the most important issue at hand—namely, the American Civil War. Slavery was not the only factor that contributed to this frustration of American aims to conduct a largely unilateralist foreign policy in its early years. Nor was it the only reason why America frequently found itself unable to achieve its foreign relations goals. But it was among the most significant reasons, and one that has not yet been thoroughly explored by scholars of US foreign relations. *Chained to History* seeks, then, to address the substantial impact of slavery in early American foreign relations to the critical extent that it warrants; to demonstrate slavery's central role in the history of America's early relations with the world.

"No one likes to speak about slavery." So observes the German historian Michael Zeuske.[12] Yet one cannot speak about early American foreign relations without assessing the role played by slavery. Bonded labor was, in fact, a significant factor in every one of America's foreign policy priorities in the period leading up to 1865, when the Thirteenth Amendment finally abolished slavery throughout the reunified republic. The example of the Congress of Panama illustrates this well in the case of Adams and Clay's desire that America assume the role of leader of the newly declared republics of the Western Hemisphere. Advocates of slavery had frustrated the Adams-Clay attempt to take a significant step in this direction. The president and his secretary of state considered participation in Pan-Americanism to be very much in the national interest. But the national interest is never static; it has to be negotiated among various sectors of the nation, and they have different priorities. For many slaveholders and their allies, a threat to the institution of slavery was not merely a threat to their own economic interests; it was, in fact, a threat to the nation itself. They thus acted according to this definition of the national interest.

Thus, slavery significantly influenced American policies for assuring US security in what had become a rather dangerous neighborhood for the new nation. When, for instance, slavery appeared to be in danger in neighboring Spanish-ruled Cuba, policymakers and opinion leaders in the United States concluded that the very security of their nation was at stake. In the minds of these men, a threat to slavery in America's neighborhood was an existential threat to America. Only by understanding this point can one begin to understand the deep desire, and extensive efforts, to acquire the island colony.

The promotion of commerce was closely tied by Americans to the issue of national security from the days of George Washington and Alexander Hamilton. For this reason, the United States from the beginning insisted on the right of neutrals to trade with all nations in a time of war. Britain, for its part, declined to accept this principle.[13] The result was a protracted dispute between the Anglo-American nations over the issue. This conflict significantly affected efforts at slave trade suppression: both nations proclaimed a strong desire to eradicate the trade yet could not overcome the hostility left by past British actions. This interaction of slavery with American foreign policy priorities complicated the matter until the Lincoln administration finally settled the issue.

Additionally, American responses to the Haitian Revolution were complicated by the countervailing desires to oppose slave rebellion and to maintain a profitable trade with Haiti. Here one sees a fundamental element running through the story of slavery and US foreign relations: issues related to slavery rarely determined American actions. Rather, they interacted with other goals, issues, and priorities, thus brining about policy that could not have been easily foreseen. The decision of slaveholding American statesmen to aid Black revolutionaries in Haiti was just the most striking example of this complex process of negotiating among conflicting policy priorities in order to arrive at decision that worked in favor of American interests.

Territorial expansion on the North American continent provides another example of slavery's impact on a primary US foreign policy priority. Jefferson sought to acquire Louisiana in part due to fears of an antislavery contagion emanating from the French colony. Texas proved irresistibly attractive to many slaveholders for its rich cotton lands and its ability to contribute slave-state members to the Senate. Florida ceased being a threat to slaveholders in the Southeast only after it joined the United States. In all of these cases, the institution of bonded labor was a positive pull in the direction of greater territorial expansion.

Perhaps the most sacred of precepts in early US foreign relations was freedom from European entanglements and its corollary, American unilateralism.[14] Important variations on this theme were composed by Presidents George Washington, Thomas Jefferson, James Monroe, and James K. Polk. The message to Europe was consistent; the execution, however, was not. Nor could it be, as long as the United States remained a slaveholding republic. Slavery was a transatlantic concern, and its existence forcefully drew the United States into transatlantic relations. From the carrying off of slaves by Britain during the American Revolution to the role of slavery in the diplomacy of the American Civil War, Americans could not retain anything like a "splendid isolation" from Europe. America's status as a slaveholding society was enough to prevent that.

Slavery thus shaped early American foreign relations from the beginning of the nation until the eradication of the institution itself. Future scholarship of the diplomacy of that period can thus benefit significantly from integrating the discussion of slavery into the narrative of US external relations. Indeed, in fact, the institution's impact was so pervasive that it is difficult to see how it could be left out.

What has thus far been missing from the scholarly literature is a single, synthetic volume that addresses the full sweep of the interconnection of slavery and US foreign relations from the American Revolution until emancipation in the 1860s. This book seeks to fill that lacuna. Its goal is to integrate previous scholarship that has appeared on the issue, while simultaneously breaking new ground through research in the primary source documentation that sheds light on a still-neglected topic. In doing so, it seeks to situate its topic in the broad international framework in which United States foreign relations with regard to slavery was both conceived and conducted.

At a book launch in 2008, the eminent intellectual historian James Turner made an insightful observation. Turner remarked that he hoped that no work of history was ever "definitive." By this he meant that no scholar should have the last word on any important subject of investigation; that any significant book would enhance a conversation rather than end it. In that spirit, *Chained to History* makes no claim to being the proverbial "last word" on its subject. Indeed, I hope that it will arouse interest in further scholarship on a highly significant aspect of America's early international relations. A torrent of works would be welcome. But if it serves in some degree to re-center slavery as a key element in American foreign relations up through the American Civil War, *Chained to History* will have made a worthwhile contribution.

CHAPTER 1

"Things Odious or Immoral"

Britain, Spanish Florida, and Slaves Unfettered

A painting by Benjamin West hangs in the Winterthur Museum in Delaware. A visitor might easily walk past it without noticing the five men in thoughtful poses forming a semicircle around a table, on which rests a lengthy document. If the visitor is struck by the painting at all, it may be because so much of it is unfinished. At the right side of the canvas there is an empty space where two more men were to be depicted, one sitting and one standing. The painting, begun by West in 1783, was supposed to portray the commissioners who signed the preliminary peace between Britain and the United States, thus ending the fighting in the War of the American Revolution. The traditional story is that the painting was never finished because the British commissioner, Richard Oswald, refused to sit for West. Who would want to be memorialized for a shocking defeat, after all?

Also noticeably unfinished is the man standing behind the legendary Benjamin Franklin, commissioner Henry Laurens. Perhaps it is fitting that Laurens's portrait is the least complete of all of the commissioners portrayed. He had arrived quite late in Paris, having only recently been released from prison in London and, as a result, he had the least input of all the American diplomats in the agreement: the most significant contribution that the South Carolina slaveholder made was but a single clause in the accord. That clause, however, was to sow discord between the two nations for years into the future, to provoke an American sense of grievance against successive London governments that would not really be set aside until 1826, and then only through the good offices of Tsar Alexander I of Russia. That the emperor in St. Petersburg needed to be enlisted to bring an end to the conflict went to show how far it had gone.

Slaves and the Treaty of Paris

The treaty that brought the War of the American Revolution to an end left much unresolved. One of the most refractory of the unsettled issues was the disposition of slaves who had come into British lines during the war. Article 7 of the 1783 Treaty of Paris provides that the British should withdraw forces from the United States "without causing any Destruction, or carrying away any Negroes or other Property of the American Inhabitants." The clause was added at Laurens's suggestion.[1] During the course of the war, the British had "carried away" large numbers of slaves who had escaped to their lines. The Americans wanted them returned, or, at the very least, their erstwhile owners compensated. Laurens had not been alone in his solicitude for the interests of the American slaveholder. Oswald remembered Franklin threatening to sell off German prisoners of war—allies of the British in the fight against the patriots—unless the slaves carried away by the British were either "restored or paid for."[2] Laurens's clause seemed to the American commissioners to require the return of slaves currently in British hands. But the British, it turned out, saw it quite differently. There followed one of the most significant diplomatic conflicts in early Anglo-American relations.

This antagonism over the status of slaves taken by the British began early on. Britons were well aware of both their own need for troops and of the southern colonists' need for labor to maintain the wartime economy. In April 1775 the royal governor of Virginia, Lord Dunmore, threatened to emancipate the slaves in that colony. Then, months before the colonists declared their independence, Dunmore struck an early, jarring blow in the battle over the status of American slaves. On November 7, 1775, he issued his well-known proclamation regarding patriot-held slaves. On board HMS *Fowey* off the coast of Norfolk, Virginia, he declared "all indentured servants, negroes, or others, (appertaining to rebels,) free, that are able and willing to bear arms, they joining his Majesty's troops, as soon as may be, for the more speedily reducing this Colony to a proper sense of their duty to his Majesty's crown and dignity."[3] Slaves "appertaining to rebels" who managed to escape to British lines, and who then served in the British military, were to be accorded their freedom. Those belonging to loyalists were not granted this option.

The proclamation caused grave concern among the patriots in the southern colonies. A committee appointed by the Virginia General Assembly prepared its own declaration in response to Dunmore's proclamation. Approved by the assembly on December 13, 1775, it denounced the "unlawful and wicked step" taken by slaves who had run to the British lines, and offered a pardon to those who would surrender to a commander of Virginia's forces.[4] Two days later, George Washington described Dunmore as "that arch-traitor to the rights of humanity," who needed to be "instantly crushed." This step was "indispensably necessary" due to "the negroes; for, if he gets formidable, numbers of them will be tempted to join who will be afraid to do it without."[5] Washington's aide-de-camp, Alexander Hamilton, went so far as to advocate that the patriots themselves arm slaves and "give them their freedom with their muskets." He worried that "if we don't make use of them in this way, the enemy probably will."[6]

On the last day of June 1779, the British commander in chief, General Henry Clinton, issued an emancipation proclamation of his own, freeing patriot-owned slaves who escaped to British lines, even if they did not take up arms for the king.[7] Thus women, children, and the elderly could also expect freedom if they managed to escape to the redcoats. A large number of slaves took advantage of the British offers of manumission. Over the course of the war, as much as 5 percent of slaves in the southern colonies escaped to the British, including several belonging to George Washington himself.[8] Given the number of slaves who had escaped to freedom, it comes as no surprise that the Americans wanted them returned at war's end.

On May 6, 1783, Washington met with the commander in chief of British forces in North America, Sir Guy Carleton, in Orangetown, New York. Among other matters, the two soldiers discussed the "delivery of all Negroes and other Property of the Inhabitants of these States in the Possession of the Forces or Subjects of or adherents to his Britannic Majesty."[9] In addressing the British preparations for the rapid evacuation of American territory, Carleton noted that he "considered as included in the Preparations for the final Departure of the British troops the previously sending off of those Persons who supposed that from the part they had taken in the present War it would be most eligible for them to leave this Country." Among these were, he added, "a Number of Negroes." Washington "thereupon expressed his Surprise" at what he took to be a British action that contravened the Treaty of Paris. Carleton replied that "by *Property* in the Treaty might only be intended Property *at the time* the Negroes were sent off," contending that "it could not have been the intention of the British Government by the Treaty of Peace to reduce themselves to the Necessity of violating their Faith to the Negroes who came into the British

Lines" under Dunmore's proclamation. To return them to their masters would be to deliver them up "some possibly to Execution and others to severe Punishment which in [Carleton's] Opinion would be a dishonorable Violation of the public Faith pledged to the Negroes." He raised the possibility of compensation for the slaves carried away if this should, in the future, "be declared an Infraction of the Treaty." To this end, Carleton had directed that a register be kept of all slaves removed by his forces.[10]

Washington responded by reiterating his conviction that the actions taken by the British with regard to the slaves were "a Departure from both the Letter and the Spirit of the Articles of Peace." He was further concerned about the difficulties raised by the issue of compensation for slaves carried away. In part, his objection concerned assessing the value of a slave, and additionally in ascertaining a slave's identity. The register could not record a slave's worth, since this consisted "chiefly in his Industry and Sobriety," and any slave could give a false name or the "wrong Name of his former Master." Carleton's response was that a former slave, once guaranteed his freedom, would "have no inducement to conceal his true Name or that of his Master." As he saw it, the matter of compensation "must be adjudged by Commissioners to be hereafter appointed by the two nations."[11] Neither of the generals had given an inch on the matter, and Washington was obviously not satisfied with the exchange. Additionally, Carleton's standpoint "quickly became the official British response to repeated American demands for restitution or compensation."[12]

The British had objections of their own to America's failures to live up to the Treaty of Paris. A fruitless diplomatic back-and-forth failed to resolve the question of which nation had been the first to violate the pact. Delegated by Congress to respond to British accusations, Secretary of Foreign Affairs John Jay wrote a lengthy report, which he submitted in October 1786.[13] According to Jay, there was "no doubt but that Britain has violated the 7th Article" of the treaty. He spoke of three classes of slaves, the first being those "as in the course of the War were captured and disposed of as booty by the Enemy." Such slaves were legitimately the property of the British. In words that could not have given solace to the slaveholding members of the Continental Congress, Jay opined, "By the laws of war all goods and Chattels captured and made booty *flagrante Bello* become the property of their Captors. Whether men can be so degraded as under any circumstances to be with propriety denominated Goods and Chattels, and under that idea capable of being booty, is a question on which opinions are unfortunately various, even in Countries professing Christianity and respect for the rights of mankind. Certain it is that our Laws assert, and Britain by this Article as well as by her practice admits, that Man may have property in Man." Jay thus concluded—against his will, it appeared—that "it is fair reasoning that this like other moveable property is capable of changing Owners by capture in War." The secretary was unable to devise a "construction of the Article" that would deny the right to such property to the British.[14]

When it came to the other two classes of slaves, however, matters were very different. The second set of slaves were those who "belonged to and remained with American Inhabitants within the british [sic] lines," and they "seem clearly to be within the design and meaning of [article 7]." But it was the final class that had caused by far the most difficulty between the two nations. These were the slaves who, "confiding in proclamations and promises of freedom and protection, fled from their Masters without, and were received and protected within, british Camp and lines." Jay concluded that these slaves also fell under the provisions of article 7, since they "still remained as much as ever the property of their Masters. They could not by merely flying or eloping extinguish the right or title of their Masters; nor was that title destroyed by their coming into the enemy's possession, for they *were received, not taken* by the enemy; they were received not as Slaves but as friends and freemen; by no Act, therefore, either of their own or their friends, was the right of their Masters taken away." Thus, carrying them away was an "infraction" of article 7.[15] Jay's argument was worthy of one of the most prominent legal minds that the new nation had to offer: war booty must be taken as property. Yet since the British received the runaway slaves not as chattels but as free human beings, they did not fit into the first class of slaves. As such, their owners' titles to them remained intact, and carrying them away was a violation of the treaty. The secretary's reasoning was so far, so good for American slaveholders.

Had Jay left it at that, few American slaveholders could have found fault with his reasoning. Yet he went on, and in a manner that could only be disconcerting to American slave owners. The secretary could also understand the situation of this third class of slaves in a different light, one "less unfavorable to Britain than it appears to his Countrymen in general." Jay was indeed aware that he was "about to say unpopular things; but higher motives than personal considerations press [me] to proceed."[16] A slaveholder himself, and one of the cofounders of the New York Manumission Society in 1785, Jay had opinions on slavery that would indeed be "unpopular" in certain circles.[17] He began his disquisition with a hypothetical case: what if, he asked, France and Algiers should go to war, and France then invited American slaves in that Barbary state to flee to the French lines, under the promise of freedom and protection? And what would Congress, "and indeed the world," think and say if France, in concluding a peace with Algiers, should return those American slaves to their masters? The answer seemed to Jay so clear that he did not even state it. He then went on to ask if there was "any other difference between the two cases than this, Viz. that the American Slaves at Algiers are *white* people, whereas the African slaves at New York were *black* people?"[18] The answer was obvious to the secretary in this matter as well.

Following this line of reasoning, Jay then wondered how far "an obligation to do wrong may, consistent with morality, be so modified in execution as to avoid doing injury, yet do essential justice," with "essential justice" clearly meaning not returning freed human beings, regardless of skin color, to bondage. He then dilated on the matter of justice for the slaves versus injury to their owners: "By this agreement Britain bound herself to do great wrong to these Slaves; and yet by not executing it she would do great wrong to their Masters." This put London in a dilemma, "for as on the one hand, she had tempted and assisted these Slaves to escape from their Masters, and on escaping had received and protected them," and it would then be "cruelly perfidious" to return them to their former bondage. Yet it would, on the other hand, be an act of bad faith to conclude a treaty obliging them to do just this and then not follow through. All was not lost, however. Jay saw a way for Britain to "extricate herself from these embarrassments." The British could "do substantial justice" to the slaveholders by "paying them the value of those Slaves. In this way, neither could have cause to complain; for although no price can compensate a Man for bondage for life, yet every Master may be compensated for a runaway slave."[19] Jay's fellow slaveholders could not have been expected to warm to this analysis. Yet on the final point, it was difficult to fault the secretary's reasoning: the British were simply not going to return thousands of freedmen to slavery. Restitution for violations of article 7 would come either by financial compensation or not at all.

Yet southerners, "scandalized" by Jay's words in his October 1786 report, were concerned when, in 1794, President Washington chose Jay to negotiate with Britain over the issues still bedeviling Anglo-American relations. The British proved to be "immovable on the subject" of compensation for slaves carried away.[20] Thus, the Treaty of Amity, Commerce, and Navigation, commonly known as Jay's Treaty, was concluded without resolution of, or even reference to, this issue. In an exchange of letters with the secretary of state, Virginian and slaveholder Edmund Randolph, Jay explained and defended his actions in London. Regarding the question that "naturally" arose concerning which side had violated the peace treaty first, the two nations found themselves at loggerheads. The American position was, of course, that the carrying away of slaves who came to the British lines constituted the first violation. But, as Jay wrote Randolph on September 13, 1794, the British had a very different interpretation. From the British perspective, slaves "who came into the possession of the British army, became, by the laws and rights of war, *British* property;

and, therefore, ceasing to be *American* property, the exportation thereof was not inhibited by the stipulation in question." To extend the stipulation to slaves who "under the faith of proclamations" had fled to the British army was *"unnecessarily"* to give it "a construction which, being *odious*, could not be supported by the known and established rules for construing treaties." Jay reported that he had responded with "the several remarks and considerations" that he had presented in his report to Congress, though he did not clarify which remarks, some of which would seem to validate the British interpretation of the clause in question. He concluded laconically that "on this point we could not agree" and moved on to other matters. There would be no settlement of the issue, and it thus "became advisable to quit those topics" that were insoluble in the current negotiations.[21]

Randolph was less than convinced by the envoy's logic. Writing Jay on December 3, the secretary remarked that he was "extremely afraid that the reasoning about the negroes will not be satisfactory. Indeed, I own that I cannot myself yield to its force." He then added his concern that, if the matter of the slaves were to be left out of the treaty entirely, "will not some quarters of the Union suppose themselves neglected?"[22] Randolph's objections went, however, beyond the matter of the sensibilities of the southern states. His argument hinged on an interpretation of the relevant section of article 7, by which, he asserted, Britain had surrendered its rights to the slaves as booty of war:

> It will not be denied that rights, even in moveables acquired in war, may, by the treaty of peace, be renounced. In this instance, there was a great reason for such a renunciation. Negroes were not, like moveables in general, difficult to be distinguished. They carried an infallible mark. British debts were stipulated to be paid, and the States in which the mass of them lay, depended for their payment, principally, on the culture of their soil, and for the culture of their soil, on this species of labor. As property, the British Government could not have been tenacious of negroes; and it may, therefore, be supposed that, in this view, they were so indifferent as to be the more easily given up.

Randolph followed this with a close textual analysis of the article 7 "carrying away" clause before opining that liberty given in war may be lost in a peace treaty.[23] This reasoning led him to the conclusion that article 7 "called for the reenslaving of some of those he conceded had been legitimately freed by the war."[24] In response to such arguments, Jay could only repeat that the Americans and British "could not agree about the negroes. Was that a good reason for breaking up the negotiations?"[25]

It was a fair question. Yet, as Randolph foresaw, southerners did not react well to the exclusion of the slave issue from Jay's Treaty. The attacks on the treaty were highly partisan, with Republicans sensing an opportunity to score political points by attacking an unpopular pact advocated by their Federalist rivals. Additionally, the faultfinding was broad based and extensive, with slavery as only one of many factors raised in opposition to the treaty. Yet, as Randolph had told Jay, the "anxiety of many parts of the United States, upon this subject" were worth consideration.[26] Indeed, the exclusion of the slave issue from the treaty proved to be a bounteous well from which Republicans—especially from slave states—could draw abuse of Federalist diplomacy. In the spring of 1796 the gloves came off in the House of Representatives, as Republican members sought to deny the funding necessary to implement the treaty with Britain.[27]

Republican John Nicholas of Virginia called for a discussion of the "merits of the Treaty" on April 16, 1796. In his opening remarks he conceded that some concessions had to be made in treaty negotiations, and that "sacrifice of private interest becomes sometimes unavoidable." Yet the claim to the return of American-owned slaves went beyond such interests, since it went to the heart of whether the United States had violated the Paris Treaty. It was not the most significant issue on its face, but Jay's Treaty offered such a "uniform surrender of the interests of the United States as to compel a calculation." On the question of which nation was first to violate the treaty, Nicholas had no doubt: Britain had done so with regard to the slaves carried away by their forces. Even before the treaty had come into force, "Britain, by carrying away the negroes, put it out of her power to execute the contract which she had made."[28] Breaking a treaty's provisions before it was even binding would thus have to rank as a first violation.

William Branch Giles, another Virginia Republican, added that the British themselves had "acquiesced" in the American interpretation of the clause in question "until the negotiation of the present Treaty." Among the evidence that Giles adduced was the fact that American commissioners were permitted at war's end to "make a list of the negroes in the possession of the British," as well as the fact "that there were resolutions of Congress claiming compensation for the property carried away in contravention of the Article in the Treaty of Peace, perhaps without even the intimation of a doubt as to the construction."[29] Thus, both the Americans and the British had understood article 7 to require, if not return of the slaves taken by the British during the war, then at least compensation of their masters. What had changed now was Jay's Treaty, which had failed to formally establish this interpretation.

But Federalists called into question the existence of the interpretive consensus so confidently asserted by Giles. Connecticut's Zephaniah Swift was "surprised that any person could ever have entertained an opinion that they were entitled to compensation" for the slaves in question. Article 7 served only to prevent the British "carrying away any negroes and property that should be taken in the future, and could have no reference to those captured during the war and before the Treaty, the property of which had vested in the captors."[30] Yet the most extensive, and formidable, defense of the treaty by a Federalist came from outside Congress. The following summer, a series of essays on the Jay's Treaty debate appeared under the pen name Camillus, which belonged to the leader of the Federalist faction—Jay's fellow New Yorker, Alexander Hamilton. The essays had their roots in remarks in defense of the treaty drafted for Washington in early July. In the third of his essays, Hamilton forcefully addressed the case made against the treaty by its opponents. In his view, the "opposers of the Treaty seem to have put invention on the rack, to accumulate charges against it in a great number of cases, without regard even to plausibility."[31] This tortured reasoning, he thus implied, pertained to the Republican case with regard to article 7.

Rejecting the Republican assertion that everyone agreed on what the article meant until Jay arrived in London, Hamilton asserted, "As to the negroes, the true sense of the article in the treaty of peace, which respects them, is disputed." The plain fact was that the terms of article 7 "admit of two constructions." One could assert that

> no negroes or other articles which *had been* American property should be carried away, the other, that the evacuations were to be made *without depredation*, consequently that no new destruction was to be committed, and that negroes or other articles, which at the time of the cessation of hostilities, *continued to be the property* of American inhabitants, unchanged by the operations of war, should be foreborne to be carried away.

The latter interpretation—which was London's understanding—was based on the laws of war that allowed war booty to be "vested in the captors the moment they acquire a firm possession." Like other property, except ships, slaves "were liable to become booty—and belonged to the enemy as soon as they came into his hands." Once in the enemy's possession, a slaveholder was "free either to apply them to his own use, or to set them at liberty," and "if he did the latter, the grant was irrevocable, restitution was impossible." Once liberty was "granted to a human being," nothing in international, or even British, law would authorize the return of that person to the state of slavery.[32]

Hamilton continued his defense of the British interpretation. Given the language of the treaty stipulation in question, which related to "negroes or *other property* of the *American* inhabitants," the slaves in question, no longer being property of Americans, "were therefore not within the stipulation." No one would, he asserted, demand the return of a captured horse, ox, or piece of furniture after seven years of war, and, "consequently the reasoning which proves that one is not included, excludes the other"—namely, the Black person taken as booty.[33]

Hamilton's most powerfully argued point followed: "In the interpretation of treaties, things *odious* or *immoral* are not to be presumed," and retuning to slavery a human being to whom one had solemnly promised liberty was "as *odious* and *immoral* a thing as can be conceived." Thus, the "general interests of humanity conspire with the obligation which Great Britain had contracted toward the negroes, to repel this [i.e., the American] construction of the treaty, if another can be found." As to arguments regarding the intent of the American negotiators, it was "not enough for us to be persuaded, that some of the negociators [*sic*], who made the peace, intended the article in our sense." Rather, the sense of the treaty's words must be found in the treaty itself. If there was ambiguity in the treaty, then "the odiousness of the effect" would "incline the scale against us." Unlike the treaty's article 7, Hamilton's words did not lend themselves to different interpretations. Returning a freed person to a state of slavery violated a fundamental moral principle, and the treaty could not have been meant to require it.[34] Hamilton had thus, "in print, declared that the British had no power to reenslave anyone." This was especially problematic, since the treaty, as Hamilton noted, made no mention of compensation.[35] The Senate had ratified Jay's Treaty, but with not a single vote to spare. Hamilton had thus won the day, if only narrowly. The owners of the slaves carried away by the British were not as lucky: they never received compensation. Perhaps fittingly for these men, the loss of slaves proved to be the price of their own liberty.

In the Wake of 1812

That was not, however, the end of this issue. In fact, "the years between 1815 and 1828 witnessed an almost eerie replay of the debates" that followed the American Revolutionary War.[36] The War of 1812 would revive the issue of slaves escaping to British lines, and then removed from the United States. As before, the two nations would be unequal to the task of finding a mutually acceptable solution to the issues that this "carrying off" raised. In the end, only an agreement to arbitrate brought the matter to a conclusion. It was thus the Russian emperor, working from a French text, who decided a matter of English grammar that had bedeviled the two Anglophone nations. It was not a glorious page in diplomatic history.

The role of slaves and slavery in the War of 1812 has increasingly intrigued historians. The desire to protect American slavery has been suggested as a potential contributing cause of the war; Jasper M. Trautsch wonders if "the escape of American slaves to British ships prior to the war [made] some Southern Congressmen opt for open conflict to protect their slaving interests."[37] There is no question that, when the war came, it raised significant issues about slavery for slaves and masters alike.[38] Slaves once again chose to risk escape to British lines and the freedom that awaited them there. Again, the issue posed a seemingly insoluble irritant in postwar Anglo-American relations. The peace commissioners meeting at Ghent did no better than those at Paris had in clarifying the issue of slaves who had fled to the British. As article 1 of the Treaty of Ghent explained, "All territory, places, and possessions whatsoever taken by either party from the other during the war, or which may be taken after the signing of this Treaty . . . shall be restored without delay and without causing any destruction or carrying away any of the Artillery or other public property originally captured in the said forts or places, and which shall remain therein upon the Exchange of the Ratifications of this Treaty, or any Slaves or other private property." This language in the Treaty of Ghent was "surprisingly similar to the much-debated wording of Article 7 in the Treaty of Paris."[39] Indeed, it proved equally open to different and debatable constructions. There thus followed another unavailing attempt to solve the dispute though bilateral diplomacy.

John Quincy Adams took the lead in pressing the American case. America's minister to the Court of St. James's, Adams was neither a slaveholder nor a defender of the institution of bonded labor. But he was a determined advocate for his country's policies and interests. He thus pressed the British indefatigably on the issue of compensation for refugee slaves. Secretary of State James Monroe informed Adams of the difficulty arising with Britain over the interpretation of article 1, and the actions taken by Britain subsequent to this interpretation: "I'm sorry to have to state that the British naval commanders have construed the stipulation in the treaty not to carry off with their forces the slaves whom they had taken from our citizens differently from this government." From Monroe's perspective, the difference of interpretation of article 1 appeared to be "so decidedly in favor of the United States, that it has excited surprise that it should have existed." He informed London's chargé d'affaires in Washington, DC, Anthony Baker, that the British were contending that no slaves "ought to be restored except such as were, at the time of the exchange of the ratification of the treaty, in the forts and places where they were originally taken." This interpretation would limit their number indeed, since none of the escaped slaves seemed to fall under this definition.

Monroe was having none of it, and told Adams, "The United States have a right either to the restitution of all these slaves, or to compensation for the loss." He followed this with instructions to Adams to seek the return of the slaves or else redress for their owners.[40] It is worth noting that the Americans were willing from the start of the negotiations to accept compensation for the slaves taken by the British. Perhaps they had learned from previous experience that the erstwhile masters were never going to get them back.

If Baker's words were any indication, they were correct in this assumption. He now raised the issue of the intentions of his nation's treaty negotiators. His "belief" was that article 1 meant that "the prohibition against carrying away slaves and private property should be taken in connection with the restoration of territory, places, and possessions." If King George III's negotiators at Ghent had thought that "the words were susceptible of the construction now given to them [by the Americans], and that a claim would be founded upon them" for the return of the slaves who had found refuge on British ships, then the insertion of such words "would have been decidedly objected to, and others proposed." Lacking instructions from his government on the matter, however, Baker promised to forward the letter to London and to the relevant British naval commander.[41] With this exchange a lengthy diplomatic impasse between the two countries had begun. The British military was willing to discuss some facets of the issue with the three American commissioners who had been delegated to acquire "an account of all slaves and other private property of citizens of the United States, which may have been removed from the Chesapeake, or any of the shores or islands thereof, since the date of the ratification of the treaty." Absent British willingness to return the slaves, the commissioners were clearly seeking to gain a list of the slaves that could be used to ascertain a fair price for compensation.[42] On April 13, 1815, one of the commissioners, Virginian Thomas M. Bayly, wrote to John Clavelle, the captain of HMS *Orlando*, who was responsible for the British ships harboring the escaped slaves from the Chesapeake Bay region. Aware that the captain was soon to depart with his ships, he sought to discover Clavelle's "determination respecting the restoration of the slaves and other property, public and private, which were captured from the United States and citizens thereof, during the war," and which were now in the possession of the British in the Chesapeake. The Briton's response was firm: "I beg to state that my determination is not to restore any slaves, private or public property, captured before the exchange of ratifications of the treaty of peace," in line with instructions he had received from Rear Admiral Sir George Cockburn, his commanding officer.[43] It did not look good for the return of the "slaves or other property": once they had departed the Chesapeake for British possessions, it would be exceptionally difficult to reclaim them, regardless of the final diplomatic disposition of the question.

In fact, it was nearly impossible. In May 1815 commissioner Thomas Spalding was sent to Bermuda as the agent appointed by President James Madison to demand "the restoration of all public or private property, and particularly all slaves," taken in contravention of the American interpretation of article 1. His May 22 interview with Bermuda's governor, Admiral Cockburn, did not go at all well. Spalding reported to Monroe that Cockburn "would not permit me to proceed to detail any of the reasons for my mission, though very ready, as he said he was bound in candor to do, to declare against the American interpretation of the first article of the treaty; and vehemently added, that he would rather Bermuda, and every man, woman, and child in it, were sunk under the sea, than surrender one slave that had sought protection under the flag of England."[44] This would have been an extreme solution to the problem. But it also provided an indication to the Americans of how set the British were in their refusal to return freed Blacks.

Spalding was nonetheless tireless in advocating for the American interpretation of article 1. On the same day as his unsatisfying meeting with Cockburn, he penned a lengthy letter to British rear admiral Edward Griffith, then the naval commander for North America. In his missive he hit on one of the central aspects of the American interpretation of the article in question—namely, whether or not it applied to private property. It was the American position that the wording of the clause referring to property "which shall remain therein after the exchange of the ratifications of this treaty" clearly related only to public property. The stipulation regarding slaves thus stood on its own, and was not governed by the prior clause's reference to time and location. In fact, Spalding asserted, the words could not be applied to private property, except by "a strange perversion of language, and, by being so applied, the whole quality of the article becomes changed; and instead of being liberal and friendly, becomes limited, illiberal, and unfriendly." The US government was thus "greatly surprised" to discover that British officers had "adopted the extraordinary principle, that if either public or private property, or slaves, were removed a single mile from the place of capture, they were not restorable, though still within the limits of the United States."[45]

Griffith, then also in Bermuda, responded the following day. He was blunt. The matter was one to be settled by the governments of the two nations, and not by officials at lower levels. "I consider it," the admiral added, "entirely out of my province to enter into negotiation or discussion with you" on the matter of the freed slaves. He concluded his response with a bit of advice for Spalding: it would be "a loss of your time waiting here . . . or visiting any other British islands or settlements for the purposes set forth in your said letter; for I can venture to assure you that there is not any authority at either competent to deliver up persons who, during the late war, placed themselves under the protection of the British flag."[46] Given Cockburn's and Griffith's dismissals, this line of diplomacy was plainly at a dead end.

This did not mean that American attempts to gain compensation for the lost slaves were over. Rather, they moved to another level. If Griffith could do nothing about the issue, British foreign secretary Lord Castlereagh most assuredly could. On August 9 Adams addressed a rather lawyerly letter to Castlereagh. He proposed that the British minister in Washington be authorized to negotiate either the "restitution of the slaves conformably to the treaty" or payment of compensation, "which, in the event of their not being restored, I am instructed by my Government to claim." In large part Adams rested his claims on the intentions of the American peace commissioners at Ghent. Looking at the conference protocol, Adams asserted that the American plenipotentiaries "did not assent to" the application of the disputed phrase—"originally captured in said forts or places, and which shall remain therein upon the exchange of the ratification of this treaty"—with regard to slaves and private property. By a fair reading of the clause, Adams asserted, the British forces "were bound not to carry away any slaves, or other private property of the citizens of the United States, which had been taken on [American] shores."[47]

Adams was a highly gifted advocate. Yet Castlereagh remained unconvinced by his line of reasoning. The British secretary and the American minister met that August, discussing, among other matters, Adams's letter of August 9. As reported by Adams in a lengthy note to Monroe, Castlereagh responded to the American case by stating that the British interpreted the stipulations of article 1 regarding slaves "very differently." From the British perspective, the wording "applied only to the slaves in the forts and places which, having been taken during the war, were to be restored at the peace." Adams replied that the American negotiators had assented to this reading of the clause with regard to "artillery and public property . . . but not with regard to slaves, which we thought should, at all events, be restored, because they ought never to have been taken." The secretary was unimpressed by Adams's line of argument, however, premised as it was on the intentions of those who negotiated the treaty. As Castlereagh saw it, the "ultimate construction must be upon the words of the treaty as they stood." Having said that, he could not resist adding his own comments on the negotiators' intentions: the British commissioners would never have agreed to a stipulation that slaves, "who, from whatever motives, had taken refuge under the protection of the British forces, should be delivered up to those who, to say the least, must feel unkindly towards them, and might treat them harshly." Were this in fact the meaning of the disputed wording, the British negotiators would have proposed something else, though he did not know what.[48] It appeared that a plea based on intentions cut both ways. Nothing fruitful could come from this line of argument.

Nor was much to be expected from Adams's assertion that slaves, being private property, were "by the usages of war among civilized nations" and not to be carried away. As Castlereagh observed, a slave was not the same as a table or a chair, and "a living human being was entitled to other considerations." Seeing where the discussion was going—that is, nowhere—the American shifted ground. If Britain felt itself bound to "make good the promises of her offices to the slaves," then it might at least "be willing to do an act of justice, by compensating the owners of the slaves for the property which had been irregularly taken from them." As Adams reported it, Castlereagh "manifested no dissatisfaction at these remarks." Perhaps there was a way out of this conundrum after all. It was becoming obvious that London would under no circumstances return even one freed slave to a state of bondage, but maybe the British would agree to fair compensation for their loss.[49] In early September, Adams sent Castlereagh a list of 702 slaves carried away from Georgia by British forces. He thus proposed that the two nations make arrangements for compensation of their masters, "if it should be deemed expedient rather to make this compensation than to restore the slaves to their owners." The approach appeared to suggest that the United States was willing to be reasonable about all this. But three weeks later, Adams found himself writing Monroe that the foreign secretary had still not responded.[50] Perhaps extracting funds from London was not going to be much easier than obtaining the return of the slaves themselves.

The secretary of state, nevertheless, remained optimistic. "It cannot be doubted," he wrote Adams in mid-November 1815, "that the British Government will make a just indemnity to the owners for the slaves who were carried from the United States by the British officers, in violation of the treaty of peace." It is difficult to see how he could be so sanguine, however, given that the British had never admitted to violating the Treaty of Ghent. But he was apparently feeling domestic pressure from the affected slaveholders to gain them some fair compensation, informing Adams that a "vigorous effort on our part to obtain justice is claimed, and expected by them."[51] The Virginian kept up the diplomatic drumbeat. Only four days later he wrote Adams that it was "important that the principle be first established that the British will pay for the slaves carried off in violation of the treaty. The manner of liquidating the claims is the next point to be arranged." Monroe opined that the "appoint-ment of a board of commissioners, with full power to investigate every case, is thought to be most eligible—indeed, the only one that could do justice to the parties."[52] One might say, charitably, that the secretary of state was "think-ing ahead," since London was far from having conceded that Britain had committed any treaty violation at all in removing the slaves in question.

Adams, on the front lines of Anglo-American diplomacy, was more pessi-mistic than was his superior in Washington. Meeting again with Castlereagh early in 1816, he referenced a letter he had received from the secretary for war and the colonies, Lord Bathurst, the previous October. Bathurst had engaged in a rather thorough examination of the American interpretation of article 1 and found it to be lacking. Britain would thus persist in its own reading of the treaty's provisions. Adams told Castlereagh of his concern that Bathurst's let-ter "seemed to intimate that the Government had taken its final determina-tion of the matter; that I hoped it was not so; I hoped they would give it further consideration; it had been the cause of so much anxiety to my Government; it was urged so constantly and earnestly in my instructions." Castlereagh re-sponded evasively, though perhaps accurately, that he had not seen Bathurst's letter, but that he would have it located, and would "examine" it.[53] Thus, once again, two of the most practiced diplomats of their time could make no pro-gress on resolving this major matter of dispute in their countries' bilateral re-lations. The question, then, was whether anyone could.

After much back-and-forth that led nowhere, Washington decided that the time had come to take a new approach to resolving the issue. Thus, in May 1816 Monroe wrote to Adams, informing him that Madison was "willing to refer the question to the decision of some friendly power; which you will propose [to the British]." The issue was, the secretary emphasized, "too important to be neglected. It is impossible that the opinion of the British Government can be more decided than that of The United States." Adams delayed approaching Castlereagh on the matter until the end of the summer. At the time of Mon-roe's letter to Adams, the British foreign secretary was deeply involved in par-liamentary politics that "absorbed his strength as well as his time." It must have made an impression on the American minister when, on April 9, he arrived for an 11:30 a.m. meeting with the foreign minister, only to find that he was still asleep. Perhaps it is for this reason that Adams held off approaching him re-garding arbitration. In mid-September, Adams finally informed Castlereagh of the American proposal, adding that, given the differences between the two nations, "no better mode can be adopted for settling them in a satisfactory manner."[54] The foreign minister responded promptly and apologetically: private business in Ireland would take him away for a time, and the seasonal absence of a number of British ministers from London would preclude a timely response to Washington's proposal. But once the government was reassembled in London, he would take it up with the ministers. Despite this foreseen delay, Castlereagh's reply was far better than an outright rejection of the American initiative and potentially boded well for an end to the protracted impasse.[55]

It would, however, take two years to come to an agreement in favor of arbitration. London and Washington had other irons in the diplomatic fire, the most significant of which was the dispute over the Canadian-US border. The simmering discord would be alleviated by the Anglo-American Convention of 1818, which set the border west to the Oregon Territory. Largely forgotten now, article 5 of the convention stipulated that the two nations would submit the dispute over article 1 of the Treaty of Ghent to "some friendly sovereign or state to be named for that purpose." No arbiter was specified, since no one had yet agreed to serve. But the Russian, Alexander I, was acceptable to both parties.[56]

It was more of a challenge to find an American minister to help conduct the negotiations. In 1820 Monroe, now president, made the decision to appoint a southerner, someone who "would be especially vigilant regarding the slave-owners' interests." A number of names were mentioned. Secretary of War John C. Calhoun recommended former South Carolina governor Henry Middleton, a wealthy slave owner who spoke French. Monroe—though preferring a different candidate, South Carolina's Joel Poinsett—decided on Middleton.[57] Now, with a minister selected and Adams at the State Department, the Americans were ready to press their case in St. Petersburg.

Acutely aware of the arbitration's significance, Secretary of State Adams drafted extensive instructions for Middleton.[58] The process occupied approximately two weeks of the his time in June and early July 1820, and the instructions were thus not completed until after Middleton had departed for Europe. As a result, Adams had two of Middleton's sons who had stayed behind deliver them to their father when the family reconvened in London.[59] In his general instructions to the minister, Adams summarized the American and British positions on the issue of slaves carried away and gave Middleton precise direction on how to respond to the London government's arguments. When the British, for example, objected that "it could not be supposed they would agree to an Article which would oblige them to deliver up slaves who during the War had taken refuge under their protection," the American reply was "that if that had been an objection to their agreeing to the Article it should have been made before the signing of the Article."[60]

This was a fundamental difference between the Americans and the British, and did not come down to the matter of the correct parsing of a sentence. "The substance of this argument of the British side," noted Adams, "is that they could not fulfill their promise to the United States and the owners of the Slaves, without violating prior engagements to the Slaves themselves." To this line of argument Adams responded that it was "obvious . . . that our rights cannot be affected by any engagement of Great Britain to the Slaves, as her officers did carry them away, thereby fulfilling all their engagements to them. She is bound by the engagement of the Treaty with us, to indemnify all the owners of slaves, for the property of which they have thus been deprived by her act." Adams wanted to avoid bringing this issue to the tsar. It was "desirable," instead, "that the question submitted to the decision of the Emperor of Russia should be simply *whether* by the terms of the first Article of the Treaty of Ghent, the British forces were bound to evacuate all captured Forts, Places, and Possessions within the United States, *without carrying away any slaves or other private property.*"[61] The American goal was thus to keep the issue before the tsar limited to the correct reading of article 1. Any other issue was a distraction, and Adams was convinced that the United States had the stronger case on this central point of difference.

The secretary was, in addition, operating on the presumption that London would want to keep Alexander's purview limited in the matter of compensation should he decide in America's favor. Thus the British would seek, as would Washington, "to narrow down as much as possible the subject to be referred to the Emperor." The final indemnity should thus be decided not by the tsar but by a three-person commission, with commissioners appointed, respectively, by the president, the king, and the tsar. This commission would "sit in the United States" and would "determine definitively upon all claims" brought before it.[62] Regarding those matters that were brought to the tsar for decision, Adams called for careful and thorough consideration: "In whatever form the decision of the Emperor shall be made and communicated, the parties have agreed to consider it final and conclusive *on all the matters referred.*—You will therefore take special care, that the matters referred shall be so comprehensive, that the decision shall have nothing unsettled for after controversy—The President relies upon your zeal and intelligence that nothing will be omitted for doing justice to this interest."[63] Lest the South Carolina slave owner forget, Adams reminded Middleton that his diplomatic mission in St. Petersburg was "an affair of particular delicacy" and "a subject involving deep interests of property of many of our citizens." Thus there was "an earnest solicitude that every justice due to them may be done as well in the zeal as in the assiduity with which it will be pursued."[64] Once again, domestic political considerations had to be taken into account in the conduct of international relations.

In a November 4, 1820 letter, Adams augmented his instructions to Middleton. According to the secretary, "we give full credence to the declaration of Lord Castlereagh, that his personal disposition would be to carry into immediate execution the determination if it should be in our favor and that he would afford any felicity depending upon him for that purpose." Should disagreement arise, however, over "the means of execution," the United States wished to retain the right to have the case settled by the arbitrator. Adams proceeded immediately to ridicule British attempts to gain the high ground in the Anglo-American dispute over the freed slaves. The British claimed the right to emancipate privately owned slaves as a right of war. But this was deemed "utterly incomprehensible on the part of a nation whose subjects hold slaves by the millions, and who in this very treaty recognize them as private property. No such right is acknowledged as a Law of War by writers who admit *any* limitation." For this reason, Adams expected that the tsar would not "recognize the right of emancipation as legitimate warfare."[65]

For his part, the American minister agreed with Adams's assessment of Castlereagh. Stopping in London on his journey to Russia, Middleton had met with the foreign secretary in August. Afterward, he wrote glowingly of Castlereagh's congenial attitude. The two discussed several matters related to the subject of the coming negotiations in Russia, "in all of which his Lordship's ideas appeared to co-incide entirely with mine."[66] Yet well before receiving Adams's letter of November 1820, Middleton had independently come to the conclusion that the British and the Americans might "differ on the necessary means of giving effect" to America's rights in the dispute. Fortunately, Castlereagh continued in his congeniality, raising no objection to Middleton's suggestion that irresolvable disagreements over execution of the final arbitral decision should also go before Tsar Alexander.[67]

More difficult to reach was agreement on a joint statement (*projet*) to be presented to the tsar. But Middleton reported to Adams in mid-September that he and the US minister to London, Richard Rush, had "come to an understanding with his Lordship upon the substance of a joint note" to be addressed to the Russian sovereign. Castlereagh thus agreed with the American desire to submit the question regarding right of compensation for the slaves to the tsar "unencumbered by any other matter." He also assented to the American proposal that, should Alexander rule in favor of the United States, a commission would meet in Washington to address claims for compensation. This British concession could not, however, be open ended: the foreign secretary insisted that "before any Commission shall actually sit to take cognizance of such claims, that their precise extent and nature should be ascertained by the American government." When disagreement arose between the English-speaking powers as to the best method of adjusting the American claims, Castlereagh agreed that they should be submitted to the tsar for his "consideration and arbitration."[68] This all was progress, and it seemed to bode well for the US cause should the tsar rule in the Americans' favor. Working against American interests, however, was the low cost of bonded labor in Russia: since no "average value" had yet been set for the slaves carried away by the British, the issue might be referred to the tsar. If so, Tsar Alexander's perception of their value could be "highly disadvantageous to the U.S."[69] This was, of course, not within the power of London to control, and thus Middleton and Rush had achieved most of the Monroe administration's goals for the London phase of the negotiations.

The final disposition of the arbitration had, however, to wait several months due to the tsar's lengthy absence from St. Petersburg to attend the Congress of Laibach. Alexander finally returned to the Russian capital on May 26, 1821. On that very day, Count Nesselrode sent a circular to the foreign diplomatic corps, informing them that he had taken over direction of the Russian Foreign Office, a position he had shared with Ionnis Kapodistrias since 1816.[70] It was he who now would lead the Russian side in the negotiations over compensation for the slaves. Middleton addressed a note to the foreign minister on June 21, reassuring him that the United States would view "the decision of this friendly power as final and conclusive." He added that the tsar was empowered to authorize "all steps necessary to give effect to the decision which may occur as a result of the good offices [*qui pourra avoir lieu par suite des bons offices*] of his Imperial Majesty."[71] London and Washington had agreed on this last point when drafting the Anglo-American *projet*, which was then transmitted to the Russians.

Tsar Alexander issued his decision on July 12, 1822, but both parties to the dispute had received word of its contents in the months leading up to its formal proclamation. Middleton told Adams in early May that the tsar was preoccupied with more pressing problems than the Anglo-American dispute over slaves. Thus, the announcement was delayed until midsummer.[72] The tsar decided as follows:

> That the United States of America are entitled to claim from Great Britain a just indemnification for all private property, which the British Forces may have carried away from the Places and Territories of which the Treaty stipulates the Restitution, in quitting the same Places and Territories.

That The United States are entitled to consider as having been so carried away, all such Slaves as may have been transferred from the above mentioned Territories to British Vessels within the Waters of the said Territories, and who, for this reason, may not have been restored.

But that, if there should be any American Slaves who were carried away from Territories of which the 1st Article on the Treaty of Ghent has not stipulated the Restitution to The United States, The United States are not entitled to claim an indemnification for the said Slaves.[73]

When the text of the decision was finally issued, both sides could find positive and negative elements. Perhaps this was a predictable result, since Moscow hoped to maintain good relations with both of the Anglophone maritime nations. Harold Edward Bergquist, for his part, asserts that Alexander was seeking to "exacerbate relations between England and the United States as well as earn American gratitude for his government." Overall, he was successful in the latter goal according to Russian historian Nikolai N. Bolkhovitinov, who concludes that Russian-American relations benefited from the ruling.[74] The tsar was at least reasonably successful in the former, since his ruling guaranteed both an Anglo-American dispute over its meaning, as well as several years of contentious negotiations before the two nations could agree on the amount of compensation the British would pay.

As to which side came out better from the ruling, there is no consensus. The unanimous ratification of the agreement by the Senate in January 1823 certainly indicates a high level of American satisfaction with the award.[75] Charles Webster, furthermore, concludes that the tsar's decision, "based on an interpretation of the text of the Treaty and not the principle involved, was given in favour of the United States." More recently, James Oakes has asserted that the tsar "resoundingly" endorsed the *British* interpretation of the Treaty of Ghent. As a result, "the British read the czar's decision as a vindication," though the Americans "acted as though the emperor had ruled in their favor."[76] According to Bergquist, the award "at first appears to be highly advantageous to the United States." But he then goes on to quote Adams on the rather confusing nature of the decision's wording, which "is expressed in language needing explanation more than the paragraph of the article which was in question."[77] In fact, the ambiguity of the Russian ruling is its most significant feature, since this meant that Britain and the United States would have to work out the details of the settlement themselves. Britain owed the United States *something* as a result of the arbitration. What this meant, however, was yet to be determined. Again, this vagueness allowed St. Petersburg to avoid a breach with either party, which was almost certainly the goal.

The ambiguous result of the arbitration also led, predictably, to Anglo-American diplomatic discord. The amount of the award was, by bilateral agreement, to be set by a commission that was to convene after the ruling was made known. Yet the American and British commissioners were unsuccessful on agreeing on specifics, including the American demand for interest payments on the value of the slaves carried away. Thus, "the entire commission process broke down."[78] Finally, separate negotiations in London—conducted on the American side by former Treasury secretary Albert Gallatin—resulted in an agreement that the British would pay a lump sum for the 3,601 slaves that the Americans claimed to have unjustly lost. The amount was set at a quarter of a million pounds, or $1,204,960 at the going exchange rate. The negotiators signed the agreement on November 13, 1826, thus bringing to a conclusion a diplomatic vexation, concerning one article of a single treaty, that had aggravated relations between London and Washington for almost a dozen years.[79]

For the British the agreement cleared away what must have seemed more an annoyance than anything like a major foreign policy crisis. Foreign Secretary George Canning, who succeeded Castlereagh after the latter's tragic suicide in 1822, certainly had bigger things to worry about: with the outbreak of the Greek War of Independence, Istanbul had to be more of a concern than Washington. It was well to be done with the matter. For the Americans, on the other hand, this was a significant foreign policy achievement. The United States had finally gained a measure of satisfaction from London on an issue that had been simmering since 1775. It had done so, moreover, by asserting the right of Americans to "property in man." Despite the reference to "Negroes or other property" in the Paris Treaty, it is impossible to imagine a decades-long American diplomatic effort to gain restitution for any other form of misappropriated property—for, say, horses or furniture. Washington had asserted, on the world stage, the significance of bonded labor for the new nation and its citizens. It had also asserted that American foreign policy would be directed, when necessary, to securing the interests of slaveholders—a category to which many of America's early diplomats belonged.

Yet even Pennsylvanian Benjamin Franklin demanded the return of American slaves, while Massachusetts's Adams—no friend of slavery—was indefatigable in his pursuit of compensation for the evacuated slaves. Both American ideas of justice and the new nation's international stature depended on compelling Britain to compensate slaveholders for their lost property; to abide by the American interpretation of the Paris and Ghent treaties. This policy imperative did not, however, place the republic on the side of the angels. The eminent diplomatic historian Samuel Flagg Bemis ends his treatment of the post-Ghent diplomacy in quite an interesting way, writing of "this whole affair of securing 'justice' for the slave-owners injured by loss of their human property."[80] The quotation marks around "justice" are instructive. Perhaps the settlement was "just" in the sense that a treaty was, for practical purposes, interpreted according to American lights. But Hamilton, as Camillus, had a point about the odiousness of the whole business.

Spanish Florida and Negro Fort

American concern regarding escaped slaves was not, however, confined to the realm of US relations with Great Britain. Escaped slaves, and the threat that they posed, also played a significant role in Washington's policy toward Spanish East Florida in the wake of the War of 1812.[81] This was most starkly demonstrated by the destruction of the so-called Negro Fort at Prospect Bluff on the Apalachicola River. The fort had been evacuated by the British in 1815. But prior to departure, the British commander had provided the Black and Native American residents in the area with weapons with which to defend the fort. General Edward Nicolls was a convinced abolitionist who wanted to prevent American expansion into the Floridas. But the arming and provisioning of runaway slaves, maroons, and Choctaw so close to Georgia in fact proved an invitation to Americans, hungry for land and terrified of armed ex-slaves in the years after the Haitian Revolution.[82]

Washington's concern regarding escaped slaves is amply demonstrated by the documentary evidence. On March 15, 1816, Secretary of War William H. Crawford instructed Major General Andrew Jackson to bring this issue to the attention of the Spanish authorities in Pensacola. "Secret practices to inveigle negroes from the frontiers of Georgia, as well as from the Cherokee and Creek nations," the secretary informed the general, "are still continued by the negroes and hostile Creeks. This is a state of things which cannot fail to produce much injury to the neighboring settlements, and excite irritations which may ultimately endanger the peace of the nation. . . . The principles of good neighbourhood, require the interference of the Spanish authority, to put an end to an evil of so serious a nature." If the Spanish governor of Florida were to fail to take appropriate action, then "it will be incumbent on the executive to determine what course shall be adopted in relation to this banditti." If the Madison administration determined "that the destruction of the fort does not require the sanction of the legislature, measures will promptly be taken for its reduction."[83] American resolve to eradicate the threat posed by Negro Fort was not to be doubted. Jackson passed the word on to the Spanish governor in April, asserting that, among the Blacks at Prospect Bluff, there were "many" who had been "enticed away from their masters, citizens of the United States." Spain was obliged "to destroy or remove from [America's] frontier the banditti; put an end to an event of so serious a nature, and return to our citizens, and the friendly Indians inhabiting our territory, those negroes now in the said fort, and which have been stolen and enticed from them." This was not a matter merely of the return of property but of national security. The American government, thus, would not allow the threat on its southern border to persist. The situation, Jackson noted, "will not be tolerated by our government, and if not put down by Spanish authority, will compel us in self-defense to destroy" the inhabitants of Negro Fort.[84]

Jackson was even more vigorous in his instruction to Major General Edmund P. Gaines, who was tasked with leading the force that would attack the fort. Jackson wrote that he was convinced "that this fort has been established by some villains for the purpose of murder, rapine, and plunder, and that it ought to be blown up regardless of the ground it stands on," Spanish sovereignty over Florida apparently being irrelevant in this case. If Gaines agreed with this assessment of Negro Fort, then he should "destroy it, and restore the stolen negroes and property to their rightful owners."[85] Gaines must have agreed, since the destruction of the fort proceeded on July 27, 1816. During the Battle of Negro Fort, the overwhelming majority of the fort's defenders were killed when hot shot from a US Navy gunboat set off an explosion in the fort's magazine, creating a massive explosion. Captain Daniel Todd Patterson exalted to the secretary of the navy that the "service rendered by the destruction of this fort, and the band of negroes who held it, and the country in its vicinity, is of great and manifest importance to the United States" and especially to the bordering states. Now that Negro Fort was destroyed, slaves had "no longer a place to fly to, and will not be so liable to abscond."[86] This "threat" to American security by the fort was no more.

Yet Florida nevertheless remained an asylum for fugitive slaves. The victory over Negro Fort had not changed this fact.[87] What would do so was—American hoped—the successful negotiation of the Adams-Onís, or Transcontinental, Treaty of 1819, by which Spain ceded the Floridas to the United States.[88] The Americans had multiple motivations for wanting to acquire the peninsula, one of which was to prevent the flight of fugitive slaves across an international border. As for Spain, "antagonizing the Anglo plantation society to the north was no longer a viable defensive strategy but rather a dangerous provocation of an awakening regional power."[89] Adams was as committed to this issue as to that of recovering slaves with whom Britain had absconded; as Matthew J. Clavin notes, "to defend an emerging slave-expansion-at-all-costs policy, Adams applauded both the destruction of Negro Fort and the death of hundreds of its defenders."⁹⁰ Whatever his later qualms about the institution of slavery, even the eminent New Englander was eager to serve its interests at this time.

Conclusion: Policy in the Interest of Slavery

These episodes demonstrate that American foreign policy had been, in a question involving slavery, oriented toward the interests of that institution and of those who profited from it. This would not be the last time. But it was not always easy for Americans to shape policies that served those interests. At least as regards the matter of compensation, it was clear from the time of the American Revolution that the goal was to gain satisfaction from London. The next in the wave of Atlantic revolutions would present the Americans with no such clarity. When slaves rose up in the French colony of Saint-Domingue, US policymakers were certain that the uprising posed a threat to the institution of bonded labor in America. They were equally certain that American foreign policy would, once again, need to be directed toward the protection of American slavery. But the issues surrounding this earthshaking event in their neighborhood were so complex that it was exceptionally difficult to determine how to accomplish this goal.

CHAPTER 2

"'Tis Ill to Fear"

American Responses to the Haitian Revolution

It might have seemed an easy call. A New World nation that had recently thrown off the rule of a European colonial power might have been expected to look favorably upon a neighbor seeking to do the same. One did not have to look hard to find the commonalities of two novice nations in the world of international politics: their birth in the time of Atlantic revolutions, their intertwined commerce, and their difficult relations with the former mother country. Both, as Alyssa Goldstein Sepinwall has noted, even had a military officer who led the revolution and became "both a civilian leader and a national icon."[1] On the face of it, the two nations should have become fast friends. At the very least, the elder might have been expected to accord recognition to its younger revolutionary sibling.

Yet the nation that would come to call itself Haiti proved to be a special case, and deciding how to respond to its revolution was not at all an easy call for three successive US administrations. There was no single reason why Haiti posed such a challenge to the Americans wrestling with the revolution in what they called Santo Domingo. International politics of the great powers, as well as trade interests, complicated the picture for American policymakers, who wanted to avoid conflict with Britain, alienation of France, or loss of markets. But troublesome issues also presented themselves to the United States soon after Haitian leaders declared independence in 1804, as the Latin American republics, one by one, began seeking their independence from Spain and Portugal. Washington, DC—by then the seat of the US federal government—generally looked favorably upon these new neighbors and did not hesitate to accord them recognition when their time came. By contrast, the United States granted recognition to Haiti only in 1862, almost six decades after Jean-Jacques Dessalines had declared his nation sovereign.

The most significant difference was, of course, the dual nature of the Haitian Revolution as an anticolonial revolution *and* a slave uprising; a revolution in which the enslaved sought to throw off their masters and French domination. The United States was a republic, but it was—in Don E. Fehrenbacher's noted terminology—a slaveholding republic. The success or failure of a slave uprising so close to the United States could not but complicate the reaction of Americans to the events in Saint-Domingue. Relations between the United States and Haiti thus proved no "hymn of fraternity." A bilateral relationship that would have been challenging to husband in the international context of the time was made much more so by the domestic and international politics of slavery.[2] The result was a complicated, convoluted, and at times contradictory response from a government still feeling its way through an international sphere that was both promising and threatening. Slavery was viewed as a national security issue; a slave rebellion in the neighborhood did not make it less so. While the emergence of new republics from the ashes of Spain's American empire could be viewed as a positive benefit to the security of the United States, it was more difficult to think the same of Haiti.[3] This revolution was bound to be different.

A Slave Revolution

There is much that is striking about the revolution in Saint-Domingue. One of the most arresting facts is that it came as such an incredible surprise abroad. As Michael Zeuske notes, the shock of the revolution was "so extreme, so incomparable with anything else known" that observers were either bewildered or, in fact, struck dumb. Slave resistance, even insurrections, were a fact of life in the Atlantic world. But slave revolts, while alarming, had never posed a threat to the existence of the slave societies themselves. The revolution in Saint-Domingue would prove to be different—even if this was not recognized immediately—and not just by virtue of the extreme brutality of the fighting that it entailed. Anthropologist Sidney Mintz has observed that the Haitian Revolution, more so than those of the thirteen colonies and France, entailed universal claims of a sort which made it particularly disruptive:

Of the three revolutions, American, French, and Haitian, the Haitian represented the most terrifying reality for its time. To be sure, it was revolutionary in those days to insist on the right to be represented politically
if one were taxed; or to deny the absolute rights of monarchy. And many
persons gave their lives for their beliefs. But that was not the same as ar-
guing that "human" rights apply to *everyone*—that there was a *universal*
definition of who was human—and meaning it. To take that stand
would mean, among other things, that rape, flogging, or sale of someone else's children was a crime, no matter on whom it was inflicted. . . .
Though we cannot be sure they knew it, the Haitian rebels were engaged in an endeavor more radical and more modern even than turning
a colony into a sovereign nation.[4]

If they succeeded in their revolution, the implications would, indeed, be dangerous for the United States and the Atlantic slave-holding empires.[5] The Haitian Revolution thus presented "a dramatic challenge to the world as it then
was," to quote Laurent Dubois.[6]

On the night of August 22–23, 1791, slaves on Saint-Domingue's Plaine du
Nord rose up against their masters. The rising was massive, with as many as
100,000 slaves involved in the north. Slaves "went from plantation to plantation, killing whites, burning houses, and setting cane fields alight," and reports
of infanticide, murder, and rape swept quickly through the region. The rebellion soon spread to the South and West Provinces. The insurgents quickly grew
in strength, while the French forces that were meant to suppress them proved
inadequate to the task. The Saint-Domingue slave rebellion had begun.[7]

The full significance of the rebellion could not have been apparent in those
summer and early autumn days of 1791, either in Saint-Domingue or in the
United States. Yet whatever the implications might be, President George Washington's administration initially wanted none of it. As Timothy M. Matthewson has noted, the developments in Hispaniola threatened American interests.
He adds, in an understatement, that President Washington, Secretary of State
Thomas Jefferson, and Secretary of the Treasury Alexander Hamilton "did not
like slave revolts." That US interests were engaged by the rebellion in Saint-
Domingue cannot be gainsaid. US trade with the colony was extensive by the
eve of the rebellion's outbreak, with Saint-Domingue being America's second
largest trading partner, behind only Great Britain itself. Since US leaders viewed
commercial intercourse as a vital element of national security, any threat to
the trade with Saint-Domingue represented a threat to the nation itself.[8]

As to America's principal policy shapers not caring for slave revolts, this was
also crystal clear. America was a slaveholding society; Jefferson and Washington

were both Virginians who owned other human beings. And while the thinking of the founders with regard to slavery was complex, their thinking on armed slaves rising up, killing their masters, and setting plantations alight was not. The fear that slave rebellion might spread from Haiti, a near neighbor, was rather a nightmare for early Americans watching events in the Caribbean. South Carolina's governor, Charles Pinckney, for example, worried that the slave revolt could "become a flame which will extend to all the neighboring islands, and may prove not a very pleasing or agreeable example to the Southern States."[9] Trade was very important. But so too, indeed, was the security of the American South. Both issues, then—trade and containment of the "contagion" of slave rebellion—would shape US policymakers' thinking regarding Saint-Domingue from 1791 on. Region, party, and economic interest all came to play their roles in the American response to what would emerge as a historic event in the Atlantic world.

The initial response from the Washington administration to the slave rebellion was to help the French suppress it, even at considerable expense. The French, short on funds, quickly sought American financial aid to help them in their efforts to put down the rebellion. Washington responded favorably, and his words clearly indicate his thoughts. In response to a request for aid from Jean de Ternant, the French minister to the United States, Washington wrote on September 24, "Sincerely regretting, as I do, the cause which has given rise to this application, I am happy in the opportunity of testifying how well disposed the United States are to render every aid in their power to our good friends and Allies the [French] to quell 'the alarming insur[rec]tion of the Negros in Hispaniola' [and] of the ready disposition to effect [it,] of the Executive authority thereof." Ternant certainly sought to make Washington's decision easier to reach. On the same day that Washington wrote his words, Ternant wrote him a "summary" of events on Saint-Domingue in which he spoke of the slaves' goal of "killing without exception all the whites of the colony." This intelligence may well have shocked Washington. Yet the president had already decided: his initial response was to aid in the suppression of this dangerous and regrettable uprising. Washington's reaction was thus what might have been expected from an American slaveholder of the time. As Matthewson summarizes, "Washington responded because he objected to the blacks' self-assertion and their spirit of autonomy or independence."[10]

Washington had decided to aid France with cash and arms. Race and slavery were an essential part of this decision, but there were other factors to consider as well. One was, of course, trade. The administration needed to do what it could to maintain access to trade with Saint-Domingue. Secretary of State Jefferson feared that the upheaval in the colony might lead to the colony "falling under any other power"—by which he meant Great Britain. Jefferson was apprehensive that the slave rebellion might lead Saint-Domingue's whites to look to Britain for their salvation and thus seek a more independent course. Hence, he wanted to make it clear that the administration "conceived it to be strongly in our interest that they should retain their connection with the mother country." The fear that Britain could, in the future, monopolize the trade of such an important commercial partner made US aid to France imperative. Ternant, concerned about the implications of direct American negotiations "with the richest and most important of [France's] colonies," perhaps found such sentiments on the part of the United States' chief diplomat reassuring.[11]

France wanted money from the United States. On September 21, 1791, Ternant wrote Hamilton, telling the Treasury secretary of "the most urgent need [*le plus pressant besoin*]" now facing the government in Paris. Requesting $40,000 in credit, paid against America's debt to France, he reiterated that the situation was "urgent." Hamilton could not have responded with more alacrity—or, apparently, sympathy. "Regretting most sincerely the calamitous event announced in your letter of this day," he wrote Ternant, "it is with real pleasure, I find myself in condition to inform you" that the sum would be paid by the US Treasury to France. The next day Hamilton informed Washington of the correspondence with Ternant, transmitting to the president Ternant's letter. In informing Washington of his actions, the secretary echoed his own words to Ternant: the slave revolution was an "urgent and calamitous case." Two days later, from Mount Vernon, Washington indicated to Hamilton that the secretary's actions met with his "entire approbation." Given Washington's absence from Philadelphia at the time, and the pace of communication in the late 1700s, the decision to aid France in its efforts to suppress the uprising of the enslaved in Saint-Domingue could not have come more quickly than it did. The administration's policy—*American* policy—appeared to be clearly and firmly set against the rebellion.[12]

Still, commercial interests were never far from the minds of the key members of Washington's cabinet. In early January 1792 Jefferson expressed his dismay at the daily reports from Saint-Domingue, and perceived that "nothing indicates as yet that the evil is at it's [*sic*] height." Yet he could not help but ask one of the commissioners sent by the white Dominguans to the United States about US flour shipments to the colony. As Rayford Logan noted in his history of Haitian-US relations, Jefferson "planned to obtain every possible advantage from France's difficulties." Hamilton, likewise, "saw in the insurrection an opportunity to exact additional commercial privileges with the colony." By 1795, in fact, the French minister to the United States, Joseph Fauchet, was quoting

Jefferson as saying, "The force of events hands over the French colonies to us; France enjoys the sovereignty over them and we, the profit from them."[13]

Despite American aid, the situation in Saint-Domingue continued to deteriorate for France. The Washington administration would provide France with over $700,000 in aid between 1791 and 1793, and US merchants kept up the supply of food, weapons, and ammunition. But the aid was insufficient to allow the French to quell what had become a three-way civil war between whites, mulattoes, and Blacks. By the end of 1791, "white power was largely broken" in the South and West Provinces. In late March of the following year, Ternant provided Foreign Minister Claude Antoine de Valdec de Lessart with a wrenching assessment of the situation for the whites in the colony. Saint-Domingue was "still in a violent state of revolution," wrote the minister, adding a note about "the confusion or rather anarchy of the powers there."[14] Rent by divisions and dissentions, the white Dominguans could not respond effectively to the insurrection that faced them, no matter how much aid the United States provided.

In any event, whether that aid would keep coming came into question due to a turn in the French Revolution. The National Convention of France "suspended"—but did not depose—King Louis XVI on August 10, 1792. This suspension of the monarchy did not, in any way, end the French government's need for American aid, but the change in the regime caused Hamilton to question how much help the administration should be giving. In a letter to Washington dated November 19, the Treasury secretary discussed Ternant's request for "an additional supply of money for the use of the Colony of Santo Domingo . . . which I regard more and more as presenting a subject extremely delicate and embarrassing." The American Treasury *could* provide at least some of the funds that the French requested. But Hamilton questioned the propriety of doing so with the king suspended and the situation in Paris unclear. Should the king be restored at some future point in time, "no payment made which might be made in the Interval would be deemed regular or obligatory." Hamilton nevertheless advised that money should be made available: aid to Saint-Domingue that sought to alleviate the suffering of the colony "would be so clearly and act of humanity and friendship, of such evident utility to the French Empire" that no French government could, in the future "refuse to allow credit" for it.[15]

Still, it was an embarrassing situation, since it was not clear, at least to Hamilton, if there was "now any organ of the French nation which can regularly ask the succor." Hamilton thus recommended to Washington that "*as little as possible* ought to be done," and that "whatever may be done should be cautiously restricted to the single idea *of preserving the colony from* destruction by

Famine." Finally, the administration must present its aid in such a way as to "avoid the explicit recognition of any regular authority in any person." If—and only if—these conditions were met, Ternant's request would be granted. Jefferson himself, in any event, was cautious at this time regarding the diplomatic niceties of providing aid to a government that still had not formally requested it.[16]

Developments in Saint-Domingue made the question of the form of US aid moot. The possibility of a negotiated settlement between whites and Blacks in the colony had seemed real enough in late 1791. Peace commissioners sent from France met with leaders of the Black rebels, whose initial demands were modest: amnesty for themselves in return for their followers' return to the plantations. The refusal of the colonial assembly to accept these terms—planning instead to slaughter the rebels once they had disarmed—guaranteed the end for white rule in the colony. As Thomas O. Ott summarizes it, "The last chance of the whites had collapsed under the weight of their own vengeance." Perhaps even this chance had been illusory. As Dubois suggests, the deal envisaged might well have "provoked open hostilities between the 'multitude' of insurgents and their leaders."[17] One thing was certain: it was no longer a matter of US aid to prop up the white plantation elite's power in Saint-Domingue. By 1793 that power was forever broken.

The collapse of white power was the result, in large part, of divisions among whites in Saint-Domingue. So, too, was the declaration of general abolition of slavery that came on August 29, 1793, by the Jacobin commissioner Léger-Félicité Sonthonax. Sonthonax and his fellow commissioners had engaged in reform of the slave system on the island, issuing an order that accorded some protections to the enslaved while still retaining the system of slavery. But even this went too far for the white planters, who came quickly to rally behind the new governor, François-Thomas Galbaud du Fort. In his effort to rally the support of the Black insurgents in the ensuing power struggle, Sonthonax first proclaimed the manumission of those Blacks who fought on his side against Galbaud's forces. By August he was compelled by the expectations of his followers to proclaim the end to slavery in the North Province. Soon, his fellow commissioner, Étienne Polverel, would do the same in the South and West Provinces, "at which point," Philippe R. Girard observes, "all slaves of the colony became officially free under French colonial law." The slaves of Saint-Domingue had, at least for the time, succeeded in their primary goal. This could not have been expected to sit well with many of their neighbors to the north.[18]

The impact of the "first general, immediate emancipation" of slaves in the Americas "would continue to be felt for decades, especially in the slave South,"

Matthewson notes. The "contagion" of slave insurrection was much feared in the United States, and more so after the slaves were successful in gaining their freedom. Ashli White observes that the very equation of slave rebellion with contagion helped to frame uprising of the enslaved as a "malevolent force of nature." This helped, in turn, deny agency to the slaves, since "disease did not have a political agenda, nor did it control its own actions." This framing might have reassured some proslavery Americans, who did not want to think of US slaves as having agency. But the horror of the contagion—the spread—of slave insurrection to Saint-Domingue's neighbors indicates that the slaveholding powers of the hemisphere had some inkling that perhaps the slaves had an agenda of their own—one that translated across the borders of the different slave cultures. One could still seek to dismiss the relevance of the revolution, attributing it, as White notes, to "circumstances on the island." But this hardly allayed the fear.[19]

Scholars have addressed the issue of the fear of the Saint-Domingue "contagion" spreading to the American South. And there is ample evidence that this fear was real. Often cited as a clear early statement of this fear is South Carolina governor Charles Pinckney's letter to the colonial assembly from September 1791, in which he stated, "When we recollect how nearly similar the situation of the Southern States and St. Domingo are in the profusion of slaves—that a day may arrive when they may be exposed to the same insurrections—we cannot but sensibly feel for your situation." There is, again, no doubt that Americans—and especially southerners—viewing events in Saint-Domingue feared the export of slave insurrection to the United States. Matthewson is correct when he notes that the founders' commitment to emancipation did not extend to "slave self-emancipation or black domination of whites. The prospect of immediate emancipation was horrifying to them." The policy taken by the Washington administration toward Saint-Domingue can only be understood in light of this analysis. Nor was the fear of Dominguan-inspired slaves taking matters into their own hands a chimera. For instance, observers at the time, and numerous scholars today, hold that Gabriel's Rebellion in Virginia in 1800 was inspired by the insurrection in Saint-Domingue.[20]

While merchants in the Northeast might respond to the insurrection by seeing trade opportunities, southerners perceived "first and foremost a dangerous example for local slaves." Yet even for leading southerners, this seemingly existential fear had to be balanced with other fears, other opportunities. In his careful study of Jefferson and Haiti, Arthur Scherr concludes that Jefferson, "always cognizant of the importance of the balance of power in the Americas and dreading British domination, was more concerned about this than with the possibility that Southern slaves might imitate their Caribbean counterparts in insurrection." Slavery remained a national security issue. But as developments in Saint-Domingue were becoming part of the broader struggle of the wars of the French Revolution, even this interest had to be viewed in that context.[21]

Thus, a major turning point—for Saint-Domingue and for US policy regarding the colony—came in 1793 with the British invasion of the island. Perhaps the invasion was motivated in part by a fear that echoed that of the Americans—namely, the horror at the spread of slave insurrection from Haiti. While the Americans fretted about the southern states, the British were particularly concerned about Jamaica. The island was an easy sail from the western ports of the South Province. In this sense, the invasion was "both an aggressive and a defensive act," to quote the leading scholar of the British invasion, David Patrick Geggus. Geggus holds, however, that "British policy towards Saint-Domingue in 1793 was essentially aggressive and not inspired by fear for Jamaica's safety." The government thought it had taken good care to defend the island. Ott notes that the desire to gain a diplomatic bargaining chip and the traditional British wartime policy of taking colonial possessions of its enemies mixed with the perceived need to protect Jamaica. With Britain and France at war again in 1793, London's decision to invade France's colony seems overdetermined.[22]

Writing from Paris in mid-February 1793, the American minister plenipotentiary to France, Gouverneur Morris, had reassured Secretary of State Jefferson that the French colony was almost certainly safe from attack: "Many suppose that the french Colonies will be attack'd but this I do not beleive. It is indeed far from improbable that a british Garrison may be thrown into Martinique but as to St. Domingo it would require more Men than can be spard to defend it and as much money as it is worth."[23] That September, Britain proved Morris wrong, in part: the British did invade Saint-Domingue. But, as Morris had foreseen, the invasion's prospects for success were slim and its costs were great. The battered invasion force left the colony in 1798. Yet the period of British occupation brought with it developments in Saint-Domingue that American policymakers would have to reckon with.

Had it come at an earlier point in time, the British invasion and occupation of the French colony could have been viewed as a threat to American interests in the Caribbean, and a major threat at that. Coming as it did, however, in the context of both improving relations with the British and of a general souring of relations with France, the governing Federalists were able to take this British move in stride. Jay's Treaty of 1794, ratified in 1795, was lambasted by Republicans as a sellout to Britain and a provocation of America's French ally that failed to address major areas of US conflict with Great Britain. The failure of Jay's Treaty to deal with British carrying off of American slaves has been addressed in chapter 1. What is most significant for the study of US relations with Haiti is that the treaty largely ended fears of a slide to war with Britain just at the time when Britain was intervening significantly in Saint-Domingue. In this heated international context it was useful to the government in Philadelphia to observe "significant marks of Britain's receptivity to conciliation with the United States." American commercial expansion could now continue to grow in peace, including commerce with that important trading partner, Saint-Domingue.[24]

During this period American merchants generally continued to run a good trade with the occupied colony, especially since British officials recognized the need for American shipping capacity. So far, so good, as American imports and exports helped sustain the British adventure. But then came late December 1794, and mulatto commander André Rigaud's capture of Tiburon on the far western end of Saint-Domingue. Rigaud's victory was stunning: by the end of the battle, the British had lost not only the town, and the port closest to Jamaica, but had also sacrificed three hundred of 450 defenders. It was, indeed, a "disaster," and it presaged further troubles for the British.[25]

The leadership ability and fighting skills of the Dominguans were major reasons for the turn of events. So, too, was the outbreak of tropical disease. The British had invaded and occupied Saint-Domingue at a time that was hardly propitious for Europeans in the Caribbean: yellow fever was at pandemic levels in the Caribbean and North America between 1793 and 1798. (The US capital city of Philadelphia had been hit by an outbreak in 1793.) The fever took a massive toll on British soldiers over the course of the occupation. The losses were indeed astounding. Geggus estimates that over 12,500 of a total force of a little over 20,500 had died by the end of the occupation. This was obviously unsustainable and called for a new approach by the British to securing their interests in the region.[26]

In addition to yellow fever, the British, from 1794 onward, would have to deal with another force of nature in Saint-Domingue: the former slave—and slave owner—turned general, Toussaint Louverture. Until the spring of 1794, Toussaint had been fighting on the side of Britain's Spanish allies. His defection to the side of the French Republic seems to have come from a combination of principle, naked ambition, and Spanish mistakes. Certainly the decision by the National Convention to ratify Sonthonax's declaration of manumission made it easier for Toussaint to justify his conversion. Yet his defection came prior to that ratification. He clearly saw that the prospects for a top leadership post were better with the French then the Spaniards. Nor was Spanish arrogance toward former slaves, or the local Spanish commander's mistreatment of Toussaint's family, endearing. Toussaint made his famous volte-face cautiously, even surreptitiously. But he made it, nonetheless. And his conversion to the Tricolor was, notes Geggus, "without doubt one of the major factors in the defeat of the British." From 1794 until 1802, no figure in Haitian history would play a more outsize role than Toussaint. American policymakers, convinced of the vital interests at stake in Saint-Domingue, would now have to wrestle with the policy to be adopted toward a French colony more and more under the control of a Black leader who came into the world enslaved.[27]

That the relationship went so well, and was productive for both sides, is a tribute to Toussaint's gifts as a diplomatist as much as to the members of Federalist John Adams's policymaking team. Both sides sought mutual profit from the relationship, and they achieved it. In this sense, from the American perspective, concerns about national interest trumped those of race, at least for a time. It should not be forgotten, however, that the time was extraordinary, and threats to American interests were very real. American policymakers still held to brutally racist views of Blacks, as even a cursory reading of the contemporary sources reveals. Yet this only makes this period in the sad history of America's relations with Haiti all the more remarkable.

Both Adams and Toussaint faced difficult diplomatic realities and crosswinds as they sought to formulate policy with regard to each other. Toussaint's situation, however, was more difficult, given that he was still a French officer in what was—if increasingly nominally—a French colony. Girard has well summarized his diplomatic predicament: "His foreign policy courted France, Great Britain, and the United States, all of which happened to be hostile to one another." Toussaint had to reckon with British naval mastery of the seas, Girard notes, and maintain a supply line to American merchants, all while not appearing to take steps toward independence, which would invite French intervention.[28] It was a tall order for any diplomatist. Yet it was not beyond his skills.

The American position, if not quite so delicate, called also for quite adroit diplomacy. Relations with France were in steep decline after ratification of Jay's Treaty, and the two nations would find themselves in an undeclared naval war during much of Adams's presidency. This conflict raised the issue of Saint-Domingue's independence at high levels of the Adams administration, with Secretary of State Timothy Pickering especially interested in such an option in light of American trade interests at a time of the Quasi-War with France. At the same time, Adams was adamant that American actions in the Caribbean comport with those of the British: no blue sky could appear between the two English-speaking nations while the conflict raged with France on the high seas. The challenges were daunting, and, if not as complex as those facing Toussaint, complex nonetheless.

Congress had passed the Intercourse Act in June 1798, suspending trade with France and its "dependencies." This ban was initially interpreted as including Saint-Domingue. It hit Toussaint particularly hard, since he needed American supplies at a time when he was engaged in a domestic power struggle. André Rigaud still held power in the South Province, and was supported by the French, who saw him as less of a threat. Toussaint gravely needed aid to help him consolidate power over the colony. And that help needed to come from the United States, since, as Girard observes, "too close an alliance with England would convince black Dominguans that Louverture was preparing to restore slavery" in the colony.[29] Toussaint thus took a rather striking diplomatic initiative, and appealed directly to the president of the United States to seek redress of the situation. In doing so, Toussaint acted as if he were a head of government, approaching a peer instead of the chief general of a colonial army.

On November 6, 1798, Toussaint addressed a letter to Adams. He got right to the point, telling Adams that "it is with the greatest surprise and the most painful sorrow [la peine la plus sensible]" that American ships had abandoned the colony's ports, thus renouncing all commercial relations with Saint-Domingue and denying it the "commodities and comestibles" of North America. He was thus approaching Adams to discuss with him the "appropriate means to reestablish navigation and to again have the American flag arrive in our ports." Seeking to appeal to Adams's perceptions of American interests, Toussaint noted that a resumption of trade was as much in America's benefit as that of France's colonies. He added the promise that Americans would always be respected as a friend and ally of France. With an eye clearly fixed on the problem with this promise—namely, French aggression in the naval Quasi-War—the general sought to reassure Adams that he would give protection to "the ships of your nation that make their way [se rendront] into the ports of the French Republic in this colony."[30] A former slave—who led an army of the formerly enslaved—had thus approached the white president of the slaveholding republic with a request that stressed the mutual benefit to be had from cooperation of the two regimes. It was a bold move indeed.

Delivering the letter to Philadelphia was Joseph Bunel, a white Dominguan who served as Toussaint's personal representative on the mission to seek redress for the trade embargo. The choice of a white emissary must have seemed a foregone conclusion to Toussaint, aware as he was of the racism that existed at the highest levels of the American government. But whatever the color of his representative, the fact remained that this person would be speaking for a Black leader and former slave. Toussaint was, in this regard as well, taking a chance that probably seemed a long shot. Yet Bunel found a positive reception, and an administration that was, Logan notes, "well disposed to grant his request." In part, this derived from America's own trade interests, which Toussaint had stressed in his letter to Adams. It also derived from the closely related desire on the part of the Adams administration to explore the idea of Saint-Domingue's independence. Strikingly, and in contrast to the policy of the previous administration, Adams's chosen diplomats were willing to give serious thought to the benefit the United States would harvest if Toussaint should declare independence from France. No one at the time could have missed what this meant: the permanent end of slavery in Saint-Domingue. Even more significant, from the point of view of American diplomacy it would mean that America would likely establish relations with a Black head of state in its own back yard. Toussaint, as it turned out, never declared independence. But the American administration's willingness to treat a former slave as, potentially, a head of state in the Americas was strong stuff indeed.[31]

Bunel was received by Timothy Pickering, Adams's first secretary of state. Pickering was, by late 1798, of the opinion that Toussaint and his associates would soon and successfully "assume the direction of affairs of the island," and he expressed himself clearly as supporting a "prompt" resumption of trade with the ports of "that island." Pickering described Toussaint as "amiable and respectable," and a leader well disposed toward "peace toward Great Britain and her [dependencies?], as well as toward the United States." Pickering here expressed none of the horror, suffered by some, that a nation led by a former slave would launch a direct attack on slavery in the Caribbean or the United States. According to his biographer, Pickering—like the British government—"feared the effect of the revolution in Santo Domingo, particularly as an example to the Negroes of the American South." Yet the secretary of state also appeared horrified by the prospect of France ever cutting off trade between Saint-Domingue and the United States. And he expressed the confidence that Toussaint posed no such threat.[32]

Writing from London, the American minister to Great Britain, Rufus King, summarized British perceptions of American policy toward Toussaint. The British foreign secretary, Lord Grenville, had "remarked to [King] concerning a supposed inclination *on our part to encourage the Establishment of a Black Republic in Santo Domingo.*" Nor was this the first that King had heard about this supposed inclination on the part of the Adams administration. Grenville and King had spoken of the matter as early as July 1798, after the British minister to Philadelphia, Robert Liston, had spoken about Saint-Domingue with Pickering. King reported to Pickering that Grenville had *"heard with horror from Mr. Liston that in a conversation between you and him, you had intimated an idea that our government might be disposed to countenance the establishment of a Republic of Blacks in Santo Domingo.*" King denied any knowledge of the policy, but added, perhaps not terribly helpfully, *"that I should prefer to see one or two Republicks [sic] in So. America."*[33]

Perhaps Grenville could be forgiven for not being so solicitous of the establishment of republics in the New World, and especially not one run by former slaves in the near vicinity of Jamaica. British policymakers hoped for rather different developments in the Caribbean. The British, defeated by Dominguan forces and tropical disease, were ready to end the occupation. But this did not mean that they were ready to give up on their policy goals for the colony. General Thomas Maitland, who was to oversee British evacuation, took the lead. He hoped, in Girard's words, to "salvage something from Britain's disastrous invasion of Saint-Domingue." In order to salvage what could be salvaged, Maitland sought to deal directly with the general who had inflicted defeat upon his nation. Toussaint was receptive. In late August 1798, the two concluded a secret agreement, after a period of negotiation. By the terms of the convention, the British promised not to "meddle in any way with anything that deals with the internal and political arrangements of the isle of St. Domingue." In return, Toussaint gave his word that he would "take no part in any way in the internal and political arrangements and government of the isle of Jamaica." Maitland was, thus, able to achieve a major British goal—namely, a pledge from Toussaint not to export slave rebellion to the valuable British colony. In return, the British were willing to give Toussaint a "free hand" in his own domain. Additionally, the British would provide aid to Toussaint, including weapons and powder for use in his war with Rigaud in the South Province. Maitland wrote London that the supplies were vital, since Toussaint's victory or defeat "undoubtedly in a considerable degree depends upon their arrival." Now the British would be supplying the force that had handed them an ignominious defeat. In doing so they acted not out of magnanimity but self-interest. The only choice now was between Toussaint and the pro-French Rigaud. In the future the former could be relied on to seek to cultivate good relations with the Americans and British, due to his need for trade and aid. Rigaud's triumph would hand a victory to the French in the strategically important Caribbean. It was not much of a choice.[34]

The Adams administration, for its part, continued its focus on trade with Saint-Domingue. During the Quasi-War with France this proved particularly challenging, especially since the United States had embargoed trade with France and its possessions. Yet Bunel's and Toussaint's efforts at cultivating the Americans showed signs of paying dividends. In February 1799, Edward Stevens was confirmed by the Senate to be the American consul general in Saint-Domingue. That title was relevant, since Pickering had now elevated the rank of the emissary in Saint-Domingue from that of consul, indicating the seriousness with which the administration took the post—and relations with Toussaint. In the most thorough treatment of Stevens's diplomatic career, Ronald

Angelo Johnson stresses the significance of the decision to send a representative of this rank to Cap Française: "Stevens's duties were those of an accred-
ited diplomat to the Louverturian government, not a consul," Johnson
concludes. "Adams expected Stevens to cultivate a strengthened bilateral relationship with a revolutionary government that the president believed would
eventually become the second sovereign state in the western Atlantic world."
Johnson makes a convincing case that the appointment of Stevens—at this
rank—was more significant than has previously been acknowledged; aware as
he was of the racist attitudes that prevailed in the United States, Adams had
essentially appointed a minister to a Black regime, while still using the phrase
"consul" to tamp down the reaction to his doing so. Adams planned on taking Dominguan-US relations quite seriously.[35]

It must be noted that this did not necessarily mean that the Americans were
enthusiastic about seeing an *independent* Saint-Domingue. On this matter there
was not a consensus within the administration. But in the context of worsen-
ing relations with France after the infamous XYZ Affair, an independent Saint-
Domingue was looking more and more attractive to some Americans. Chief
among these was Pickering, who, in Gordon S. Brown's words, wanted Toussaint "to become an instrument of policy, aimed at France." Pickering was
positively disposed toward the Dominguan leader and, if not pushing for independence, was certainly "actively resigned" to it. Writing to Rufus King on
March 12, 1799, Pickering was cautious, but perhaps King could read between
the lines: "We meddle not with the politics of the Island. Toussaint will pursue what he deems the interest of himself and his countrymen. He will probably declare the Island independent. It is probable that he wished to apprise
himself of our commerce, as the necessary means of maintaining it. Neither
moral nor political considerations could induce us to discourage him: on the
contrary, both would warrant us in urging him to the declaration."

Knowing full well that the Adams administration was actively seeking to
expand commerce with the French colony, Pickering had said that this commerce would be necessary for Toussaint to maintain independence. He could
not have come much closer to calling for independence, and he expected a declaration from Toussaint after the general had defeated Rigaud. Yet Pickering
was no firebrand on the issue of Saint-Domingue's independence. Writing the
president's son, John Quincy Adams, in April, he again insisted that the United
States did not "intermeddle with Toussaint's politics." He expected a declaration of independence. But whether Toussaint took that route, or whether he
"govern[ed] it as a colony of France," the same commercial relations would
be maintained. In any event, since the president's son was positively disposed
to independence, there was no reason for the secretary to argue the case. For

Pickering, a Saint-Domingue in the hands of Toussaint was infinitely prefer-able to one held by France. He wrote King in March that "if left to them-selves . . . the Blacks of St. Domingo . . . will be incomparably less dangerous than if they remain the subjects of France," adding, "France with an army of those black troops might conquer all the British Isles [in the Caribbean] and put in jeopardy our Southern States."[36]

Most members of the administration, however, did not share Pickering's separatist enthusiasm. One rather prominent skeptic was the president him-self. Adams was not as certain as Pickering was that Toussaint would declare independence. In fact, he believed that Toussaint was not sure either. "Tous-saint," he wrote to Pickering, "has puzzled himself, the French Government, the English Cabinet, and the Administration of the United States. All the rest of the World knows as little what to do with him as he knows what to do with himself." For Pickering, the great fear was France at the head of a Black army of liberation. But for the president, the concern was for America's ties with British policy in the Caribbean. And the British did not share Pickering's de-sire for an independent Saint-Domingue, which could serve as an example to Britain's possessions.[37]

Adams could not have made himself clearer on this last point. If unsure about Toussaint's policy, he had no doubts about his own in this regard. He wrote Pickering in early July, making it clear that "Harmony with the English, in all this Business of St. Domingo is the thing I have most at heart." He went further at the end of that month, telling the secretary that "a good understand-ing with the English is of more importance to Us than the trade of St. Do-mingo, which I'm afraid will be found to have been too highly estimated." Not that Adams was a fawning British sycophant. In fact, as Arthur Scherr has noted, the president was not beyond dropping hints of his distrust of the Brit-ish. For example, Adams wrote to Secretary of the Navy Benjamin Stoddard in June 1799 concerning events in the Caribbean. Even while stressing to the secretary the need for working "in concert" with the British in Saint-Domingue, he felt compelled to add, "The English in my opinion have made much mis-chief for themselves as well as for us in that island." Given the power of the Royal Navy, and the state of Quasi-War with France, America could not risk alienating Britain over Saint-Domingue. That did not mean that Adams had to trust them.[38]

Adams and Pickering may have disagreed about matters relating to policy toward the Caribbean, but Adams was the president. Playing the role of the good soldier, Colonel Pickering largely followed the lead of his commander. In instructions written for Stevens in April 1799, Pickering did not depart from Adams's prescription of priorities. Pickering emphasized to the consul that "we desire perfect harmony with" the British. One must always bear in mind that "the security of the British possessions and commerce in the West Indies, especially in relation to St. Domingo, is closely interwoven with our own." In a telling passage, the secretary instructed Stevens, "On our part, we consider the prospect which has been opened to us of a lucrative trade to St. Domingo, is to be ascribed in a great degree to the operations of the British; and that the continuation and protection of that trade rests chiefly on the Naval superiority of Great Britain. We are bound then, by a direct regard to our commercial interests, and considerations of political safety against what may justly be called a common enemy, to act in perfect concert with Great Britain in all this business respecting St. Domingo." The secretary was here singing from the president's hymnal.[39]

As concerned as he was regarding independence, Adams was equally convinced that trade with Saint-Domingue was in America's interests—provided, of course, that this trade was conducted in cooperation with Great Britain. Toussaint had written to Adams in November, asking that trade be reestablished between Saint-Domingue and the United States. To do so, Adams would first have to do something about the embargo that the United States had imposed on trade with France and her possessions. If an exception were to be made for Saint-Domingue, it would have to pass Congress. This, then, was the background for the well-known Toussaint's Clause. The administration asked Congress for an extension of the embargo, with the proviso that the president could declare an exception to the act covering those places "with which a commercial intercourse may safely be renewed." The nickname given to this clause reflected the universal understanding in Congress that the clause would be invoked in the case of Saint-Domingue. Debate thus focused on this French colony.[40]

Federalists in Congress—in both the North and South—strongly advocated for the passage of the measure. Republicans were generally less enthusiastic. Pennsylvania's Albert Gallatin took the opposition's lead, resulting in a debate that was more partisan than regional. Adverting to possible independence for Saint-Domingue, he observed that the colony "is known to consist, almost altogether, of slaves just emancipated, of men who received their first education under the whip." These were a people, he added, "who have been initiated to liberty only by that series of rapine, pillage, and massacre that have laid waste and deluged that island in blood." Now, Gallatin said, he would like to see emancipation "when it can be properly effected, but no man would be more unwilling than I to constitute a whole nation of freed slaves, who had arrived to the age of thirty years, and thus to throw so many wild tigers on society." Having thus dismissed the humanity of the slaves who had liberated themselves by equating them with feral predatory animals, Gallatin helpfully added that "they might also become dangerous neighbors for the Southern States, and an asylum for renegadoes from those parts." The Republican leader on the issue had made it quite clear: taking a step that helped Toussaint gain independence would have the result of unleashing wild beasts on the American South.[41]

The Federalists were not shaken to the core by Gallatin's tocsin. The bill passed both houses of Congress and, on February 9, 1799, Adams signed it. The American administration had made what was, in the context of the time, the rather remarkable decision to open trade with a regime led by Blacks who had freed themselves from slavery. The US government, Scherr notes, was in no way moving toward recognition of an "independent black regime" on Hispaniola.[42] Still, it was a high point in US relations with what would become Haiti. But, once again, it was not possible to execute even so magnanimous a policy without the cooperation of the British; Adams had been correct about this. Thus, coordination with Great Britain had to be guaranteed before the terms of the Toussaint Clause could be put into effect. And to achieve this, Adams and company would need some quality diplomacy. Stevens was able to provide it.

Edward Stevens—a St. Croix native, physician, and childhood friend of Hamilton—developed a quick liking for the Black general whose background could not have been more different from his own. In correspondence with Pickering, the consul general praised Toussaint's "penetration and good sense" and commended his "humane and mild Conduct" in what had become a brutal civil war with Rigaud. Such was his conduct, in fact, that "Whites of the Colony . . . now look up to him as their only Shield against the cruel Tyranny of Rigaud." Where Gallatin saw mad beasts, Stevens saw a capable and moderate leader. Johnson rightly highlights the striking nature of the relationship between these two men. The seemingly routine gesture of a handshake between the two was, in fact, a significant event in the context of the time: "Shaking hands with a black person as a sign of mutual honor and respect represented a gesture unthinkable to most white Americans." Adams had chosen well.[43]

To prepare the way for Toussaint's Clause going into effect, Stevens negotiated with Maitland and Toussaint. As Brown emphasizes, the Adams administration—and thus Stevens—was trying to "straddle the horns of a dilemma." It wanted to open trade with the colony, but at the same time to tamp down on the dangers of privateering and the spread of slave revolt. The Maitland-Toussaint convention of June 13, 1799, cleared the way for the opening of trade by addressing all of these points. Of particular importance, Stevens wrote Pickering, was the insertion of the "Clause which I deemed so essential to the Security of the Southern States of America." By the terms of the agreement, Toussaint pledged that "there would be no expeditions against any possessions of His Majesty or the United States of America by the Troops of Saint-Domingue." With this promise, along with agreements regarding the suppression of privateering, Toussaint's Clause could now be put into effect. Thus, on June 26, Adams issued the proclamation. After some confusion, it actually went into effect on August 1. The resumption of trade was now an accomplished fact, and all sides had gotten what they most wanted.[44]

What Toussaint had most desired was supplies for his forces to allow them to take the battle to Rigaud. The agreement gave him this. In the view of Stevens, aid to Toussaint also benefited the United States. The consul general had no doubt that Toussaint's victory over Rigaud was in America's best interest. In writing Pickering, Stevens stressed the brutality of Rigaud, and compared the mulatto general quite negatively to the Black former slave with whom he had just treated. He added, "It will readily occur to you, Sir, that if Toussaint should prove unsuccessful, all the arrangements we have made respecting Commerce must fall to the Ground. The most solemn Treaty would have little weight with a man of Rigaud's capricious and tyrannical Temper. This circumstance points out the absolute necessity of supporting Toussaint by every legal measure." Stevens added that it might be useful if the US Navy would send some ships to the "South side of the Island" to help the Royal Navy choke off aid to Rigaud and his forces. Stevens was, to put a fine point on it, calling for US military intervention to aid Toussaint in the bloody civil war against Rigaud.[45]

The US Navy began to take active steps to interdict ships supplying Rigaud. But American intervention did not stop there. In an oft-noted intervention, the navy assisted Toussaint in his assault on Jacmel by bombarding Rigaud's fortifications. In March 1800 Toussaint, with the help of the American navy, took Jacmel, thus "pav[ing] the way for a complete victory for Toussaint's troops in the south."[46] While this intervention has been commented upon extensively, it bears again noting that the United States had engaged in its first foreign military intervention in order to aid a Black leader at the head of a Black army. The former slave seemed the better bet to help protect America's significant interests in the (increasingly nominal) French colony. The fact that American military and commercial intervention could well help solidify Toussaint's inclination—if he had one—to declare independence was a risk that Adams and company were willing to take. Racism against the Blacks, however, informed their thinking on this matter, with the presumption being shared at the highest level that, as Secretary of the Treasury Oliver Wolcott put it, "it is very problematical whether the Blacks will ever maintain regular habits of industry under the government of their own Chiefs." Secretary of State Pickering, seemingly the administration's most enthusiastic cheerleader for independence, shared Wolcott's assessment of Saint-Domingue's Black population. Toussaint, he wrote King, "cannot form a 'black republic'—the blacks are too ignorant." Alas, Toussaint had to take allies where he could find them.[47]

The question soon arose as to whether Toussaint could find them at all. The Adams policy toward Saint-Domingue had emerged within the context of an undeclared naval war with France. The Quasi-War had increased Toussaint's diplomatic leverage, as Saint-Domingue became, quite literally, a battleground in the conflict. He could not have desired a quick rapprochement between Paris and Washington, the new national capital of the Americans. Yet peace between France and the United States was hammered out at the end of September 1800. The Convention of 1800, also known as the Treaty of Mortefontaine, put an end to the Quasi-War. France was then engaged in the War of the Second Coalition, and needed no additional enemies. From the American perspective, the end of the 1778 alliance with France reduced the chances of being dragged into this European war. Both sides benefited from the conclusion of bilateral hostilities.

But Toussaint did not. News of peace between Paris and Washington struck him, in Logan's words, like a "thunderbolt," and "the wily general probably concluded that the United States would become less friendly since she no longer needed his assistance against France." Probably aware of the impact that the news from Mortefontaine would have in Saint-Domingue, the new secretary of state, John Marshall, sought to assuage Toussaint's fears, writing him on November 26, "Be Assured, Sir, of our sincere desire to preserve the most perfect harmony and the most friendly intercourse with St. Domingo, and that we shall rejoice at every occasion of manifesting this disposition compatible with those fixed principles, which regulate the conduct of our Government." Whether Toussaint found the Virginian's words reassuring has not been recorded. It is, however, rather doubtful that Toussaint was feeling confident about his future relationship with the United States, given that a slaveholder, Jefferson, had just been elected to the presidency. Any reassurance from the outgoing Federalists had to be weighed against concern that policy would change in Washington, both because of the Franco-American peace and the election of a southern Democratic-Republican.[48]

Had Toussaint had access to subsequent scholarship on Jefferson and Haiti, his anxiety would have known no bounds. The standard interpretation of Jefferson's Haitian policy notes a significant reversal from the cooperative and respectful policies implemented by Adams and the Federalists. Jefferson's primary motivator, it is alleged, was a fear that the contagion of slave revolution would spread. Thus, anticipating American security policy of a century and a half later, he adopted "containment" as his strategy. Dubois writes, for instance, that "Thomas Jefferson would ultimately move toward a policy of containment. With his eyes on Louisiana, he was clearly interested in limiting French power in the area, but he was also concerned about limiting the impact of the revolution on North America." A new administration of slaveholding southerners had moved into Washington and brought with it new priorities. Marshall, of course, had been a slaveholder as well. Yet under Adams he had sought to continue the policy of engagement. James Madison, Jefferson's secretary of state, did not. Johnson notes that Madison "began to dismantle Marshall's plan for closer relations with Saint-Domingue within weeks of Jefferson's inauguration." The shift, it would appear, was hardly short of radical.[49]

Scherr, however, challenges the received wisdom. He observes, correctly, that Jefferson allowed trade with Toussaint—including the trade in arms—to continue. In fact, Scherr concludes, "little difference existed between Jefferson's policy as president and that of Adams." This should not come as a complete surprise to careful students of the literature on the United States and the Haitian Revolution: Matthewson—a major target of Scherr's revisionism—grants that Jefferson's "sense of imperial priorities proved to be stronger than his racial concerns." Jefferson, indeed, sought to "contain" the spread of a Louverturian-type rebellion to Hispaniola. But so had Maitland, and, by association, Stevens. Jefferson's initial policy was not so much a radical departure as a nuanced shift from that of Adams, one that was likely to have occurred in some form under any administration holding office immediately after the Mortefontaine convention.[50]

Even before his election to the presidency, Jefferson showed signs of flexible thinking on the issue of American relations with Toussaint. While the Republicans generally, for instance, opposed Toussaint's Clause, Jefferson had come to be resigned to it. Writing Madison in early February 1799, he observed that the clause was designed "to facilitate the separation of the island from France." If so, he continued, then the Toussaint-Maitland agreement was "the best thing for us. they must get their provisions from us. it will indeed be in English bottoms, so that we shall lose the carriage. but the English will probably forbid them the ocean, confine them to their island, & thus prevent their becoming an American Algiers." Jefferson's analysis of relations with Saint-Domingue was focused on trade benefits and piracy, not race. It is instructive, as well, that he assumed "containment" would be seen to by the British. Again, Jefferson was showing himself broadly resigned to the Adams policy.[51]

After his election in the so-called Revolution of 1800, Jefferson continued his focus on trade and containment as the two pillars of American policy toward Saint-Domingue. Soon after taking office in March 1801, he met with the British minister to the United States, Edward Thornton, and spoke of the "establishment of a free and open trade for the subjects of [Britain and the United States], and the prevention of all maritime exertion on the part of the Negroes."[52] The suppression of the Blacks' "maritime exertion" would have the dual benefit of preventing the proliferation of both piracy and dangerous ideas. If London and Washington could agree on such a policy toward Toussaint's regime, then American interests should be well provided for.

To see to American interests in the colony itself, Jefferson removed Stevens and replaced him with Tobias Lear. The president's decision to downgrade the post from consul general to general commercial agent was hardly designed to reassure Toussaint. Nor was Toussaint pleased to find that Lear bore no letter addressed to him from Jefferson. As Lear explained in a letter, "I handed my Commission to the General, who asked me if I had not a letter for him from the President, or from the Government. I told him I had not, and explained the reason, as not being customary in missions of this kind, where I should be introduced by my Predecessor, and exhibit my Commission as evidence of my Appointment. He immediately returned my Commission without opening it, expressing his disappointment and disgust in strong terms, saying that his Colour was the cause of his being neglected, and not thought worthy of the Usual attentions." Lear sought to explain the reasoning behind this decision as a matter of protocol. But Toussaint, accustomed to corresponding with high-level members of the Adams administration, was not placated. He sent Lear, and his papers of commission, away until the next morning.[53]

The following day Toussaint reiterated his frustrations. This diplomatic snub would "hurt him in the eyes of his Chief Officers, when it was found that he was not thot. [sic] worthy of having a letter from the President or Government. . . . He appeared to be much hurt." But Toussaint was not in a position to allow relations with the United States to deteriorate, at least not if he could help it. Expressing again to Lear the "mortification he felt" at the shabby treatment he was receiving, he nevertheless accepted the representative's papers, stressing his "desire to preserve harmony and a good understanding with the United States." Still, these were worrying times for the general, who must necessarily have wondered what the power change in Washington boded for him and his future. For Toussaint, this was not so much a matter of slights as survival.[54]

Toussaint continued to seek to maintain the positive relationship—economic and diplomatic—that had flourished under Adams. But it would be a challenge, even for this new master of the diplomatic game. Jeffersonian Republicans were less solicitous of international trade than were the Federalists of the Northeast. Nor had Jefferson's fear of the exportation of slave rebellion from Saint-Domingue ever been fully assuaged. Gabriel's slave uprising in Jefferson's home state in 1800 gave him further reason to worry about this. So, too, it seemed, did Toussaint's invasion of the Spanish-held eastern two-thirds of His- paniola the following January. For one seeking evidence of the danger a free and potentially independent Black regime posed to the southern states, the evidence kept mounting.[55]

But the real threat to Toussaint's survival came not from Washington but from Paris. First Consul Napoleon Bonaparte had overthrown the Directory in November 1799. As Ott notes, the Directory had "planned to restore French authority in Saint-Domingue." Thus, Napoleon inherited the policy upon which he would act. And with his dream of an empire in the east shattered by his defeat on the River Nile, The first consul now looked to the west. As a first step, this meant restoration of French control over Saint-Domingue. For Tous- saint and his followers, an attempt by Napoleon to return the colony to met- ropolitan control was fraught with threats—and not just to their own power. In January 1800 Napoleon had issued a proclamation stating that slavery would never be reestablished on the colony. And in a further attempt to reassure his fellow general, the first consul named Toussaint captain general, thus going "so far as to acknowledge Toussaint's *de facto* military and political control of the colony." But at the same time, slave traders and planters, in France and the West Indies, respectively, were pressing Napoleon to restore slavery on the island. To seek to restore slavery to Saint-Domingue, however, was to play with fire; Toussaint had still not declared the colony independent. Yet a French at- tempt to restore slavery would leave the free Blacks with no real option but to seek independence from France. Toussaint's relationship with emancipation and labor was complicated, but a restoration of plantation slavery on Saint- Domingue was, for him, not an option.[56]

Napoleon's decision to wage war on Toussaint was made in early 1801. Yet he was in no position to launch any sort of seaborne invasion while the Royal Navy blocked his sea-lanes. A British peace feeler in May was, thus, a godsend for the first consul: peace with Britain would open up the opportunity to send the invasion force that was now assembling in Brest. The diplomatic process that would lead to the Treaty of Amiens in the following year provided the respite that he needed. Napoleon could, furthermore, rest assured that he would have the support of both Britain and the United States in his attempts to reduce Toussaint. At least, he assumed that that was the case.[57]

Napoleon made such an assumption because Charles-Maurice de Talleyrand-Périgord had been told so by Louis Pichon, the French minister

to Washington. Pichon met with the US president on July 19, and they engaged in a rather frank discussion of American policy toward Saint-Domingue.
During the conversation, Jefferson indicated that his administration would not
aid Toussaint. Pressed by Pichon as to whether the United States would cooperate with France in reducing Toussaint and regaining control over the colony,
Jefferson responded that it would, provided that France first "make peace with
England." If this were to happen, "nothing would be easier than to furnish
your army and fleet with everything, and to reduce Toussaint to starvation."
The message that Pichon gave to the regime in Paris was clear: the Jefferson
administration would assist in French military efforts to defeat Toussaint and
reclaim control over the colony.[58]

One must, however, take Scherr's analysis of this discussion seriously. The
report of the conversation utilized by scholars is Pichon's, and, thus, so is the
reporting of Jefferson's words. Indeed, Jefferson's promise was more "cryptic"
(according to Scherr) than Charles Callan Tansill would present it. Jefferson
may well, as Scherr concludes, have been "seeking to divert Bonaparte's search
for allies against Louverture from the United States to a most unlikely partner, the British." Much has been made of Jefferson's "starvation" comment.
A more productive line for scholars is, no doubt, to look at what Jefferson actually did rather than on what he allegedly promised to do.[59]

Madison's January 8, 1802, instructions to Lear become important in this
context. One presumes that Madison was well briefed on Jefferson's Saint-
Domingue policy. And in these instructions, one in fact finds something of a
shift toward France, though nothing indicating that American intervention on
France's side was imminent. Madison began by telling Lear of the confused
reports regarding British aid to France in her effort to reconquer Saint-
Domingue. The reports included one of a "supposed understanding between
the British and the French governments in pursuance of which the latter was
to be aided by the former in the means of transporting an effectual force to
St. Domingo. Such a cooperation however has not been indicated by any event
['overt' in the letter book copy] proceeding on the British side although it is
not improbable that a complete subversion of the example so much dreaded
by G. Britain may be favored by her." Madison's words are not exactly clear,
but presumably he meant the "subversion" of the "example" that a Black-run
country would present for Britain's empire.

Madison went on to note that there was no confusion about a second, related matter: the French were planning on sending an expeditionary force con-
sisting "of a large body of troops" to Saint-Domingue. He then instructed
Lear as to what approach to take in this situation: "In the present uncertainty
nothing better can be done for the direction of your conduct than to assist your

discretion by observing 1. That it is equally inconsistent with our duty and policy to take any step that would controvert or offend the authority of the French republic over St. Domingo or have the appearance of intermeddling in any manner in its affairs [and] 2. That as far as these considerations will permit it is desirable on the part of the United States to avoid every unnecessary irritation or umbrage to the people of the island." France and its interests were thus to be given priority by the American representative, with every effort, as far as possible given this priority, to avoid giving "unnecessary" offense to the residents of the former colony. No mention was made of American intervention; indeed, the goal seems to have been diplomatic caution at this point.[60]

This nevertheless indicated a clear theme in Jefferson's policy: the preference for France above Toussaint. As Tansill notes, "Jefferson was committed to a policy of co-operation with France against the black dictator, and the Department of State permitted [the United States'] official relations with Santo Domingo to decline to a vanishing point." The desire to see France balance out British power in the Caribbean was certainly a factor leading the president and his secretary of state to such a policy. So, too, however, was the nature of Toussaint's regime as a functionally independent government of the formerly enslaved. The administration feared the implications of such a regime. The 1800 Gabriel Conspiracy in Jefferson and Madison's native Virginia was likely not far from their minds. Jefferson and Virginia governor James Monroe worked under the assumption that the Haitian example had helped inspire this conspiracy. The rebellion made it that much more difficult for Jefferson to separate his fears of slave rebellion in the American South from his policy toward Toussaint.[61]

What is so stunning is that Jefferson's policy reversal came so soon after the Gabriel Conspiracy. But Jefferson had policy priorities in addition to preventing the spread of slavery. Most significant among these was the acquisition of Louisiana; as rumors of the retrocession of Louisiana by Spain to France began to reach Washington, the Napoleonic vision of an empire in the New World became more of a threat to American interests than Toussaint and his freed slaves. Jefferson proclaimed that the transfer of Louisiana to France "was very ominous to us."[62]

In assessing the potentially ominous implications of a French reconquest of Louisiana, United States slavery was much on the minds of the Republicans. Pennsylvanian and Madison correspondent Tench Coxe summarized the threat that French intervention in Louisiana posed. The French forces that arrived in the territory "will come thro the strainer of St. Domingo, and will keep up an extensive constant intimate connexion with the great Negro state. They are free. They are military. Their habits of subordination and labor are broken." The impact of a French "establishment" in Louisiana would thus be ominous indeed, since American contacts with the new French entity "may diffuse St. Domingo views among our blacks. Our southern states, a main republican limb of our sincere republican body, may thus be doubly affected." Coxe goes on to paint a fearful picture of the republican United States practically encircled by antirepublican elements. The French were rumored—correctly—to be preparing to send a large force to suppress Toussaint and his forces; as Coxe noted, "If they go, thro St Domingo, to Louisiana or half of them with the most dis[t]inguished Secret anti republicans of the French Army, and are combined with a black corps under some officer from thence of note, the sensation in the Southern states will be serious—and extensive. English, Spanish, Indians, St Domingo blacks, Manumitted Louisiana blacks, french Antirepublicans from Nova Scotia round out west to St Mary's will not be well. Tis ill to fear. Tis well to be aware of the worst and to watch symptoms & facts that may occur." In case Madison missed the point, Coxe reminded him that it "is impossible to be too much on our guard against the consequences of a large detachment of republican blacks from St. Domingo to *Louisiana*, accompanied by the sudden emancipation of the blacks *there*." French plans thus posed a threat to slavery in the American South. Madison had expressed—if more succinctly—a similar concern to Robert Livingston the previous September, indicating the seriousness with which the administration took this threat.[63]

Perhaps it was ill to fear. But the French were coming, and Toussaint was preparing to meet them. He would have under his command perhaps as many as thirty thousand soldiers to meet a French force of roughly comparable size under the leadership of General Charles Victor Emmanuel Leclerc—Napoleon's brother-in-law. Napoleon considered the force sufficient, for, notes Ott, "he was so contemptuous of the blacks that he believed that a small French army could sweep them aside in a few weeks." Napoleon instructed Leclerc to indicate a willingness to work with Toussaint, in order to be able to land his forces on the island. He was, later, to go back on this, deporting the Black leaders and reestablishing colonial rule over Saint-Domingue. Thus, Napoleon was, in Girard's words, "relying more on deception and collaboration than brute force." Included in Napoleon's plans was a reassurance from the first consul himself that the French would not restore slavery on the island. Taking this approach, Napoleon could convince himself that things would go better for the French invasion force than they had for the British.[64]

The Jefferson administration's response to the Leclerc expedition was one of grave concern. It certainly worried about the costs to American trade of a new French mercantilist regime over Saint-Domingue. Even more disturbing was the implication for Louisiana. The colony of Saint-Domingue would always be dependent upon imports of food, lumber, and other needs that its coffee, cotton, and sugar plantations could not provide—products that the United States had been shipping, to great financial benefit. And if Saint-Domingue was not to get these commodities from the United States, it nevertheless had to get them somewhere. For Napoleon, Louisiana would be the granary that would keep the colony supplied with the goods that it could not produce for itself, thus allowing a return to the glory days of the rich export economy of the colony. As Ott has observed, mercantilism and the Louisiana issue were thus tightly bound, as Napoleon "seemed to be striving to make Louisiana and Saint-Domingue a closely correlated economic unit." Had Napoleon been seeking to devise a policy that threatened America's perceived vital interests, he could hardly have done better.[65]

As early as late October 1801—and thus a month prior to Leclerc's departure for the New World—Rufus King was sending warnings from London. "It is confidently believed," he informed Madison, "that a considerable Expedition composed of land & Sea forces, is preparing in france, and will soon proceed to St. Domingo, and perhaps to the Mississippi." The prospect of seeing a French army in Louisiana was extremely alarming. It became even more so when reports of the size of the French force began filtering in. Lear wrote to the secretary of state from Cap Français on February 12, 1802, and delivered the distressing news. He reported that a force of thirty-two ships of the line and fourteen frigates had already arrived with forty thousand troops. As if this were not bad enough, another twenty-five ships and twenty thousand soldiers would be arriving in the future. As he summarized, "This is certainly an immense naval Armament for *this Island*." The "immense" size of the force itself thus raised the uncomfortable question of its ultimate goal. And this, the Americans assumed, was Louisiana.[66]

The Jefferson administration thus adopted the policy of allowing the United States to become the arsenal for the formerly enslaved Blacks of Saint-Domingue. Far from helping to starve Toussaint, the administration kept his forces well supplied. As Matthewson observes, the French expedition to Saint-Domingue "led Jefferson to conclude that the black rebels would be less dangerous under Toussaint's leadership than under the rule of the French." Jefferson had not changed his thoughts on slave revolts. But he was willing to provide for the needs of the former slaves who could bog down Leclerc and, thus, prevent his moving on Louisiana. It was a significant change.[67]

The aid to Toussaint's forces was significant. And it was frustrating to the French. Not long after his arrival, Leclerc expressed this frustration to the minister of the marine in Paris. It was the United States, he complained, that was bringing to Saint-Domingue "the guns, the cannons, the powder and all the munitions of war. It is they who arouse [*excité*] Toussaint to defense." In Leclerc's mind, there could be only one conclusion: the Americans were seeking the independence of all of the Antilles in order to "have exclusive commerce" in that region. Not long after, Pichon lectured Madison that a slaveholding nation like the United States had an interest and obligation to avoid providing munitions and supplies to the "rebel blacks." Clearly, the French already perceived American provisions to be helping Toussaint and his forces.[68]

With American aid in hand, Toussaint's forces were able to put up significant resistance to Leclerc's troops. But neither Toussaint nor Leclerc would be present for the last act of the drama. On June 6, 1802, Toussaint was captured by French officers. He was soon put aboard a ship and deported to France, where he died in prison the following year. Leclerc died in November 1802, succumbing to yellow fever like so many of his troops. In all, disease would kill over half of the troops sent by France to subdue the colony. The French forces, like the British before them, proved unable to subdue the former slaves of Saint-Domingue. By the autumn of 1802, Ott notes, "nature, neglect, stupidity, and black resistance combined to pull the 'colony' in the direction of the rebels."[69]

The chief culprit in the category of stupidity was Napoleon's decision to restore slavery in Saint-Domingue. As the Blacks perceived the direction that the first consul was moving, they came to equate their continued freedom with their future independence. And on the first day of the new year, General Jean-Jacques Dessalines would take the step that Toussaint never had: he proclaimed Haiti the second independent nation in the Western Hemisphere. The declaration of independence was, according to Dubois, "a furious attack on the brutalities of the French, and a call for the members of the new nation to reject forever the past of empire and slavery."[70] Slavery had come to an end in Haiti as the result of the struggles of the formerly enslaved. That they had succeeded in their struggle for liberation with the help of the slaveholding US republic was an irony that speaks to the complexity of the role of slavery in the making of American foreign policy.

Conclusion: The Persistence of the Slavery Issue

For decades the United States refused to recognize the independent nation that it had—if inadvertently—helped to foster. While a few policymakers, such as Pickering, had hoped that Toussaint would declare independence, the existence of a state run by self-manumitted slaves was not easy for most Americans to swallow. The fear of the example that it posed to slaves in the American South continued after 1803.[71] Like other nations, the United States "played a long game that included talking and trading with Haiti while steadfastly refusing to grant the country official recognition."[72] In fact, the issue was not resolved until 1862, the same year that President Abraham Lincoln signed the Emancipation Proclamation; that year the United States accorded diplomatic recognition to Haiti. The prospective freeing of America's slaves had thus made the matter of Haiti's example moot.

Slavery had never been the sole determinant of the American response to the Haitian slave revolution. The interconnected issues of commerce and national security were major factors in helping to determine the US course in the Caribbean from 1791 until 1803. Yet American attitudes toward slavery, interacting with these other two issues, helped shape this response in significant ways. But America's failure to extend recognition to the newly liberated nation to the south indicates that slavery would continue to be an issue for US policymakers for decades to come.

And yet, the Haitian revolution was no isolated event. It was, rather, "just one more manifestation of a growing opposition to African slavery." The legitimacy of the institution itself was, increasingly, being called into question in the Atlantic world. The most significant front in the struggle against slavery in the early 1800s would come in the form of the assault on the Atlantic slave trade.[73]

CHAPTER 3

"Separate from Foreign Alliances"
Limiting Connections and Commitments

Heinous, barbarous, detestable, inhuman, and even *flagitious*: the adjectives used in the early nineteenth century to describe the Atlantic slave trade leave little doubt that the practice was then seen as what would now be called a crime against humanity. This may come as a surprise to the contemporary reader, who, it is presumed, will view the entire practice of slavery in the Atlantic world to be a criminal enterprise and will consider all of those involved in any of its aspects as morally culpable. Yet the evidence is overwhelming: even large numbers of slaveholders—who felt justified in exercising brutal dominion over their fellow human beings—recoiled at the means by which these same people had been captured in Africa, transported across the ocean, and sold in the New World. Recent historical writing echoes this perception of the traffic as something singularly abominable. Scholars have pointed especially to the horrid Middle Passage—or Maafa, the "disaster"—as an outlier in the history of modern humans' inhumanity; as Brenda E. Stevenson notes, "Maafa has come to symbolize the violence, abuse, and horror of the Atlantic trade and, indeed, slavery itself. It is for good reason. Enslaved Africans, already traumatized in multiple ways by the time they boarded, were subject to even more barbaric treatment as they crossed the Atlantic. The devastating conditions were beyond description for some and most simply were not comparable to other oceanic travel experiences of the day." The trade's "violence, abuse, and horror" were well known at the time as well. Visitors to various slave societies in the Americas found themselves able to descant on the relative merits of this versus that slave system in terms of treatment of the enslaved.[1] But the record left by those with experience on slavers is one of scarcely mitigated atrocity.[2] It thus comes as no surprise that as the institution of slavery began to be questioned more aggressively in the Atlantic world, the first of its manifestations to come under assertive attack should be the trade in slaves.

Origins of Opposition

Thomas Jefferson began early in the verbal assault on the trade. In his first draft of the Declaration of Independence, he asserted that King George III "has waged cruel war against human nature itself, violating it's [sic] most sacred rights of life & liberty in the persons of a distant people who never offended him, captivating and carrying them into slavery in another hemisphere, or to incur miserable death in their transportation thither."[3] This act of condemnatory blame shifting did not make it into the final draft of the declaration. Yet it serves as an indicator of the contemporaneous realization that a people calling on nature's law to justify their revolutionary cause could not long continue to act so patently in violation of it.

Whether seeking to shift the blame for the trade or to make amends for complicity in it, much of the Anglo-American world was condemning it by the end of the eighteenth century. Early in the nineteenth, condemnation had turned into active legal, even military, attempts to suppress it. While not all supported the efforts, even those who appealed to its economic necessity were likely to cite "their personal moral opposition to the slave trade."[4] With such consensus that the trade was an evil—necessary or otherwise—what could possibly hamper the success of suppression efforts?

Actually, there was much that could—and did. Among the most significant impediments was hostility and mistrust in Anglo-American relations, especially in the arena of British naval policy. This suspicion amplified the already strong American desire to keep strictly limited its formal cooperation with any European power in any area except legitimate commerce. Slavery drew the Americans increasingly into the international relations of the Atlantic world. But it was in the matter of the suppression of the trade, more than on any other, that American policymakers sought to keep that involvement within tight bounds. Additionally, southerners began increasingly to fear the connection between abolition of the trade and general abolition of the institution of slavery.[5] The result was mutual frustration, much barren diplomacy, increasing enmity, and, in the end, an inability for decades to achieve what both London and Washington, DC, claimed to want: an end to the cruel trade.

The economic development of America's slaveholding regions significantly affected the domestic politics of slave trade suppression as time progressed. As a general rule, legislators from the Upper South and Border States were more likely to support the suppression of the trade than were their counterparts in the Deep South. A decline in tobacco prices, together with the depletion of soil nutrients that resulted from cultivation of that crop, led growers in the Upper South to switch increasingly to the farming of wheat. This was now a more profitable crop, and it did not rapidly lead to erosion and soil exhaustion as did tobacco. It was also not as labor intensive as cotton production, and the work was seasonal. As a result, planters found themselves with a surplus of slaves, whom they were now motivated to sell. Meanwhile, the growth in cotton production in what came to be called the Black Belt created a demand for slaves in that region. Slaveholders in the Upper South now had an economic interest in restricting supply and thus securing a higher price for the slaves whom they could sell to farther south and west. This financial incentive—added to the perception of the baleful effects of slavery on white society and a legitimate repulsion to the horrors of the transatlantic trade—helps explain these men's desire to see an end to the international trade.[6]

Banning the Trade

It is sometimes said that the US Constitution provided for an end to the slave trade in 1808. In fact, the Constitution provided that importation of slaves could not be *prevented* until that year, and that this provision was not amendable. But as 1808 approached, and the topic of the slave trade was taken up by Congress, the regional fault lines already began to appear, even if less vociferously than would later be the case. When in December 1803 South Carolina's legislature voted to once again allow the importation of slaves, Congress quickly took up a bill that would tax each African imported. Representatives who were hostile to slavery used this opportunity to declaim not only against the reopening of the trade—South Carolina was now the only state to allow importations—but also against slavery itself. Representative David Bard of Pennsylvania gave voice to such thoughts, proclaiming that slavery, and not just the trade, "is radically unjust, and violates the principles of morality." Slavery also, he added, affected America's standing in the eyes of other nations. Americans had denounced "tyranny and oppression." Yet what would foreigners think of the Republic's character "when they examine our census and find that we hold a million men in the most degraded slavery?" What, indeed, should other nations conclude, but that "we possess the principles of tyranny, but want the power to carry them into operation, except against the untutored and defenceless African"?[7] Slavery damaged foreign perceptions of the United States, and especially so in light of its clear contradiction of America's revolutionary rhetoric. While some members thought the tax was an unfair burden on a single state, "not a single voice was raised in defense" of South Carolina's act. In fact, "by all its existence was deprecated."[8]

Given this consensus in Congress, it was clear that Charleston would not long be open to slavers: 1808 was fast approaching, and, with it, an almost certain ban on importation. The president was also urging Congress to act, calling in December 1806 for legislation that would end the trade on January 1, 1808. As Matthew E. Mason notes, "In contrast to his record on slavery in general,' in fact, Jefferson proved effective and decisive in his opposition to the international slave trade."[9] The trade thus became illegal on the first day that the Constitution allowed.

The 1807 legislation was actually the culmination of a "congressional attack on the slave trade that had begun in 1790" with Congress's assertion of its authority to restrict American participation in the trade. The 113–5 vote indicated "an aversion to the slave trade that varied in intensity but was prevalent across most of the nation," while the near "national consensus" on the subject "seemed to promise a high level of compliance." But the promise of the legislative actions was not realized for decades. Don E. Fehrenbacher writes of "impressive legislation" but "faulty enforcement."[10]

The Failure of International Enforcement

The significant failures of enforcement frequently stemmed from the international context in which slave trade suppression had to take place if it were to be successful. Like the trade itself, the problem of suppression was a multinational, transatlantic problem. The fact that the United States was, over the course of administration after administration, resistant to participation in the British-sponsored international regime to suppress the trade may not be surprising. But Washington's refusal to do so made elimination of the Atlantic slave trade impossible. It was not until 1862 that the administration of President Abraham Lincoln would accede to the key component of the British treaty system, the right of search of US-flagged vessels. At that point, with the Union in dire peril, President Lincoln and Secretary of State William H.

Seward were less concerned with the rights of neutrals on the seas than they were with preventing European support for the Confederate cause.[11]

The British came to the slave trade suppression table at essentially the same time as did the Americans. In the same year that Congress passed the law banning the slave trade, Parliament passed the Slave Trade Act 1807, which became law in May 1808. With this act Britain prohibited slave trade with its colonies. In its first years, enforcement was not much of a problem: given the general war in Europe, Britain was able to seize the slave ships of France, and of France's allies the Netherlands and Spain, at this time. For the duration of the war, the trade was largely suppressed.[12]

But the end of the Napoleonic Wars brought with it the likelihood that the slave trade would be revived. As Reginald Coupland notes, "When at last the end of the war came in sight, it was clear that, unless something were done to prevent it, the West European Trade, especially that of France . . . would recover all of its old proportions." By this time, a peace of this sort had become completely unacceptable. Antislavery "became part of the British self-definition" at the time when Europe was moving from war to peace.[13] Something would have to be done to prevent other nations from using the cover of peacetime to reestablish their lucrative slave trades.

Initially the hope was to use a series of international conferences, set to put Europe right after more than two decades of war, to convince the other European nations to join Britain in prohibiting the trade. Going into these congresses, London could well expect that Britain would be able to exert considerable influence in this matter, as in others. Jeremy Black explains that "Britain's influence on other states rose greatly as a result of her major, and eventually successful, role in resistance to revolutionary and Napoleonic France from 1793–1815. Britain emerged from its wars with France as the preeminent global power."[14] The British foreign secretary, the redoubtable Lord Castlereagh, could well expect to carry the day on an issue of such vital importance— and clear moral purpose—at the upcoming diplomatic conferences.

Castlereagh was, in a sense, right. But he was also a realist. The British foreign secretary "foresaw from the outset that it would not be difficult to obtain from the Congress some general moral condemnation of the traffic in slaves; the difficulties would arise when it came to putting this general principle into practice." He was correct in this estimate. The Final Act of the Congress of Vienna indeed issued a general moral condemnation of the slave trade. And though it was nonspecific regarding implementation, it was not meaningless. No signatory nation could now "reject diplomatic initiatives concerning [the trade] as interference in domestic affairs."[15] So far, so good.

British policy came to be based on the creation of an interlocking network of alliances after failure of initial diplomacy to achieve specifics as to the means of suppression. Castlereagh proceeded, in short order, to achieve most of the treaties. Frustrations arose, nevertheless, with the half-hearted efforts of the signatories to actually do the work of suppression.[16] Of all the powers "abolishing" the trade by treaty, "only Britain took the requisite steps to ensure that her law was *strictly and continuously* obeyed." Particularly frustrating for Castlereagh and the British was French "nonchalance" with regard to abolishing the trade. After agreeing to do so, Paris was, in fact, doing precious little. According to Coupland, "Having conceded abolition to appease Britain, nobody in the government gave it further thought."[17] The French Navy showed "but little zeal" in pursuing a mission of which they, in the majority, disapproved.[18]

British vexation with treaty signatories was significant and persistent. But a different set of problems was to be had with the slaveholding republic on the other side of the Atlantic; a nation that had recently fought a war with Britain, and which had reason to be suspect of British motives. The causes of the War of 1812 are debatable. But what is clear is that impressment "served as the key justification for the war once it began."[19] Memories of this issue on the part of the Americans would bedevil attempts to end the trade in slaves for half a century. Thus, as much as successive administrations might have desired to end the trade, they were unwilling to take the vital step necessary to do so.

The United States had abolished the slave trade by law. But legislating against the trade and actually stopping it were two different matters. James Madison acknowledged as much in his December 3, 1816 address to Congress. The president noted that the United States had gone first in banning the importation of slaves, as well as the punishment of citizens who participated in it. And Americans could be "gratified" by the efforts that other nations were making toward suppression. With this being the case, Americans must feel, at the same time, "the greater solicitude, to give the fullest efficacy to their own Regulations." He therefore called for further action by Congress due to "the violations and evasions which, it is suggested, are chargeable on unworthy Citizens who mingle in the Slave-trade under Foreign Flags, and with Foreign Ports, and by collusive importations of Slaves, into the United States, through adjoining ports and territories." Thus, the president called upon Congress once again to act, "with a full assurance of their disposition to apply all the remedy which can be afforded by an amendment of the law."[20]

Congress indeed took up the issue, and in 1818 passed a new law that facilitated prosecution of those accused of participation in the trade. The congressional debate over the suppression of the trade is instructive, since it raised the central issue at play in the diplomacy that would follow—namely, to what extent ought the United States participate in a collaborative effort with other maritime powers to interdict the trade in slaves. On the second day of 1818, Senator George Troup, a Democratic-Republican from Georgia, rose to oppose a section of a resolution dealing with suppression of the slave trade. The senator objected to the final clause of this sense of the Senate resolution, since it called for a "concert with other nations" in pursuit of an end to the trade in humans. According to Troup, "no measure could be adopted more replete with danger to the welfare, to the very existence of this country, than a formal coalition, for any purposes, with any foreign nation whatever." Troup could not "separate from foreign alliances the idea of foreign politics and foreign wars; and the proposed measure he should view as the commencement of a system of foreign connections tending to foreign alliances, to which Mr. T[roup] expressed great repugnance."[21] The rejection of multilateralism was categorical. The problem with a unilateral approach, however, was that it was unlikely to be successful in achieving the goal of ending the slave trade.

Senator James Burrill, a Federalist from Rhode Island, made this point clearly in response to Troup. The United States, in Burrill's opinion, ought indeed to work with other maritime nations in suppressing the trade, "because it was only by such concert and co-operation that the slave trade could be abolished." It was, in fact, "impossible to put an entire stop to it without a co-operation among the nations prohibiting it; for, no matter how many nations prohibit the trade, if one or two are allowed to carry it on, the evil will still exist." The issue was decidedly not one of entanglements in foreign politics, he added. In fact, he "had no idea of [the resolution's] authorizing the slightest interference with the international affairs of other nations, or of allowing them to interfere in ours."[22]

Unfortunately for the British, they would find that the administration of President James Monroe inclined toward Senator Troup's framing of the issue. In early October 1820 the British minister to Washington, George Canning, met for over two hours with Secretary of State John Quincy Adams. His goal was to convince the Americans to accede to the right of British warships to search US-flagged vessels in pursuit of slavers. Reciprocal right of search was the basis for the interlocking system of treaties that Britain had negotiated for the suppression of the trade. Castlereagh was, however, aware that this treaty structure was doomed to fail without the participation of all of the major maritime powers. Yet the United States remained outside the system. A central thrust of British foreign policy at this time would thus be to convince the Americans to accede to the right of search.

As Adams summarized the British proposal in his memoirs, "The United States should accede to the principles of the treaties made by Great Britain with the Netherlands and Portugal, by which the vessels of either nation are allowed to be searched by the captains of the armed vessels of another, and two mixed Courts of Commissioners are instituted to try all such captures." The secretary of state then went on to delineate the American objections to both aspects of the British scheme. First, the federal government lacked all constitutional authority to establish such courts. As to the mutual right search, the administration disapproved of "the principle of allowing the search, in time of peace, of our merchant vessels by armed cruisers from another nation." The objections would appear lock solid, and especially the constitutional objection to the mixed courts. After all, what nation could speak with more authority on the proper interpretation of the US Constitution than the United States? Adams added, correctly, that the Americans were not the only holdouts: "France has been the most decisive in her objections."[23]

Yet Castlereagh, and thus Canning, were not to be discouraged by American reluctance. The British minister sought to convince the American secretary, at their October 2 meeting, that the latter's objections could be successfully addressed. Canning began by suggesting that one of the two proposed reciprocal courts might "be established within the United States"—thus, it would appear, addressing the constitutional issue. Adams brought him up short, adding that there were additional, broader reasons, for American refusal to participate in the British treaty system. The first of these was "the general extra-European policy of the United States—a policy which they had always pursued as best suited to their own interests and best adapted to harmonize with those of Europe. This policy had also been that of Europe, which had never considered the United States as belonging to her system." Since the end of the Napoleonic Wars, the great powers of Europe had "regulated the affairs of all Europe without ever calling the United States to their consultations." This was a good thing, and it "was best for both parties that they should continue to do so." After all, the United States would bring to any such deliberations "some principles not congenial to those of the other members, and those principles would lead to discussions tending to discord rather than harmony." Thus, in the interest of maintaining transatlantic good will, the Unites States must remain outside of any European diplomatic combination.[24]

Adams went on to add a second, more specific objection to Castlereagh's proposal. Britain's past policy of impressment now precluded any future American concession on the right of search. As Adams noted, "we had had one war with Great Britain for exercising what she alone claims of all the nations of the earth as a right—search of neutral vessels in time of war to take out men." During both the peace negotiations in 1814 and since, the United States had sought to come to an agreement with Britain on this matter but had been frustrated in this attempt. It remained, nevertheless, "a point upon which, more than any other, not only the people but the Government of the United States were sensitive." The secretary's rejection of the British proposal was thus categorical, as the administration was fixed in "the determination in no case to yield the right of search in time of peace."[25] Past British actions had poisoned the well. London could not now expect the Americans to concede in time of peace what it had rejected in time of war.

Canning, undaunted, sought to address Adams's objections to the concession of the right of search. He did not, he began, see "any analogy" between what the British were now seeking from the Americans and the issue that had done so much to provoke war between the two nations in 1812. After all, in the current case, the "right of search given was entirely reciprocal." The Netherlands and Portugal had seen fit to assent. These were, he implied, nations that were less capable than France and the United States of protecting their interests. Why, then, should "nations justly conscious of their power" hesitate to sign on? Adams responded forthrightly, concerned that "all concessions of principle tended to encourage encroachment." Give British naval officers the right to board ships for one thing in a time of peace and they would be "still more encouraged" to do so for another reason in time of war. As to the Netherlands and Portugal, "they might be supposed to be actuated by a sense of dependence upon or of obligation to Great Britain."[26] In reporting the results of the conversation to Castlereagh, Canning was left to seek the silver lining that he could. He was, he said, "gratified" to find that Adams willingly granted that the current measures in place for suppressing the trade were inadequate.[27] Beyond that, it was difficult to find too much encouragement for the British in Adams's line of diplomacy.

This lengthy discussion of the issues between Britain and the United States anticipated the extensive diplomatic back-and-forth between the two nations on the issue of slave trade suppression. Of course, "it seemed a little ungracious to be nursing the grievances of 1812 whenever the British Minister called." Castlereagh, for his part, had expressed the sense that, if the Monroe administration were to continue to reject the British system for suppression, then it should be invited to "point out in return how, in their judgment, the evil is to be cured—for we must hope that so enlightened a State is not prepared supinely to acquiesce in the continued existence of so flagrant an immorality."[28] Canning was thus to keep up the diplomatic effort.

In early December the House of Representatives called upon President Monroe to submit the diplomatic correspondence of the administration concerning the slave trade. Canning appears to have taken this as an opportunity to reopen the conversation and called on Adams for another lengthy conversation on the December 18, during which Adams "told him that there was no change in the President's opinions concerning the British proposals." But the secretary suggested that Canning submit an aide-memoire of Britain's recent proposals. Canning did so on December 20. In this note he indicated that "it is generally acknowledged that, a combined system of Maritime Police can alone afford the means of putting it [the slave trade] down with effect." He once again called for cooperation between the English-speaking naval powers. Such a concert, he thought, could not be rejected in light of the desire on both sides to put an end to "a practice so flagrantly immoral."[29]

The House's inquiry was not, however, to open up new vistas for the institution of joint commissions for the prosecution of slavers. In his response to Canning's December 20 memorandum, Adams at length restated the constitutional impossibility of American accession to this scheme, stressing "the incompetency of this government, to become a party to the institution of Tribunals organized like those" that Britain had created with the cooperation of the Iberian nations and the Netherlands. Such courts, furthermore, would violate the "Constitutional rights guaranteed to every citizen of the Union." No American could be "called to answer for any penal offense, without the intervention of a Grand Jury to accuse, and of a Jury of Trial to decide upon the charge." While Monroe and Adams were on firm constitutional ground in this assertion, this did nothing to help the cause of suppression. To address this problem, Adams proposed a system of joint cruising of British and American naval ships on the African coast. In granting this concession, the president and secretary of state evinced a willingness, however limited, to go beyond the strict American unilateralism that had marked their policy up to this point. American and British naval commanders off Africa could thus "be ordered, whenever the occasion may render it convenient, to cruize [sic] in company together—to communicate mutually to each other all information, obtained by the one, and which may be useful to the execution of the duties of the other, and to give each other every assistance which may be compatible with the performance of their own service, and adapted to the end which is the common aim of both parties."[30] This carefully worded concession to British importuning was as far as Monroe and Adams were willing to go in the direction of multilateralism on the slave trade front. As Adams noted, he had written the response to Canning, refusing to accede to the right of search, "in terms of the strongest character, with a view to leave no occasion for further discussion upon the subject."[31]

The only concession—the stipulation of joint cruising—was hardly likely to solve the problem of slavers hiding under the American flag. But it was something, and Castlereagh soon instructed the Admiralty to "use their best endeavours to cooperate, as far as may be in their power, with such American ships as may be placed on the Coast of Africa" for the purpose of apprehending slavers. Canning nevertheless complained to Adams just a few days after receiving the December 30 note that "the proposals in my [Adams's] note would be quite inadequate to the object proposed, the effectual suppression of the trade." To Adams it was "very apparent that Mr. Canning was in no wise satisfied with our proposed substitute; nor is it to be expected that his Government will be more so."[32]

It was not. While discussions continued regarding the number of American ships to be deployed to Africa, and the methods of joint cruising, Canning could not hold back from observing to Adams that the British government had "felt the deepest regret" to learn that the US government would not participate in the "mutual Engagements" that were required to effectually suppress the trade in Africans. Despite Adams's attempt in his December 30 letter to indicate that the time had come to drop the whole matter of the British proposals, Canning made manifest yet again that "it is not possible for His Majesty to consider the Counter-proposal, contained in your letter, as an efficient substitute for the system of measures which I have had the honour of proposing to you." Yet "such is the King's benevolent anxiety to co-operate with the Government of The United States, in whatever may tend, in the slightest degree, to mitigate the evils of the Slave-trade, that His Majesty is willing even to avail himself of the present very limited opening to a concert between the two countries."[33] His pen thus veritably dripping with regret, Canning went about his duty to facilitate the limited cooperation to which the Americans had acceded. Had he even the slightest hope, however, Adams sought to put that to rest. In his response to Canning's note, the secretary of state once again reviewed American objections to British proposals, explaining that, in fact, the US proposal for cooperation by joint cruising was "better adapted to the suppression of the Traffick than that of the British Government."[34] Joint cruising it was to be.

In early 1819 Congress had passed a law, signed by Monroe in early March, authorizing the president to deploy ships to the African coast in furtherance of the suppression of the slave trade. The bill also provided for a twenty-five-dollar-per-slave bounty to the captain and crew of the ship making the seizure, though an amendment prescribing the death penalty for slavers was removed by the Senate. The following year both houses of Congress concurred on a bill that equated slaving with piracy. Slave traders, as pirates, were now subject to the death penalty. In this sense, at least, "the American law against the slave trade [was] the most strenuous in existence."[35] In August 1821 Adams forwarded to Canning instructions that were to be issued "immediately" to

US naval ships charged with interdicting slavers on the African coast. The Americans were to cooperate with the British Navy "by all suitable means" and to engage in joint cruising "should the occasion occur in which [the American commanders] may find it mutually convenient."[36]

None of this meant, however, that the British had permanently given up their attempt to get the United States to sign on to a right of search. By year's end, Adams and Canning were at it again. The two met on December 4 and spoke for three hours. The conversation was wide ranging but, necessarily, came to the topic of the slave trade. Canning had spoken with the French minister to the United States, Baron Hyde de Neuville, about the slave trade, and found him to be foursquare in favor of suppression. Reflecting the position of his government, however, Neuville was also opposed to the right of search, even while admitting that it was the best way to end the trade. Canning used his report of the conversation with Neuville to raise the issue, yet again, of the American position on the right of search. Indefatigably, the British minister remarked that he thought that the US government "should ultimately be convinced of the necessity" of agreeing to the right of search.

Adams could not have been more categorical this time in his rejection, nor clearer on the key reason: "I said that it was impossible. There were objections of the most serious nature against the thing itself in any shape; but unless Britain would bind herself by an article, as strong and explicit as language can make it, never again in time of war to take a man from an American vessel, we never for a moment could listen to a proposal for allowing a right of search in time of peace." Lest Canning get the idea that this unambiguous rejection contained a seed of hope, Adams quickly made clear that, as far as he was concerned, negotiations with London over impressment were off the table: "We had exhausted negotiation in endeavoring to make an arrangement with Great Britain on the subject of impressment. We had failed, and were not desirous of obtaining the object by indirect means. The proposal must come from them, if they were prepared for it."[37] Both Adams and Canning well knew that the government of the Earl of Liverpool was decidedly not willing to propose an end to impressment. There seemed no room for diplomatic maneuver: London remained frustrated with Washington's refusal to accede to the right of search, while Washington despaired of ever convincing London to renounce the despised practice of impressment.

Such was London's commitment to effective suppression of the trade, however, that even the definitive nature of Adams's statements was not enough to daunt Canning and Castlereagh—not for long, in any event. Both saw opportunity in the actions of Congress. The House of Representatives had constituted a committee on the slave trade, which was in the habit of issuing reports that went against clear policy direction coming from the Monroe administration. In both 1821 and 1822 the committee had recommended adopting the right of search as an effective means of combating the trade. Castlereagh would seek opportunity where he could find it. In April 1822 he spoke with the American minister to London, Richard Rush. The foreign secretary expressed his hope that, as "unfavorable the language of the American Government was to our wishes," the 1822 report of the House Committee on the Suppression of the Slave Trade "still gave ground for hope, that, upon the principles therein laid down, some joint Measure could, in the end, be arranged between the Two Countries." In addition to previous suggestions, which had already been rejected, Castlereagh hoped at this point for joint Anglo-American "representations" to Paris, urging the French to do more to suppress the trade which "is still very extensively carried on under their Flag." Castlereagh, therefore, urged Rush to raise the matter with Adams, stressing the "great advantages which might be expected" if the two English-speaking powers were to unite in diplomatic pressure on France.[38]

Rush, complying with the foreign minister's request, wrote out a memorandum of this conversation. To the extent that Rush can be assumed to have accurately summarized Castlereagh's words, the memorandum is revealing. The Briton had taken heart from the report of the House committee, which "opened a new hope to him that The United States might accede to some System" that allowed the right of search. Additionally, he hoped that a way could be found to make the mixed tribunal system accord with the American Constitution. Finally, a joint Anglo-American approach to France "would not be without its effect in overcoming the scruples that had hitherto existed with that Power" regarding mutual search. Duly summarizing Castlereagh's fond wishes, Rush reports adding that "I had not the least expectation of my Government agreeing to the mutual Right of Search, under whatever modification or circumstances the proposition might be again exhibited, but on the contrary, entertained the most decided and unequivocal belief . . . that its objections to it in every shape would be insurmountable."[39] Rush was, indeed, correct in his assumptions. In the last weeks of his life, Castlereagh was to learn from Canning that the House did not, in fact, take up the slave trade committee's report. Nor had it done so the previous year, under similar circumstances. And at that point, in March 1821, Adams had made clear to Canning that the president "would not have changed his policy" even if Congress had voted the resolutions. Castlereagh perceived a division within the US government on the question of the right of search.[40] But with Adams directing foreign policy for the Monroe administration, there was no chance that even a more united Congress could have brought a change in policy. When Canning met with

Adams in mid-July, the secretary described Monroe as "still decidedly adverse to the Right of Search." Likewise, there was nothing to be expected from the administration when it came to a joint diplomatic approach to Paris.[41] Castlereagh never received Canning's report of this meeting with Adams; by the time his note arrived in London, the foreign secretary had committed suicide.

His successor, Stratford Canning's cousin George, proved equally persistent in attempting to bring America into the British system of slave trade suppression. Yet again, Adams proved up to the task of limiting American commitments to those it could execute unilaterally. Foreign Secretary George Canning could have been forgiven had he found the situation that he inherited dispiriting. Minister Stratford Canning's most recent meeting with Adams "present[ed] no very satisfactory prospect of the co-operation to be expected on the part of The United States, in our efforts for repressing that abominable Traffick," he observed. And the news of similar discussion in Paris was "hardly less discouraging." The foreign secretary found it "most unfortunate" that Monroe "should see anything invincibly objectionable" in the proposed right of search. After all, the right was mutual, and thus there could be no sacrifice of national dignity involved. And "what Great Britain is ready to allow, in a point so vital to her pride and to her power, may surely be allowed reciprocally by any other Nation."[42] The new foreign secretary was finding that the Americans could, indeed, be difficult.

Or perhaps it was the secretary of state himself who was the problem. Stratford Canning reported, rather boldly, to Adams in October that he had "become satisfied that [America's] compliance with the proposal of admitting mutual search depended personally and exclusively" on Adams. "I assured him," Adams explained, "he had been misinformed, as he might hereafter have occasion to know." At this, the British minister dropped the matter. Still, Canning had not been completely off base: "the slave trade was an international concern, and . . . only a system of international cooperation would be adequate to destroy it." Yet Adams stood firm in his "independent attitude, and he remained of the opinion that each nation must guard its own interests in the matter."[43] If Adams, moreover, was not the sole advocate of this position within the administration, he was nevertheless its most emphatic and important one.

Congress Intervenes

Anglo-American conversation on the suppression of the trade carried on in this manner for some time: the British urged cooperation, and Monroe and

Adams insisted upon unilateralism. America was not to be drawn into the foreign affairs of the Atlantic world any more deeply than was absolutely necessary. If the Cannings refused to despair, Stratford was at least aware of the long odds against them. His hopes that Congress would act decisively having been all but dashed in the previous two years, he nevertheless wrote to his cousin on the first day of 1823 that "I still apprehend that nothing short of a decided impulse from that quarter will produce any change in the disposition of the American Government."[44] It appeared that diplomatic overtures to the Monroe administration would be futile until pressure was placed upon the White House from without. Things looked bleak.

If Congress did not quite come riding to the rescue, it at least gave impetus to a matter that had remained diplomatically frustrated for some time. The catalyst was provided by the Virginia congressman Charles Fenton Mercer. In February 1823 Mercer introduced a resolution that read, "That the President of the United States be requested to enter upon, and to prosecute from time to time, such negotiations with the several maritime powers of Europe and America, as he may deem expedient for the effectual abolition of the African slave trade, and its ultimate denunciation, as piracy, under the law of nations, by the consent of the civilized world." The wording of Mercer's resolution might have been ambiguous with regard to the right of search. But he made clear in his remarks on the floor of the House exactly what he had in mind. "So long," he declared, "as the right of common search and punishment is withheld, so long may the flag of a single State cover this detestable commerce." The vote in favor of the resolution was, in Fehrenbacher's description, a "thunderous" 131–9. Fehrenbacher adds that the resolution gave Adams "a route of graceful retreat from his and the administration's previously held position." Pirates were, after all, *hostis humani generis*—enemies of humankind—under international law, and admiralty law before that. As such, they had no claim to protection from their native country's government, and could be apprehended by the armed ships of any nation. "With Monroe's approval," Fehrenbacher adds, "Adams instituted negotiations along those lines and drafted a proposed Anglo-American convention dependent upon British legislation declaring the slave trade to be piracy."[45]

Rush and George Canning began negotiations in January 1824, and by March 13 the two had hammered out an agreement. It was "remarkable that this convention contained a right of search provision," especially given that Rush had not secured a British renunciation of impressment.[46] It is also surprising that the agreement foresaw British naval cruising in American, as well as African and West Indian, coastal waters. And while this proved acceptable to the House of Representatives, the Senate removed the provision, along with a provision allowing "the capture of citizens of either nations [*sic*] sailing in a vessel of a third country." Due to these excisions, Parliament would, in the end, refuse to ratify the convention. The British, for their part, "viewed a convention that did not allow their navy to search suspect vessels on the North or South American coasts as unworkable." In this they had a point.[47]

By this time, Adams had begun to sour on an agreement for which he had little love in the first place, and which had been forced upon him by Congress. In May he spoke with Congressman Mercer, who told him that it was "apparent and known to every one" that legislative opposition to the slave trade convention "was merely personal, pointed against [Adams] with reference to the Presidential election, and but for that would not have existed." It was, of course, an election year, and Adams, as the likely successor to Monroe, was now under fire from political opponents. He needed little convincing, then, that the debate over the suppression of the trade had now taken on a domestic political character that, in fact, determined the direction of the debate. The secretary of state was convinced that the "only object" of the "profligate opposition" to the convention in the Senate "was to use it as a weapon to raise a popular clamor against me."[48] Partisans of Treasury Secretary William H. Crawford planned on using this convention to leverage their man into position. Additionally, as Adams was aware, "some of the Southern Senators had taken a panic at the late speeches in the British Parliament looking to the abolition of slavery, and were exceedingly adverse to forming any concert with the British Government whatever in reference to the subject of slavery." The Senate debate thus came to revolve around the question of whether there should be a time limit on the convention, or whether one of the contracting parties should be able to annul the agreement "by giving notice of days or months." This sort of agreement would be "pernicious," however. As Adams noted, "It would defeat the joint attempt to influence other nations to make the slave-trade piracy. For how absurd that we should try to prevail upon all other nations to declare it piracy, when they might retort upon us that we have shrunk from our own obligations, and made it a piracy for a term of years, reserving ourselves the right of appealing our own law!"[49] Domestic politics and fear of abolitionism thus helped derail a policy that might have aided in the suppression of the trade, at exactly the time when "American complicity in that trade was rising to a scandalous level." The United States had, for a short time, flirted with withdrawing in a significant way from its unilateralist policy toward the trade. It had done so at the impetus of Congress, acting upon the Monroe administration, which had advanced the initial proposal for the convention to London. The failure of the slave trade convention was, however, "decisive of the relations of the two countries on the question of the slave trade." The United States now "retired into the isolation from which it had temporarily emerged," with the result that "Great Britain was compelled to proceed with its system of alliances against the slave trade without the cooperation of the most important of the maritime powers, and the handicap was disastrous to her efforts."[50]

Asked at one point by Stratford Canning if he could imagine a worse evil than the slave trade, Adams responded, "Yes: admitting the right of search by foreign officers of our vessels upon the seas in time of peace; for that would be making slaves of ourselves."[51] Monroe's administration had successfully avoided any commitments that would lead to this figurative type of "slavery." But, in the process, they had assured that many more Africans would be subjected to slavery of a much more literal kind.

The Colonization of Freed Slaves

The question of what to do about the traffic in slaves across the Atlantic tested the limits of America's willingness to become involved in international connections and cooperation. So, too, would the issue of what to do with those slaves who were already in the United States. One of the persistent themes in America's exterior policy well into the Civil War was that of colonization of freed slaves. From early on in the history of the republic, the question of what to do with manumitted African Americans posed a conundrum for those who wished to see an end to slavery. Many Americans would, over the course of several generations, come to conclude that Blacks should be free, but that they should be so somewhere else. Colonization thus became a leitmotif for those so inclined, despite the fact that it was unclear precisely how to send so many human beings abroad and, even if the logistics could be worked out, where to send them.

Attempts to work out these problems brought successive administrations into contact with the world in new ways. But in this case, what stands out is the limits of the US government's willingness to engage in a diplomacy that would make extensive colonization a reality. Slavery pulled the United States into the international sphere in many ways. In this instance, however, Washington sought to keep commitments and involvement limited. American policymakers were, furthermore, largely successful in doing so. Yet their admittedly limited efforts on behalf of colonization of Black Americans resulted in some of the first US involvement in sub-Saharan Africa. Furthermore, as a result of this involvement, Washington would once again face potential conflict with London, this time over a matter that the British viewed as a vital imperial interest.

Searching for a Cure

The roots of colonization ran deep. In his "Notes on the State of Virginia," written in 1781–82, Thomas Jefferson discussed a scheme he had proposed for the manumission of the state's slaves. As part of the plan, freed slaves would "be colonized to such place as the circumstances of the time should render most proper." According to Jefferson, there was ample reason to assume that the two races could not live side by side in freedom. Indeed, any experiment in cohabitation of the races in freedom was likely to result in genocide: "Deep rooted prejudices entertained by the whites; ten thousand recollections, by the blacks, of the injuries they have sustained; new provocations; the real distinctions which nature has made; and many other circumstances, will divide us into parties, and produce convulsions which will probably never end but in the extermination of the one or the other race." It was better, in his estimation, to deport Blacks when they reached their majority to some faraway place and "declare them a free and independant [sic] people." It is important to note that Jefferson's vision for colonization implied a diplomatic responsibility, since the American government was to "extend to them our alliance and protection, till they shall have acquired strength."[52] This last proposal, at least, went further than American policymakers proved willing to go.

Jefferson was hardly alone in his enthusiasm for colonization at this time. In 1790 his fellow Virginian, Fernando Fairfax, likewise called for the deportation of freed African Americans "to a distance from this country." Fairfax in fact proposed that Congress establish a colony in Africa, to which freedmen from all states could be sent. Africa had the dual advantages of being the "native climate" for Blacks, as well as being very far away from America. Christianity and commerce would both be the beneficiaries: American Blacks could bring the Gospel to Africa, while (white) Americans would gain from trade with a tropical colony.[53] Just two years earlier, James Madison had advocated for an American colony in Africa, also with the goal of sending freed slaves abroad.[54] Clearly, the idea that colonization could provide a solution to the problem of slavery, and especially of manumission, had garnered much support among some of the most elite of southerners by the late 1780s. Colonization seemed to offer a way out of what would otherwise be an insoluble dilemma; by means of it, the new republic could be rid of both slavery and the free Blacks that an end to that institution would necessarily produce. The revolution in Haiti served to increase elite interest in finding a way of removing Blacks—especially freedmen—to a place far from the United States.[55] The ideas that Jefferson, Fairfax, Madison, and others advocated were, however, just that—ideas. There was as yet no concrete plan for how to achieve such a monumental objective as the removal of roughly nine hundred thousand people to distant shores. Nor was there any organization—public or private—that could engage in this work, however it was to be accomplished.

The founding of the American Colonization Society (ACS) in 1816 gave a new impetus to the colonization movement. In 1815, with the end of the War of 1812, "the colonization issue burst forth once again."[56] Additionally, the founding of Sierra Leone—a crown colony from 1808 onward—as a refuge for London's "Black poor" had given added impetus to the idea of colonization in Africa. The fact that this British colony was not open to American merchants only heightened the interest in an American establishment on the west coast of Africa.[57] In addition to being an outlet for poor Blacks from Britain and a trade station for that nation, Sierra Leone gave the British government, after 1807, a place to take "recaptured" Africans taken from slavers.[58] This last point was quite significant: as the United States entered the fight against the slave trade in the Atlantic, the question of what to do with recaptured slaves would give Washington a concrete reason to become involved in sub-Saharan Africa. It would thus give the fledgling ACS an opportunity to influence the foreign policy of the American government.

Influential advocates of colonization came together in December 1820 to give form to the new ACS. Among their numbers were such luminaries as Henry Clay, Francis Scott Key, and John Randolph of Roanoke. The conferees chose Bushrod Washington, a Supreme Court associate justice and nephew of George Washington, as president of the society. From the beginning, ACS leaders agreed that the success of their enterprise would require the support of the federal government. Two weeks after the December meeting, Randolph was already introducing a resolution in the House, calling for governmental financial assistance. The appeal was rejected by the House Committee on the Suppression of the Slave Trade.[59] Yet members of the society were hardly discouraged by this early rebuff. Over the course of the coming years, they would indefatigably lobby Congress and successive administrations to aid their cause.

President James Monroe, himself an advocate for colonization, soon appeared to rally to the cause of governmental aid to the society's efforts. A founding member of the ACS, Charles Fenton Mercer of Virginia, introduced a bill in the House that became the Slave Trade Act of 1819. Officially titled An Act in Addition to the Acts Prohibiting the Slave Trade, it became law on March 3. As a result of the Slave Trade Act, the president was "authorized to make such regulations and arrangements as he may deem expedient for the safe keeping, support, and removal beyond the limits of the United States, of all such Negroes, mulattoes, or persons of color, as may be so delivered and brought within their jurisdiction."[60] The act thus addressed a lacuna in American anti-slave-trade law: it required American naval forces to seize slave cargoes but did not clearly specify where those interdicted slaves were to be taken.

Precisely what the act actually allowed the president to do in relation to this problem was, however, not spelled out, allowing for a variety of interpretations. ACS leaders expressed the conviction that Monroe was now authorized to purchase land in Africa for the resettlement of freed slaves. In their zeal, they "badgered" Attorney General William Wirt in an attempt to gain an official interpretation of the law favorable to their plans for establishing an African colony.[61] But Wirt, a Marylander and a "strict constructionist," was less than convinced. Nor was the rest of Monroe's cabinet swayed. Adams was particularly opposed to an interpretation of the law, and indeed the Constitution, that would allow the federal government to establish a colony in Africa. On March 12 the secretary told Monroe that he "thought it impossible that Congress should have had any purchase of territory in contemplation of" the March 3 act. Adams believed that the ACS plan "obviously imports the engrafting of a colonial establishment upon the Constitution of the United States, and thereby an accession of power to the National Government transcending all its other powers." Yet it is clear that Monroe was earnestly seeking a way to interpret the law more flexibly, given his interest in colonization as a means of bringing about manumission of slaves. "The important object now," he told Adams, "was to remove these free blacks, and to provide a place to which the emancipated slaves might go: the legal obstacles to emancipation might then be withdrawn, and the black population in time be drawn off entirely from Virginia."[62] He therefore called a meeting of the cabinet to advise him on the matter.

Later that day, Adams met with a delegation from the ACS. He was treated to a lecture on the acquisition of Louisiana and settlement in the Oregon Territory, which, he was told, "placed beyond all question the right of acquiring territory as existing in the Government of the United States." The secretary responded "with all possible civility" that "the late Slave-Trade Act had no reference to the settlement of a colony." The purchase of Louisiana and the establishment of a settlement on the Columbia River were in no way precedents for the establishment of a colony in Africa, being as they were "in territory contiguous to and continuous with our own." These examples did not justify "the purchase of countries beyond the seas, or the establishment of a colonial system of government subordinate to and dependent upon that of the United States." The delegation left understanding, said Adams, "that they will have no aid from me."[63]

At the March 16 cabinet meeting, the secretary of state's interpretation of the act prevailed. Wirt, Secretary of War John C. Calhoun, and Secretary of the Navy Smith Thompson all concluded that the March 3 act authorized no colonial ventures in Africa. Monroe "accepted the decision, telling the Colonization Society that he was powerless to aid it."[64] The attorney general followed up in October with an initial opinion that advanced a very narrow interpretation of the 1819 act. According to Wirt, no portion of the monies appropriated by Congress for execution of the act could be used to purchase land for a settlement; to transport freedmen to Africa; to purchase goods for a settlement; or to pay an agent for the colony. If Congress had intended for the US government to cooperate with the ACS in its efforts, Wirt concluded, then the act was "altogether inadequate."[65] It was clear that the role of the federal government in this matter would remain limited, despite the presence in the White House of a strong supporter of ACS goals who was himself disposed to give a "liberal interpretation" of the act.[66]

Still, even the limits that the executive placed on itself were in flux at this time. Treasury Secretary William Crawford—Adams's cabinet rival in this and other matters—sought to loosen the administration's interpretation of the act, and under "Crawford's hammering, Wirt grudgingly altered his opinion," bringing it more in line with the desires of the president. The federal government still could not establish a colony. But it now could take steps to help settle and support rescued Africans in a "station" that, in the near future, would be established privately by the society. Included in Wirt's new opinion was the authority to establish an agency to assist in the settlement of the freed slaves.[67]

Despite Wirt's desire for delay until Congress should clarify its intention, Monroe moved forward on the basis of this second reading of the March 3 act. On December 17, 1819, the president sent a special message to Congress addressing his administration's interpretation of the act. According to this interpretation, Congress had "enjoined on the Executive to cause all negroes, mulattoes, or persons of color, who may be taken under the act, to be removed to Africa," and only to Africa. The president, furthermore, was "authorized to appoint one or more agents, residing there, to receive such persons." The administration interpreted Congress as saying that the executive should see to it that shelter and food were provided for the newly freed Africans: "Should they be landed without such provision having been previously made, they might perish." Nor could it have been "the intention of the law to preclude" the appointment of an agent or agents competent to see to these vital provisions. Monroe would thus appoint and send to the coast of Africa two salaried agents for this purpose. But, perhaps as a sop to Adams, the agents would be given "an express injunction to exercise no power founded on the principle of colonization, or other power than that of performing the benevolent offices above recited, by the permission and sanction of the existing Government

under which they may establish themselves." Because Congress "took no action" after having received Monroe's message, the president's interpretation
of the act became the basis for future administrations' policies toward what
would become Liberia.[68]

On the recommendation of the ACS, the Reverend Samuel Bacon was com-
missioned as US agent in Africa on January 8, 1820. Additionally, Dr. Samuel A. Crozer was chosen as both the agent of the ACS and as the government's
physician for the expedition to Africa.[69] Crozer's double role indicated early
that distinctions between the functions of the government and of the society
on the African coast were not to be as clearly drawn as Monroe had seemed
to imply, nor as Adams must have wished. The navy secretary, nevertheless,
gave strict instructions to Bacon on this matter. Thompson wrote the new
agent, "It is to be distinctly understood that you are not to connect your Agency
with the views or plans of the Colonization Society, with whom, under law,
the Government of the United States has no concern. You are not to exercise
any power or authority founded on the principles of colonization, but to confine yourself to that of performing the benevolent intentions of the Act of
Congress of the 3rd of March 1819, which will govern you in all other respects."[70] Thus, Bacon's official instructions provided for a distinction that, in
practice, would be exceedingly difficult to maintain. They also warned against
acting in any way as colonialists in what certainly looked like a colony. The
administration's goal was to make clear that the colony in Africa was not an
American colony, but rather a *private* colony established and run by a private
organization, the ACS. Yet the "entire mission was under the sponsorship of
the United States government and under the command of Federal Agents."[71]
If nice distinctions in responsibility were this difficult to discern when the expedition departed, they became even more so on the ground in Africa.

Early Efforts at Settlement

The first expedition ended in unmitigated disaster, with the agents and numerous colonists dying in rapid succession from tropical disease. This left them just
enough time to come into conflict with British authorities at Sierra Leone. The
agents and colonists arrived first at the British colony, before proceeding to
their geographical objective: Sherbro Island down the coast. In February the
agents met with the governor of Sierra Leone, Charles McCarthy, hoping to
receive aid including small craft for transit to Sherbro. McCarthy was clearly
concerned about the prospect of an American-sponsored colony being established close to Great Britain's. "We could perceive," Bacon wrote Thompson,

"that a great excitement had been produced by our arrival," adding that "had not a fair and clear discrimination been made between the acts of the Colonization Society and those of the Government . . . we should have been turned aside from this delightful part of the country to seek an asylum in the midst of an active slave trade between the Gallinas and Cape Coast. Again, had we come and settled here without first visiting Sierra Leone, we should have been disturbed according to all human probability."[72] In fact, despite Bacon's interpretation of the situation, it is likely that McCarthy was unimpressed by the distinction the Americans made between the purview of the ACS and that of the federal government agents.[73] The agents from the New World were now encountering the international problems that arose from European colonial rivalry on the west coast of the African continent. The British had an interest in maintaining an exclusive trade with Sierra Leone, and together with the desire to exert political leverage in West Africa, they could not have looked without suspicion at an American establishment in their backyard. The Americans could thus expect only minimal help from the uneasy officials at Freetown. The British might have been less concerned had they foreseen the futility of the initial American attempt at colonization. Indeed, "neither the British nor the Americans had learned much from the disastrous mistakes of New World colonization." They had once again chosen unsuitable, "unhealthful" sites for settlement; they had once again failed to take the natives of the place, and their cultures, into consideration.[74] The results were regrettable to the sponsors of the colony, and lethal to the expedition.

The calamity of the first attempt at settlement did not stop the ACS or the administration from trying again. In November 1820 Jonathan B. Winn and Ephraim Bacon (Samuel's brother) were chosen as the new government agents. The ACS sent the Reverend Joseph R. Andrus, with Christian Wiltberger as assistant agent.[75] The navy secretary made clear, in his instructions to Winn, that "the Africans who may be captured & landed at Sherbro or elsewhere ought not to be supported at the expense of the United States longer than can be avoided," a term that Secretary Thompson estimated to be less than one year. If Winn found the recaptured Africans were becoming "troublesome and insubordinate," he was to communicate "with the European Agents at Sierra Leone, Gambia, or other places on the Coast of Africa, who may be duly authorized to cooperate in similar arrangements." Above all, Winn was to operate with "rigid economy in fulfilling the duties enjoined."[76] The administration clearly wanted to keep its support of the Africans limited, both in duration and expense.

Thompson's presumption that Winn's European counterparts would be willing to aid the American colony in the event that his charges became refractory again reveals a failure to understand the interests and policies of the European colonial empires. In his report to Thompson on April 19, 1821, Winn indicated that relations with the British were not ideal. The American and ACS agents had recently met with the acting governor of Sierra Leone, Alexander Grant, and other high officials from the colony's administration. Though friendly toward the Americans, "they told us that they considered they were in duty bound frankly to state that the establishment of an American settlement so contiguous to theirs at Sherbro, would be considered as clashing with the feelings, interests, etc. of the people of their Colony." The Britons were quite clear on the fact that they did not want to see the American colony become contiguous with their own, and advocated for more suitable and healthful sites down the coast.[77] American government agents could continue to insist that the settlement that they were founding was not a colony of the US government. The British would, however, continue to act as if it were.

Once again, there appeared to be little for the Europeans to worry about. Disease took its toll on the second expedition as it had on the first. Bacon left the coast in mid-June, along with his wife, for "health reasons." In July the fever took the life of Andrus and, the following month, Winn and his wife. With the news of Crozer's death, the government had sent a new physician, Dr. Eli Ayers, to Africa. Ayres was also appointed as agent for the ACS, thus mingling responsibility to official Washington with that to a private body.[78] Ayres arrived in Sierra Leone on November 21, and proceeded to Fourah Bay, where the American expedition was temporarily located. He then "took over control of the Settlement," moving it to the apparently more salubrious Cape Mesurado and promulgating a code for the punishment of mutiny, insubordination, and the like.[79] The colony now took the name of Liberia, and the first permanent settlement, Monrovia, was named in honor of the president who had sponsored the enterprise.

Monroe may well have felt honored by the gesture. But the connection of the federal government to the colony remained strictly limited. In fact, the US government "at all times refused to take any responsibility in regard to the Settlement."[80] American government officials would continue to seek governmental aid for the colony, especially in times of significant need.[81] Yet Monroe's administration, and those that followed it, refused to take on significant political responsibility for the colony that they helped to sustain. Lawrence C. Howard thus overstates the case when he asserts that the period from 1822 to 1828 "is marked by the steady assumption of responsibilities for the operation of the colony by the United States government."[82] What is striking in terms of US foreign relations is the refusal of successive American administrations to treat Liberia as a full-fledged colony of the United States. The issue has been blurred by the extent to which the federal government acted in partnership with the ACS in helping to establish the colony, and then in assisting in its survival and growth. David F. Ericson notes that the ACS "may have been a private organization, but its African colonial enterprise was not a private project." Indeed, he observes, the "public-private partnership established to pursue the project was not only one of the first of its kind in the history of the American state; it was the longest lasting and most well-funded partnership during the 1791–1861 period."[83]

Still, the partnership was limited. This was particularly so in the realm of international politics. Washington never viewed developments in Liberia as vital to the security of the nation, as it did with regard to, say, Haiti, and would in the future with regard to Cuba. Significantly, the US government "did not acquire sovereignty over Liberia, either under derivative title or by occupation, or by operation of law. On the contrary, the United States always disclaimed such rights, and refused to incorporate Liberia as a colony or to assume a legal protectorate over that country." The settlers and the ACS would have "hailed with joy" an American decision to extend a formal protectorate over the new colony, but this was not offered. Above all, Washington "remained obdurate in its refusal to undertake any political commitments in this foreign field." Domestically, Americans remained divided on the matter of the connection between colonization and abolition, and the federal government did not want to raise this issue too specifically by taking on responsibility for a colony of freedmen. In the field of foreign relations, the US government was unwilling to risk "complications" with the European powers, which increasingly defined their African colonies as vital in terms of high politics.[84] The extent of the American government's partnership with Liberia was to be bound by these considerations.

Politics Intrude and Gurley Arrives

As has been noted, domestic political considerations played a significant role in determining the attitude of the federal government toward the colonization project. Nicholas P. Wood sees in the Missouri crisis of 1819–20 a watershed for the ACS, and thus for federal sponsorship of the society's project. The conflict over the admission of Missouri into the Union as a slave state "destroyed the cross-sectional trust essential for a federal colonization program." As a result of the crisis, "cross-sectional support for the ACS in Congress collapsed. During the rest of the antebellum period, colonizationists were unable to mobilize a congressional majority in favor of greater federal support."[85] This development was potentially disastrous for a movement that was predicated on garnering financial aid from the federal government.

The ACS found itself in a difficult position. At its board meeting in February 1824, General Robert Goodloe Harper acknowledged this difficulty, saying that the choice was between abandoning Liberia or else appealing to the federal government for relief aid. At this point, "There was frank admission by the Society of its inability to support the colony. The fact was that this condition had existed from the beginning although the Society had permitted the allusion [sic] to exist that the settlement had been launched under their efforts. Actually, the Society had never been in a financial position to handle the expenses of the settlement."[86] Nor, by 1824, were things going well on the ground in Africa. In April, as ailing US government agent Jehudi Ashmun was leaving to recuperate at Cape Verde, colonists robbed him of his money and belongings while he lay on a stretcher.[87] The society was losing control of its colony, and desperately needed both financial assistance and better administration.

The Monroe administration intervened, sending a warship to Cape Mesurado to help quell the rebellion. At the head of the expedition Monroe placed Ralph R. Gurley, who was delegated by the ACS to restore the society's control over the fractious colony. Together with Ashmun, Gurley drafted a new constitution for the colony and began the practice of allowing colonists to hold offices within the Liberian administration. Gurley's intervention helped to save the experiment, and it also helped the ACS regain control of Liberia. In June 1825 he was rewarded with appointment as the society's secretary.[88] Gurley proved gifted at fundraising, and helped restore the society to some semblance of fiscal stability. During this period, Secretary of the Navy Samuel L. Southard approved aid to the colony—with the obligatory adjuration to be frugal.[89]

There can be little question that the colonial experiment in Liberia would have failed during the critical years of 1823–24 were it not for timely intervention of the US government. Federal aid, though quite limited, was vital to the colony. It was, therefore, a cause for concern for the ACS and its allies when Andrew Jackson was inaugurated president in 1829. One of the most prominent advocates for colonization had long been Jackson's nemesis, Henry Clay, a founding member of the ACS. Legitimately committed to the cause, Clay had also sought to use colonization to his political advantage. Thus, as the election of 1828 approached, Jackson supporters began to view the ACS as a "political engine" in the ambitious Kentuckian's machine. In Jackson's Tennessee, Clay was, it was said, "considered . . . to be its leader and to be making use of it for political purposes—for gaining popularity in the North."[90] Colonizationists might well anticipate that the much-needed aid from the federal government could be curtailed, or perhaps even eliminated, once Jackson took office.

In fact, Jackson adopted a less generous approach to Liberia than had his predecessors. An audit by the Department of the Treasury in 1830 had revealed the high cost to the government of the settlement when compared with the number of Blacks of any type actually settled in Liberia. It also advocated a much narrower reading of the March 3, 1819, act than had previously prevailed. Auditor Amos Kendall opined,

> It would seem that the terms of the Act were hardly sufficient to authorize the establishment of a colony, owing allegiance to the United States, and entitled to protection, if ever Congress itself possesses a *right* to authorize such an establishment. In the simple grant of power to an agent to *receive* captured negroes, it requires broad construction to find a grant of authority to *colonize them, to build houses for them, to furnish them with farming utensils, to pay instructors to teach them, to purchase ships for their convenience, to build forts for their protection, to supply them with arms and munitions of war, to enlist troops to guard them, or to employ the Army or Navy in their defense.*

The act, he continued, "which seems intended merely to facilitate the return of liberated Africans to their own countries and families, was, by construction, made to authorize the appropriation of the power and means of the Government to their civilization, and to their location and protection in a new community."[91] Kendall, with his report, indicted the policies of previous administrations: the actions taken in pursuit of colonization in Africa, limited as they were, had in, in his assessment, no sanction in the law which supposedly had authorized them.

In his own report to Congress of December of that year, Secretary of the Navy John Branch wielded Kendall's report to assure that "understanding the law in the limited acceptation represented . . . , it will in the future be executed accordingly, and every effort made by the Department to confine the application of this fund within the pale of its provisions."[92] To be sure, "further appropriations for the Agency were drastically limited." Jackson did not take the radical steps of ending the agency or ceasing the navy's protection of the colony.[93] He did, however, manage to frustrate attempts by Clay to gain additional funding for colonization efforts.[94] The ACS seemed to be practically moribund by 1830: in October 1829 Francis Scott Key had told an assembly of sympathetic Philadelphians that the ACS "had become involved in pecuniary embarrassments, which prevented any further active operations, and rendered it impossible to send out anymore emigrants to Africa for some time."[95]

By the end of the 1830s the government in Washington had set itself a pair of connected policy goals with regard to slavery: ending the slave trade and ridding the country of freed slaves. Yet in neither case was it willing to expend the resources necessary to achieve its aims. Even more significantly, it proved unwilling to foster the sorts of international connections that would be necessary to accomplish them. Ending the trade could come only with an agreement to cooperate with Britain in its suppression, which necessarily entailed a mutual right of search. This was far more than any American administration was willing to concede. Thus, the slave trade would continue. It was, furthermore, becoming increasingly obvious that colonization efforts would fail if left to private action alone. If colonization were to continue as a viable option, some other means of accomplishing it would have to be found. Washington could adopt external policy with regard to slavery. Without a commitment to engage more actively in the international relations of the Atlantic world, however, it could not bring that policy to fruition.

The Negro Seamen Acts

Yet another difficulty that arose to complicate the Anglo-American relationship was also intimately connected with American slavery. This time, however, the upshot for the respective governments was prolonged embarrassment rather than punctuated crisis. The initial provocation for this misadventure was the passage by the South Carolina legislature in December 1822 of the first Negro Seamen Act. Eventually, all southern states along the Atlantic seaboard and the Gulf of Mexico, from North Carolina to Texas, would enact some version of the act aimed at preventing the entry of free Blacks into their respective states. As a consequence of the strict enforcement of these acts, Afro-British sailors found themselves imprisoned for violation of state laws for the "crime" of being in the wrong place at the wrong time; and, of course, of having the wrong skin color.[96] Successive British governments attempted to gain the repeal of the laws. At the very least, they wished to see them amended so as not to apply to British subjects. Yet one US administration after another proved powerless to affect the situation. In frustration, London would turn to lobbying the governments of the southern states themselves in order to gain satisfaction. The result was one of the more peculiar episodes in the history of Anglo-American relations.

Unsurprisingly, South Carolina led the charge in banning the ingress of free Blacks. The immediate cause of the legislation was the discovery and brutal suppression of a planned slave rebellion, the Denmark Vesey Conspiracy, in early summer 1822. But these events came against the background of a long history of slave unrest in the colony, dating back well before the bloody Stono Rebellion of 1739. The fact that Blacks had made up a majority of the population in colonial South Carolina had exacerbated the situation. Nor were efforts at banning the influx of Blacks new; in 1787, the legislature had forbidden the importing of slaves into the state for sale. Granted, this prohibition probably resulted more from reasons of economics than racial fears: deeply in arrears after the Revolutionary War, the state could "ill afford the increased debt being piled up by importing slaves."[97] But fear soon became the chief motivator of whites in the state. The revolution in what would become Haiti provoked great alarm in South Carolina, along with the concomitant conviction that slave unrest in the state was a result of the "example of San Domingo." The dread of free Blacks bringing the "contagion" of slave unrest into the state led to the passage in 1794 of the first ban on their entry into South Carolina.[98] Against this background the Vesey rebellion occasioned the most stringent ban yet on free Blacks.

It was this attempt to limit the spread of the emancipation contagion to the state's slave population that occasioned prolonged difficulties in Anglo-American relations that persisted until the outbreak of the American Civil War. Although it is an overstatement to say that the difficulties "escalated into a diplomatic battle," the incident certainly did nothing to improve the already vexing relations between the British and US governments.[99] That officials in Washington were not responsible for the provocation was of little solace to either side. The episode in fact provided evidence that America's federal system of government "has within it the possibilities of embarrassment in the conduct of relations between the United States and other members of the family of nations."[100] This time, slavery was the culprit.

On December 21, 1822, the South Carolina legislature passed the most stringent of bans on free persons of color entering the state. The new law provided that

> if any vessel shall come into any port or harbor of this State, from any other State or foreign port, having on board any free Negroes or persons of color . . . such free Negroes or persons of color shall be liable to be seized and confined in jail until said vessel shall clear out and depart from this State; and that when said vessel is ready to sail, the captain of said vessel shall be bound to carry away the said Negro or free person of color, and to pay the expenses of his detention.

Should the shipmaster fail to do so, furthermore, the "free Negroes or persons of color shall be deemed and taken as absolute slaves, and sold in conformity to the provisions of the Act."[101]

This was strong stuff, and resulted in the boarding of both American and foreign ships to remove persons of color. It did not take long for the British government to protest the ill treatment of its nationals and the insult to its flag. In mid-February 1823 the British foreign secretary, Stratford Canning, sent a "brief but vigorously worded note" to Secretary of State John Quincy Adams. Canning declaimed against the "most grievous and extraordinary" treatment of Britons in accordance with the Negro Seamen Act and called on the federal government "to prevent the recurrence of any such outrage in the future."[102] Adams did not see fit to respond to his British counterpart until mid-June. But, though dilatory, he sought to be reassuring. He replied that Washington had already taken steps that Adams thought would ameliorate the situation and prevent such offenses in the future.[103]

For a time, in any event, the act was not strictly enforced. But soon a group of notables, organized as the South Carolina Association, began to press Charleston officials to apply the law stringently. Their particular fear was that contact between free Black sailors and slaves would allow "for introducing among our slaves, the moral contagion of their pernicious principles and opinions." To allow this would be "to invite new attempts at insurrection."[104] Advocates of both the Negro Seamen Acts and their diligent enforcement stressed this theme of contagion: certain dangerous ideas were contagious, and free Blacks were vectors for contamination. In fact, the "rhetorical power of 'contagion' was immense," suggesting to some "that governmental officials ought to be much more diligent in sifting through the messages being introduced from abroad."[105]

So successful were these efforts to bolster enforcement that even the ruling of Supreme Court Justice William Johnson, sitting in circuit, that the act violated the Anglo-American Convention of 1815 was insufficient to gain redress for the British; South Carolina officials simply ignored the ruling.[106] Now the government in London found itself faced with imprisoned nationals convicted "under the supposedly defunct state law."[107] This all seemed very much at variance with what Adams had promised the British. The British chargé thus asked the secretary of state to take "immediate measures . . . for securing British subjects in future [sic] a full and effectual protection against acts so unjustifiable, and so totally at variance with the Convention of 1815." Adams responded this time with a strong indication that Washington would, if necessary, meet South Carolinian obstructionism "with the arms of authority."[108]

Such "arms" never materialized, however. Decades of off-and-on, fruitless diplomacy failed to alter the situation in the South. Faced with the prospect of further slave rebellions brought on by—it was assumed—the effects of the mingling of free Blacks with slaves, the southern states proved largely unwilling to budge.[109] Nor were successive denizens of the White House eager to provoke a sectional crisis over the rights of foreign Blacks or the sanctity of the British flag.

Having failed to move Washington to act effectively, "the authorities of the Foreign Office became convinced that there was no hope of help from the Federal government." London for a time would have to be satisfied to warn its subjects of color "of the inconveniences they would suffer if they should violate the laws."[110] The British government chose, however, to make one last effort, and this time it tried going to the source of the laws themselves. In 1850 the British minister in Washington, Sir Henry Bulwer, proposed to the Foreign Office that an attempt should be made by the various British consuls to urge the legislatures of southern states to modify the acts. The consuls would thus serve as lobbyists seeking to persuade state officials to alter the laws of their respective states.[111] Yet even as the crescendo of "states' rights" was building in southern capitals in the 1850s, the conviction generally prevailed that foreign relations was the exclusive purview of the federal government. A Richmond newspaper categorically declared in early 1851 that South Carolina could have "no political existence whatever in the eyes of foreign nations." In a similar vein, a Savannah paper asserted that, if a state could negotiate with a foreign capital on the matter of the Seamen Acts, then it could negotiate with them on any matter. The federal government would thus become "a nullity, and the Confederacy resolve itself into thirty-one separate and distinct sovereignties, each possessing the right to treat with other Powers, form alliances, and declare war."[112] It was a ridiculous prospect. But the only alternative was continued frustration for Britain. Michael Schoeppner's assessment of legal cases generated by the Seamen Acts can likewise serve as a general coda to Anglo-American diplomacy on this issue: "In the end, we see that the repeated protests of the Seamen Acts' insult to British sovereignty never affected the administration of the laws. Claims of British sovereignty and Afro-British rights had no impact. Absent any military or economic threats, these legal claims were completely ineffectual."[113]

The entire episode, in fact, underlines the complexity of international relations for a slaveholding republic. The federal government would gladly have seen the affair of Britain's Black sailors swept away—or at least under the rug. But Washington could not realize this policy goal, despite the patent desire by multiple administrations to reduce Anglo-American tensions and the priority that they put on doing so. Racial slavery was intrinsically interwoven with issues of American constitutional federalism, domestic politics, transatlantic relations, economics, and law. Slavery was not the tapestry itself. But it was a vivid thread running through the whole of America's foreign relations. And like Irish poet Louis MacNeice's "woven figure," it could not undo its thread.

Escaped Slaves and Anglo-American Relations

There was certainly no shortage of slavery-related issues to complicate relations between the two English-speaking powers. One of the nettlesome controversies concerned the escape of American slaves to the Bahamas, and thus to freedom. The British government had ended slavery on the islands on the first day of August 1834.[114] In practice, this meant that a slave who managed to make land in the Bahamas was forever free under British law. Remarkably, an unknown number of American slaves risked the journey, which was a testament to the compelling appeal of freedom and the ingenuity of slave resistance. Yet what strikes one today as grounds for admiration was, to American slaveholders, a cause for great anxiety: their "property" was stealing itself away across the so-called Saltwater Railroad. If they could not get these slaves back, then they at least demanded compensation from Britain for their loss. The result was a "little-known but disruptive foreign policy dispute between the United States and Britain."[115] As with other Anglo-American disputes precipitated by slavery, this one was the cause of much frustration and recrimination, and, in the end, produced results not entirely satisfactory to the Americans.

Ideally for the American slaveholders, the British would return any slaves who made land in the Bahamas. But there was no British law against slaves running away. As a result, London would not return slaves who reached British territories. In fact, according to Foreign Secretary Lord Aberdeen, it legally could not do so. Once slaves reached the Bahamas, they "at once became free" and the government had "no legal power or authority to restore them to a state of slavery."[116] Given that escaped slaves thus had a safe haven a short distance from Florida, it is no surprise that the "lure of the Bahamas . . . represented a persistent foreign policy issue for proslavery Americans."[117] The issue led to something of an uproar with the *Creole* Affair. While it is an overstatement to declare, as does Arthur T. Downey's study of the episode, that the affair "led the U.S. and Great Britain to the brink of war," it certainly introduced further complication into an already charged bilateral relationship.[118] And though it is not nearly as famous as the earlier case of the slave uprising on the Spanish-flagged ship *La Amistad*, its impact on American relations with Britain were far more significant.[119]

The "affair" began on the night of November 7, 1841, as the brig *Creole* was sailing from Norfolk, Virginia, to New Orleans with 135 slaves aboard. Shortly after 9:00 p.m., a "portion of the slaves"—more precisely, nineteen—rose up. Led by a slave named Madison Washington, they seized control of the ship, in the process killing slaveholding passenger John Hewell, who "was employed with the officers in resisting the mutiny." Four members of the crew, including the captain, were also wounded in the melee. The self-liberated slaves then forced the crew to sail for Nassau, Bahamas, where they arrived on November 9.[120] According to British law, all of the slaves on the ship were now free.

The cry quickly went up from the mainland that the nineteen former slaves who commandeered the brig should be returned to the United States to be tried for mutiny and murder. It was self-evident that the remaining slaves who had been on the *Creole* would never be returned to slavery by the British. But the ship had been involved in the legal interstate slave trade, as opposed to the illegal international trade that the *Amistad* had been plying (as a small part of what Michael Zeuske has labeled the "Hidden Atlantic" of the period). In consequence, "most southerners believed that the slaveholders who lost their property in Nassau were entitled to compensation from the British government."[121] It thus fell to two New England Yankees to seek redress from London.

Both Secretary of State Daniel Webster and the US minister in London, Edward Everett, gave it their best shot. There was an irony to this, since southerners—"determined to use this foreign policy appointment to further a Southern domestic agenda"—had opposed Everett's confirmation to the Court of St. James's.[122] True, it went against the grain for the Boston pastor's son to play the role of advocate for southern "property rights." Everett, however, was no antislavery radical, as his biographer Matthew Mason demonstrates. Rather, his views on the issue harmonized "with the moderate brand of British antislavery thought." Believing that slavery was heading toward extinction "was part of what kept Everett from agitating the issue himself."[123] Southerners who feared a feeble assertion of slaveholders' interests from the erstwhile Harvard University professor of Greek must have been pleasantly surprised by Everett's diplomacy in London.

Following Webster's detailed guidance, Everett addressed a lengthy note on the *Creole* matter to Aberdeen on March 1, 1842. In summarizing the case of the administration of President John Tyler, Everett found that the issue called "loudly for redress." After all, the ship had been "passing from one port of The United States to another on a lawful voyage" with slaves on board who were "natives of America and belonging to American citizens." Such persons were "recognized as property by the Constitution of The United States, in those parts of the Union in which slavery exists." Anticipating a counterargument regarding the universal evil of slavery, the American diplomat quickly added that "this species of property, far from being unknown to the law of nations, or peculiar to The United States, exists in the colonies of all the States of Europe, who have colonies, excepting Great Britain, and has but recently been abolished in a portion of the colonial possessions of the British empire."[124]

Having established this to the satisfaction of official Washington, Everett went on to charge British colonial authorities with behavior "contrary to every principle of maritime law applicable to the case." Given all the violations alleged, Everett was "instructed to say that his Government will deem it a clear case for indemnification and redress." True, former prime minister Lord Palmerston had previously staked out the position that slavery "being now abolished throughout the British empire, there can be no well-founded claim for compensation in respect to slaves who, under any circumstances, may come into the British colonies, any more than there could be with respect to slaves who might be brought into the United Kingdom." But to this seemingly conclusive statement, Everett responded that the US government did not concede "that the question depends at all on the state of the British law." Nor could Everett admit that "the influence of local law can affect the relations of friendly Powers in any such case as this," adding, "No alteration of the local laws of England can increase, diminish, or in any way affect the duty of her Government and its colonial Authorities in such cases, as such duty exists according to the law, the comity, and the usage of nations."[125] Webster and Everett had put forth what can only be called a detailed and forcefully argued case for compensation.

Additionally, the Tyler administration "never called for the return of the actual mutineers."[126] Hence Webster "was frustrated by British politicians' apparently willful misinterpretation of the American position as asking for return of the actual people involved rather than monetary remuneration."[127] He must have found Aberdeen's response to Everett's March 1 note irksome indeed. The foreign secretary replied as if the Americans had demanded a return of the freed slaves, and argued accordingly. To add insult to injury, he reminded Everett of the ringing words of the Declaration of Independence, which proclaimed the inalienable right of all men to life, liberty, and the pursuit of happiness. In this case, it was British law that had "pronounced these rights to be indefeasible" and had thus "deprived Her Majesty's Government of all discretionary power by which [the former slaves'] condition could be affected." Having thoroughly dismantled the straw man, Aberdeen concluded that it was "impossible" to "acquiesce in the claims of Mr. Everett on the present occasion."[128] Everett would "gamely" continue to seek reparations from London, but he would do so in vain. Meanwhile, in the United States, North-South divisions were hardening over the issue of reparations, with southerners insistent on recompense for the slaveholders financially injured by the mutiny.[129]

In fact, the *Creole* case was soon threatening to derail the delicate negotiations between Lord Ashburton and Daniel Webster in Washington. This was yet one more cause of frustration: the issue of the *Creole* was never included in Ashburton's instructions, and the Briton thought that the whole matter was best negotiated in London rather than Washington. The two men managed to save their pact, the Webster-Ashburton Treaty of 1842, with a well-timed if vague guarantee from the British side. After more than a decade of controversy, the *Creole* Affair, along with a set of related controversies, was finally settled in 1855 by an Anglo-American claims commission that awarded payments to both sides.[130] But the ruckus over the liberation of slaves in the Bahamas had stirred domestic sectional dispute while imperiling the conclusion of a treaty that was crucial to establishing amity in Anglo-American relations. The omens were not auspicious.

Conclusion: Constrained Options

By the 1830s slavery had been the cause of multiple difficulties in Anglo-American relations and had exacerbated others. It was particularly frustrating for both sides when issues related to slavery had stymied their attempts to achieve shared policy goals (such as suppression of the transatlantic slave trade) or threatened a thaw that was in the interest of both (as had the Negro Seamen Acts). But Washington was not in a position to determine on its own America's exterior relations. On the issue of colonization, Washington would for a time cede leadership to the states. And with regard to the slave trade, the United States would have to sacrifice its long-held policy against the right of search in order to achieve a more pressing goal in the Civil War, which was also brought on by slavery.

CHAPTER 4

"Fully Meets Its Responsibility"
The Limits of American Unilateralism

With interest in colonization of free Blacks rising after Nat Turner's Rebellion, and the national colonization society in a state of seemingly terminal decline, the opportunity presented itself for someone to step into the breach. Under the circumstances, it is not surprising that the initiative now moved to the individual states. Nor is it coincidental that states began to take more assertive action toward removing Blacks soon after Turner's failed slave revolt in Southampton County, Virginia, in August 1831.[1]

On the related issue of the slave trade, no progress at all had been made in the diplomatic back-and-forth between London and Washington, DC. Furthermore, without an American concession on the right of search, it was unclear how any future progress could be made. The British government would continue tenaciously to lobby successive American administrations for at least some meaningful compromise on the issue. But it would take a cataclysm in the United States to compel the administration of President Abraham Lincoln to give in on the issue. By that point, they had more important issues to deal with, and thus other foreign policy priorities.

States Take the Lead

The Maryland State Colonization Society chose in 1833 to act independently of the national society and moved forward with the foundation of Maryland in Africa at Cape Palmas. It was soon followed by the colonization societies in New York and Pennsylvania. In the Deep South, Mississippi took the lead, and Louisiana soon followed suit.[2] The legislature of Maryland in fact resolved to remove *all* free Blacks from the state, and sheriffs were authorized to do so forcibly in the case of African Americans who refused to leave voluntarily.[3] This went against the voluntary expatriation policy of the American Colonization Society (ACS). But in the aftermath of the slave rebellion in neighboring Virginia, the Marylanders were determined to act. Maryland in Africa was generally a success, and would merge with Liberia in April 1857.[4] New York and Pennsylvania would jointly contribute the settlement at Bassa Cove, while Mississippi in Africa was established at Greenville.[5] Eventually these settlements would also be absorbed into the expanding Liberia.

The growth of Liberia raised further issues for America's foreign relations. As the colony expanded, so, too, did the potential for conflict with European imperial powers. The House Committee on Commerce released a significant report on February 28, 1843, that addressed this possibility (commonly known as the Kennedy Report). "It is vitally important," the Committee asserted, "that the territory of the colonies should be enlarged, and that their jurisdiction should become clear and incontestable over the whole line between Cape Mount and Cape Palmas, a distance of about three hundred miles; and that, in case of hostilities between this and any European country, their rights as neutrals should be recognized and respected." British merchants, the reports continued, were "claiming rights, independent of the Government of Liberia and Maryland, within their territorial limits." The Royal Navy had been called upon by merchants to shield them from the revenue laws of Liberia, while the French had "sought to obtain a cession of lands within the limits of Liberia . . . and to which the people of that colony have a pre-emptive right." This was all quite problematic; to the committee's knowledge, "neither Great Britain nor any European Government has . . . claimed political jurisdiction from Cape Mount to Cape Palmas." Since, furthermore, a "republican commonwealth" now inhabited that territory, "it is essential that they be not disturbed in the exercise of rights already acquired, or from extending their authority over the entire line of the coast . . . generally known as Liberia."[6]

The committee had come to the conclusion that the subject of African colonization had "become sufficiently important to attract the attention of the people, in its connexion [*sic*] with the question of the political relations which these colonies are to hold with our Government." In a striking line, the Kennedy Report asserted that it was the duty of the United States, "before an occasion of conflicting interest may arise, to take such steps toward the recognition of our appropriate relations to these communities as may hereafter secure them the protection of this Government, and to our citizens the advantages of commercial intercourse with them."[7] The implication of an extension of American protection to Liberia was obvious: it would be tantamount to declaring that Liberia was, in fact, an American colony.

As the committee saw it, this was not a problem. "The idea of an American colony is a new one," the report granted. But it "is manifestly worthy of the highest consideration. The committee sees nothing in our Constitution to forbid it." A colony in Africa would be analogous to the relationship that Washington had with various Native American tribes, the major difference being that Liberia "would require much less exercise of political jurisdiction, much less territorial supervision, than is presented in the case of these tribes." Liberia would, instead, "require aid towards the enlargement of territory, occasional visitation and protection by our naval armaments, a guarantee, perhaps, to be secured to them by the influence of our Government, of the right of neutrality in the wars that may arise between European or American States." With this said, the committee resolved that the secretary of state should submit a report to the next Congress on the "political relations proper to be adopted and maintained between this Government" and current and future African colonies.[8]

Such opinions emanating from official Washington proved confusing, and concerning, to other nations, which were left unclear as to the Tyler administration's position on the relationship between Liberia and the United States. In August 1843 the British government inquired, through its minister in Washington, about this matter. His government, Sir Henry Fox told Secretary of State Abel P. Upshur, had "for some time past, been desirous of ascertaining, authentically, the nature and extent of the connexion [sic] subsisting between the American colony of Liberia, on the coast of Africa, and the Government of the United States." "Differences" that arose between British merchants and the authorities of Liberia "render it very necessary, in order to avert for the future serious trouble and contention in that quarter, that her Majesty's Government should be accurately informed what degree of official patronage and protection, if any, the United States Government extend to the colony of Liberia, how far, if at all, the United States Government recognize the colony of Liberia, as a national establishment; and consequently, how far, if at all, the United States Government hold themselves responsible toward foreign countries for the acts of the authorities of Liberia."[9] With numerous merchants on the West African coast and a colony at Sierra Leone, London needed to know the nature of the relationship between Liberia and the United States.

Upshur responded with an extended narrative of the founding and early years of the colony, emphasizing the philanthropic nature of the project. The upshot of this disquisition was that the United States did not claim Liberia as its colony. He then added that America, for its part, did not "undertake to settle and adjust differences which have arisen between British subjects and the authorities of Liberia." Since the Liberians were "nearly powerless, they must rely, for the protection of their own rights, on the justice and sympathy of other powers." This might have served as an answer to Fox's inquiry. Yet Upshur continued, adding that the US government regarded Liberia "as occupying a peculiar position, and as possessing peculiar claims to the friendly consideration of all christian [sic] powers; that this Government will be, at all times, prepared to interpose its good offices to prevent any encroachment by the colony upon any just right of any nation; and that it would be very unwilling to see it despoiled of its territory rightfully acquired, or improperly restrained in the exercise of its necessary rights and powers as an independent settlement."[10] In this last paragraph, Upshur had managed to be both paternalistic and vague. He seemed, at the same time, to be claiming an American responsibility for oversight of Liberia's external policy and for the policy of other nations toward Liberia. But the nature of this responsibility was left unclear. His note, nevertheless, appears to have answered British concerns, since London sent no request for clarification.

If Upshur's note had been meant to quell conflict between the British and Liberians, however, it failed. The secretary's wording had been too equivocal, it appears, to warn off London, which continued to disregard Liberian assertions of sovereignty over trade with territories claimed by Monrovia. In this context, the House Committee on Foreign Affairs sought again to clarify the responsibilities of Washington with regard to the Liberians. Their conclusions were more restrictive than Upshur's had been: "The General Government, implicated by no legitimate State authority has nothing to do with [Liberia]; nor does the duty of protection, which the Government of the United States owes to its citizens everywhere, at all apply to the inhabitants of Liberia. They are not citizens of the United States; they exist and live under a government regularly organized, with all the powers and attributes of sovereignty, bearing politically the same relation to the United States as to Britain, and independent of both."[11] The US government had created a diplomatic difficulty for itself, with which, in the 1840s, it was now wrestling. It wanted to disavow the responsibility of the colonial power. Yet because Liberia was a nation of former slaves, domestic political concerns prevented successive administrations from

recognizing Liberia as an independent nation. It thus held an anomalous position in America's foreign policy: founded by Americans, it was not an American colony; possessing all the rights of sovereignty, it was not a sovereign
nation. It is little wonder that the British had sought clarification.

Advocates of colonization also sought clarity on the question of Liberia's
status. The ACS requested that the board of the Massachusetts Colonization
Society provide their opinion on the sovereignty of Liberia. On January 9, 1845,
the Massachusetts society responded that Liberia was, in fact, a sovereign state,
with the power to enact necessary laws "and to perform all other acts implied
in sovereignty." The "dependence of a feeble state on foreign aid and counsel" was in no way "incompatible with its sovereignty." Given this, the board
resolved "that the Government of the United States should be requested as a
powerful and friendly nation, and from a regard for the general interest of humanity to interpose its good offices for averting any such danger which may
at any time threaten the Commonwealth of Liberia."[12]

It was, however, an inopportune time to call for greater American commitment in Africa. President James K. Polk was most concerned with matters
relating to the Western Hemisphere. Thus, in articulating the little-remembered
Polk Corollary of 1845, he reemphasized the Monroe Doctrine, with its assertion that the United States had no interest in colonization outside its hemisphere, in regions of interest to European powers.[13] This policy would seem
to limit the scope of American involvement on the west coast of Africa. American ability to project power in that region was, in fact, reduced at this time
with the withdrawal of ships from the Africa Squadron during the Mexican-
American War. Furthermore, this came at a time when the British government
formally informed Washington of its contempt for claims of Liberian sovereignty: it "could not accept the slightest assumption of any sovereign powers
being present in a commercial experiment of a philanthropic society."[14] American policymakers could not, it would appear, have it both ways. Either Liberia was a sovereign entity or it was not.

Liberian Independence

Under these circumstances, the ACS decided that the time had come for Liberia to draft a constitution and to declare itself an independent nation. The
United States "chose a temporizing course, and by declining to invest the colony of Liberia with the sovereignty of the United States, impelled it to assume
a sovereignty of its own."[15] On July 5, 1847, a constitutional convention met in
Monrovia, and drafted both a constitution and a declaration of independence.

The new nation now found itself under significant pressure from Britain and then France to grant commercial concessions in exchange for recognition.[16] Independence thus failed to solve Liberia's international affairs dilemmas.

Chief among these dilemmas was now the failure of the United States to recognize the nascent republic. Slavery was, as with the failure to recognize Haiti, the determining factor in Washington's decision. With slavery taking center stage in the American political debate after the Mexican-American War, it was impossible to imagine southerners establishing normal diplomatic relations with a nation governed by free Black emigrants and former slaves.[17] The degree to which the successful functioning of such a state would undercut the narrative of Black inferiority was too much to contemplate. As with Haiti, recognition would have to wait until the Lincoln administration. In 1850, Ralph R. Gurley, the ACS secretary, submitted to the secretary of state a report on the state of Liberian-US relations. In it he argued strongly for American recognition of Liberia as an independent nation.[18] But the Whig administration of Millard Fillmore proved no more receptive than had the Polk administration.

It was not until 1862 that the US government would extend diplomatic recognition to Liberia. By then the president was Abraham Lincoln, who had a record of supporting the cause of colonization. A controversial policy in the new Republican Party, colonization found a "public spokesman" in Lincoln by 1858. In that year Lincoln advocated for colonization in the first of the Lincoln-Douglas debates. "For many white Americans," Eric Foner notes, "including Lincoln, colonization was part of a plan for ending slavery that represented a middle ground between abolitionist radicalism and the prospect of a United States existing forever half-slave and half-free." Colonization was, Foner asserts, an option that might put slavery on the path to its "ultimate extinction," of which Lincoln "had spoken but without any real explanation of how it would take place."[19] Lincoln's interest in exploring the possibility of exporting America's freed slaves nevertheless extended into his presidency, thus inducing the United States to engage in further engagement with the Atlantic world.

Continued Tensions over the Slave Trade

Meanwhile, the issue of slave trade suppression continued to bedevil the Anglophone maritime powers. The British government, though discouraged by the lack of progress with the Americans, was determined to continue with its efforts at eradicating the trade. Increasingly, its cousin across the Atlantic began to question its motives in doing so. John Quincy Adams had told Stratford Canning that a major objection to the right of search in time of peace was the proclivity of such a policy to bring "other changes" that might lead to "the dominion of the Sea, which may eventually . . . confound all distinction of time and circumstance, of Peace and War, and of Rights applicable to each State."[20] The idea of British maritime domination of the Atlantic was a nightmare to Americans, who frequently asked themselves if London's motivations in the anti-slave-trade crusade had more to do with commercial and imperial advantage than with a desire to deliver Africans from evil. Scholars have debated the same issue. Some historians have tended to conclude that economic reasons cannot explain Britain's decision in the early 1800s to seek abolition of the trade. According to Kenneth Morgan, the argument that "Britain abolished its slave trade primarily for economic reasons cannot be sustained on the evidence available." The British political class was, rather, "willing to make the economic sacrifice of abolishing the slave trade."[21]

But if antislavery was not motivated primarily by a desire to expand market share and impose handicaps on potential competitors, it was not disconnected from questions of empire. In this the Americans had a point. As Richard Huzzey has perceptively noted, "foreign and colonial anti-slavery policies were part of a global assertion of imperial power, with British policies flexible, responsive and opportunistic with different peoples in different circumstances." Huzzey thus concludes that "it is useful to see a British world system of anti-slavery, its 'gravitational field' fluctuating in power depending on the terrain, atmosphere, and individuals involved."[22] American policy toward slave trade suppression can thus be usefully viewed as an attempt to remain outside of this gravitational field to the greatest extent possible while doing what could be done to suppress the trade with this imperative in the forefront. John Quincy Adams had once spoken of the American desire not to "come in as a cockboat in the wake of the British man-of-war." While he said this in a different context, the principle remained the same: the United States could not allow itself to be sucked into the British foreign policy and imperial system, and thus to take a subservient role in determining policies that were in Britain's interest. James Monroe was, Adams wrote, "averse to any course which should have the appearance of taking a position subordinate to that of Great Britain."[23] This aversion continued after the Monroe presidency, as did American perceptions that American subordination was indeed part of the British plan.

Thus Washington's policy of maximum independence continued. This presented the problem that the British had, in fact, hit upon the only scheme that was likely to successfully end the trade, but they needed American cooperation to make it work. Yet "despite the fact that only the consent of the United States was necessary to complete the international cordon around the slave

trade, American opinion persisted in attributing British efforts to ulterior motives."[24] Anglo-American diplomacy on the suppression of the trade went into
the doldrums after the failure of the slave trade convention, and the British
continued with their attempt to construct a system of treaties that would allow for more effective suppression. But without American participation—
defined as accepting the right of mutual search—the "cordon" could not be
completed. In 1831 Mercer tried again to move the American administration,
now headed by President Andrew Jackson, to negotiate with the maritime
powers of the Atlantic for the suppression of the trade. He introduced a resolution calling on the president to begin such negotiations as "he may deem
expedient for the effectual Abolition of the African Slave-trade, and its ultimate
denunciation as Piracy under the Law of Nations, by consent of the civilized
world." In part, the timing of the resolution's introduction was determined
by the perception that France might be thereby influenced to pursue "measures more effectual than those which they have hitherto been disposed to
adopt for the accomplishment of that object." Yet Charles R. Vaughn, the British minister to Washington, saw no great hope for the resumption of Anglo-
American discussions on the topic, noting, "I have not perceived the slightest
inclination, in 2 successive Administrations, to renew the Negotiations."[25]

Yet the British minister would, in fact, try again in two years. The impetus
this time was significant progress in anti-slave-trade diplomacy with France.
In November 1831 and March 1833, London and Paris concluded conventions
on trade suppression by which, among other matters, the two powers granted
to each other the right of search. Both now sought to gain American accession to the conventions by means of a joint appeal to Washington. In August 1833, therefore, Vaughn approached Secretary of State Louis McLane
with a proposal that the Jackson administration join in the Anglo-French arrangement. McLane put Vaughn off, saying that he would need to sound out
Congress on its opinions. The delay continued, and Vaughn and his French
counterpart, Louis Barbe Charles Sérurier, decided in December that the
time had come to enjoin a response from the administration. "I think it is
time to press this Government to a decision," Vaughn wrote Lord Palmerston in December.[26]

The time was hardly ripe. Southern objections to British anti-slave-trade
crusading were growing. In fact, Southerners "were highly sensitive to the re-
percussions of any attack, no matter how remote, on slavery; and a new
factor had entered into the consideration of American diplomacy." The opposition to granting the right of search continued, but "the hostility of the
South now constituted a more intractable factor." Southerners could not help
but see in British attacks on the trade the hidden goal of abolition of slavery

itself. Hugh G. Soulsby cites historian of the South William A. Dunning, who noted the "feeling in the South that the war on the slave trade was too closely associated with abolitionism to be wholly free from peril to the institutions of the section."[27]

McLane, a native of the border state Delaware, expressed precisely this problem in a conversation with Vaughn, telling him "of the apprehension of aggravating the excited feelings of the Southern States, and that, at this time, the endeavours to get up Anti-Slavery Societies have roused the jealousy of all the Slave-holders throughout the Union, about the General Government touching in any shape the question of the Slave Trade, notwithstanding the accession to the Conventions has nothing to do with Slavery, as it exists in the States."

Vaughn warned McLane "that a subserviency of the Government to the feelings of their Slave-holders, by refusing to accede to the Conventions, will do infinite mischief to their national character in Europe."[28] Vaughn thus wrote McLane in December to ask for an answer on American accession to the conventions. He expressed the "confident expectation" that, if the United States should join the Anglo-French arrangement, the other maritime states would also accede. In appealing to the secretary of state, Vaughn reminded him of the congressional resolutions of 1821 and 1822, thus recalling a time when the American legislature acknowledged that only the right of search could end the trade for good.[29]

McLane's polite but firm response reflected the Jackson administration's resolve to continue Washington's unilateralist policy toward suppression. "In the opinion of the President," he wrote Vaughn, "these Conventions are substantially liable to the objections which, on former occasions, have been deemed insuperable." And if that was not sufficient, the added provision that the right of search should be extended to America's coasts "would have led him, under any circumstances, altogether to decline it."[30] Palmerston was, however, "unwilling to abandon hope" in the face of McLane's note. After all, even absent the right of search off the coasts of the United States, a joint agreement was worth having. The British could still police the coast of Africa and the West Indies, thus forcing would-be slavers to "run the gauntlet through the cruizers of almost all the Naval Powers of Christendom, over some thousand miles of sea, unprotected by any Flag by which they might attempt to cover their iniquity." The last point was key: the enemies of the trade needed an agreement with the United States in order to deny the slavers the protection of the American flag. Palmerston thus instructed Vaughn once again to propose accession to the Jackson administration, this time "omitting the stipulation for the extension of the right of search to the Coasts of the United

States."[31] With this uncharacteristic show of flexibility, Palmerston hoped to seal the deal.

He was to be disappointed yet again. The new US secretary of state, Georgia's John Forsyth, responded to Vaughn on October 4. It appeared, he said, that neither the British nor the French government had "comprehended the full force and effect of the Note of Mr. McLane." McLane's answer was meant to express the president's determination "not to accede to any Convention liable to the objections brought into view." He now raised the matter of the tribunals. The geography of these was simply impossible, according to Forsyth: "Beyond this Continent, The United States neither have, nor expect, nor desire to have, territory or jurisdiction." Thus, Americans accused of slaving would, when captured, have to be sent all the way back to the United States for trial. This was untenable: "Acquitted individuals might be compensated, yet the commercial enterprise of their Country be obstructed or paralyzed while the tribunals were deciding their innocence or guilt." Now that Palmerston had compromised on one issue, the Americans raised another. Forsyth could not have been clearer that this was, from the US perspective, the end of the discussion. "The Undersigned," he added, "does not intend to invite a discussion of the subject." The conversation was over, since the Jackson administration had "definitively" decided "not to make The United States a party to any Convention on the subject of the Slave Trade."[32]

The Cuban Slave Trade

The discussion was over, but the problem was not resolved. The slave trade to Cuba was picking up considerably, and "American influence, in particular, helped in the continual slave trade" to that island.[33] Cuba had been a problem for British suppression efforts, even without American involvement. London had sought to bring Spain—as well as Portugal—into its Atlantic network of slave suppression treaties. Madrid, unlike the recalcitrant Lisbon, signed a suppression treaty with Britain in 1817, but "tried to placate British demands while it procrastinated as long as possible." The loss of most of its American empire made Spain even more dependent upon the Cuban sugar industry for funds coming into its coffers. Hence, Madrid was "loath to abandon the slave trade. It was thus able to play a constant game of duplicity, which enabled it to maintain the trade until the late 1860s."[34] For their part, Spaniards detected a like hypocrisy on the part of London. The British, as Bishop Don Félix Varela noted, were the major slave traders for much of the history of the odious commerce in Africans. Yet now, with so much blood on its hands, Britain preached "leniency, with the smoking sword in its hand, and bloodstained clothing; Englishmen, the word philanthropy loses its value on your lips . . . you are poor apostles of humanity."[35]

This distrust was further exacerbated, and Spanish anxieties were increased, when Palmerston named David Turnbull as the new British consul in Havana. Turnbull, a committed abolitionist, arrived in Cuba in early November 1840. His antislavery writings may in fact have resulted in his appointment.[36] Such was the concern in Cuba that Captain General Miguel Tacón wrote his government to say that Turnbull should be declared persona non grata. Palmerston "brusquely rejected" the call for a different candidate when it was forwarded by Madrid's minister in London, and the consul made his arrival. Tacón, however, refused to recognize Turnbull.[37] Turnbull's crusade against slavery in Cuba attracted the attention of American southerners, who "raised an outcry for United States action" against him and the new captain general, Gerónimo Valdéz—the latter having taken the unexpected step of actually seeking to enforce the anti-slave-trade agreements.[38]

Not all southerners were equally panicked about the British attempt to end slavery in Cuba. The American consul in Havana, South Carolinian Robert Blair Campbell, "was less impressed by the threat to Cuba's slaveholders," and thought that the Spanish Army could deal with any slave revolt.[39] Spaniards in Cuba were, however, less certain of this capacity. The *ayuntamiento*, or town council, of Havana argued in 1841 that if Madrid negotiated an agreement with Britain allowing the latter to "decide the status of illegally imported slaves, then rebellion would be likely and the island would be irretrievably lost to the mother country."[40] The aggressive British attempt to end the slave trade, and indeed slavery, in Cuba also led Spaniards to note that London was not taking the same approach to the United States, which also was a slaveholding nation.[41]

Yet efforts to get the Americans out of the slave trade were, in fact, a British priority—and especially, in the 1830s and 1840s, the slave trade with Cuba. Palmerston was particularly, and vocally, concerned with the use of US-flagged ships in the trade to the island. In December 1836 Palmerston was already writing to the US consul in London, Andrew Stevenson, to complain of "alleged employment of vessels under the Flag of the Union to assist Spanish subjects in carrying on the Slave Trade." Stevenson promptly and properly replied that he would pass this note on to the American government, which would "omit nothing which may be proper to be done" to prevent such use of the nation's flag.[42] The issue was not, however, to be so easily resolved. The American consul in Havana was Virginian Nicholas P. Trist, a man "lukewarm in his opposition to the slave trade" who "nursed a deep resentment of British power in general and British abolitionism in particular." Trist arrived in Havana in 1833 and proved to be a constant thorn in the side of the British, who accused him of issuing papers to slavers so that they could sail under the American flag. Trist also served for over a year as consul for Portugal, and, "in that capacity, it was said, cleared many slave ships for the African coast."[43]

This was all too much for Palmerston, who wrote to the British minister in Washington, Sir Henry Fox, in April 1839 to ask him to make the secretary of state aware of Trist's actions. As Palmerston put it inimitably to Fox, "You will suggest for the consideration of that minister, whether some inconvenience may not arise from the circumstance that The United States' Consul in a port which is a great slave-mart, is also Consul for the Power, whose flag is most notoriously and extensively employed to protect Slave Trade undertakings."[44] Trist, however, continued in his position. In July, Palmerston was complaining to Fox that "the American Consul at the Havana appears . . . to have lent his seal and signature to attest untruths, and to sanction irregularities, intended to cover undertakings in Slave Trade." Once again, the prime minister called on Fox to bring this to Forsyth's attention, so that, in atypical understatement, "the American Consul at the Havana may be directed to take more care in the future not to attest documents which may be meant to cover the traffic in slaves."[45] But despite complaints from both Britons and Americans, as well as a thorough investigation of his dealings by the administration of President Martin Van Buren, Trist was able to remain in place until removed in 1841 with the change of parties in Washington.[46]

Search and "Visit"

Nor, unsurprisingly, was there progress to be made on the issue of the right of search. Fox raised the issue for reconsideration with Secretary of State Forsyth in late October 1839. Given, he said, the "regular, rapid, and frightful" expansion of the trade under the American flag since the matter had last been discussed, the British government thought the time was right to look at this issue again. If the Americans were still unwilling to accede, then they were asked "to devise some other effectual method" for ending the "guilty and sinful traffic."[47] The American response to British requests to reopen discussion of the right of search could not have been more categorical. Stevenson wrote Palmerston in February 1840 that the United States could "never acquiesce" on this subject, adding "that her flag is to be the safeguard of all who sail under it, either in peace or in war." Washington would make no exception for the suppression of the slave trade, nor for the fulfillment of treaties to which it was not a party.[48] No further negotiation on this matter was called for. Forsyth reemphasized this point in a lengthy letter to Fox on February 12, noting that President Van Buren "sees with regret . . . that Her Britannic Majesty's Government continues to think important, that The United States should become a party to a Convention yielding the mutual right of search to the armed vessels of each other" in the pursuit of slavers.[49]

American noncompliance with the British system of slave trade suppression continued to clash with London's—and especially Palmerston's—determination to wipe out the trade by means of interlocking right of search conventions. The British thus introduced an innovation that they hoped would obviate the need for a right of search agreement with the United States. The idea was that of the "right of visit," by which the British claimed the right to "visit," rather than "search," a ship in order to check its papers and determine if it was truly an American vessel. The Americans utterly rejected the distinction, and hence any steps taken by Britain to visit US-flagged ships were bound to cause controversy between the two nations. It was indeed "unfortunate that the dispute over the right of visit should have become acute at a time when the relations between the two countries were strained almost to the breaking point." Issues relating to the Maine boundary, the Oregon Territory, and Texas "now threatened to produce war."[50]

In this context, cases of British "visits" of American ships only served to exacerbate relations. In November 1840 Stevenson was instructed to lodge a protest with Palmerston concerning British "unwarrantable search, detention, and ill-usage of an American vessel and her crew, on the coast of Africa." In the course of the complaint, the minister expressed "the painful regret which the Government of The United States feels" at the fact that previous remonstrances on the issue "should have proved unavailing in preventing the repetition of such abuses, as those which have so repeatedly been made the subject of complaint against Her Majesty's naval officers." Such wrongs "cannot longer be permitted by the Government of the United States." And although Palmerston responded that the British were investigating the incident in question, the issue would continue to rankle.[51] This dynamic of British actions and American reactions could not continue indefinitely.

The basis of a solution had been attempted in March 1840 by two naval officers—one American, one British—on station in Africa. Commander William Tucker of HMS *Wolverine* at that time reached an agreement with Lieutenant John S. Paine of USS *Grampus* regarding the right of search. The Tucker-Paine Agreement provided that ships of either country could "detain all vessels under American colours, found to be fully equipped for, and engaged in, the Slave Trade; that, if proved to be American property, they shall be handed over to the U.S. Schooner *Grampus*, or any other American cruiser, and that, if proved to be Spanish, Portuguese, Brazilian or English property, to any of Her Britannic Majesty's cruisers employed in the West Coast of Africa for the suppression of the Slave Trade." Upon learning of the Tucker-Paine Agreement, the Van Buren administration declared it void and beyond Paine's authority (*ultra vires*) even to negotiate.[52] The agreement would return to the table under the following administration, to help ease the logjam. But first, issues came to a head between London and Washington.

The five major powers of Europe agreed to a suppression treaty in December 1841. The terms of the agreement stated that the slave trade would be treated as a form of piracy and that the contracting parties would be granted a mutual right of search. The treaty was, in a sense, superfluous: Britain and France had already negotiated a suppression treaty, while Austria, Prussia, and Russia were not involved in the trade or its suppression. The point of the five-power treaty thus seems to have had "only an emblematic purpose—except, perhaps, as the first step in a larger project."[53] And this "larger project" was precisely what concerned the Americans, since it could only mean that the British were seeking to establish an alliance of nations that would put diplomatic pressure on the United States to join the system that London led. Unwilling to get roped into such a multilateral agreement—and totally opposed to granting the right of search in peacetime—the Americans might find themselves in a difficult position.

One American who was determined to avoid such a diplomatic trap was Lewis Cass, America's minister in Paris since 1836. Cass was a veteran of the War of 1812 and former territorial governor of Michigan. He was also a devout Anglophobe who was "readier to tolerate the abuse of the American flag in the slave trade than to concede anything to Great Britain," convinced as he was that "British activity against the slave trade was . . . merely a screen for the advancement of maritime power."[54] Cass took it upon himself to use his diplomatic post as a war room in his struggle against the Quintuple Treaty and, thus, against the extension of the right of search. Not content to press official Paris to reject the treaty, he put pen to paper and authored a lengthy pamphlet on the subject under the pseudonym An American. Published in Paris in January 1842, his pamphlet advanced little that was new, but much that was hostile to London. Denying that the connection of the right of search to the slave trade was more than "incidental," he declared of Britain, "Naval superiority she has acquired and naval supremacy she seeks." Granting the right of search would give the British flag "virtual supremacy of the seas." Echoing John Quincy Adams, Cass asserted that "it is not African slavery, the United-States wish to encourage. It is . . . American slavery, the slavery of American sailors, they seek to prevent." British ships stationed off the African coast, and armed with the right of search, would "seriously interrupt the trade of other nations." Thus dismissing the proclaimed reason for which the British were seeking the right to search ships of other nations, Cass added a disquisition on the sad history of impressment to round out the case. He concluded that the United States, "tho she may be crushed . . . will not be dishonored." The fact that the pamphlet was reprinted in the United States under Cass's name left no doubt that its author was, indeed, the American minister in Paris.[55]

The British response came in the form of a small book, written under the pseudonym An Englishman. The Englishman in question, Sir William Gore Ouseley, was unimpressed with Cass's vehement argumentation. Hoping to "calm his evidently morbid nationality," Ouseley made the case that it was unlikely indeed that impressment would ever be used again, "even in time of war." After all, the right of search had been in place for years with the French and Germans, and yet not one sailor had been taken by the nefarious practice. He thus concluded that there could be no reason to oppose the mutual right of search "unless the covert reason be the opposition of the slave-holding interests."[56]

Here Ouseley had a point. Southerners began at this point to seriously impugn the motives behind the British antislavery crusade. Most notable among these was the "self-important Kentuckian" Duff Green. Green arrived in Europe in 1841 as President John Tyler's "personal agent," and quickly began to give support to Cass in his efforts. Green published numerous pieces in the French newspapers, and maintained, as well, a correspondence on the issue. His case, as Matthew Karp summarizes, was that Britain was using the anti-slave-trade cause as a screen behind which to develop a dominant position in the world economy: "British antislavery was, in a real sense, British imperialism." Karp in fact concludes that Green's argument came to "dominate proslavery political discourse."[57] Britain had ulterior motives behind its abolitionist moralism, and its actions threatened American interests.

While modern-day scholars do not share Green's desire to defend the institution of slavery, they do grant that British antislavery efforts were linked with imperial and commercial ambitions. It was not just slaveholding Americans who perceived this. The French, as Keith Hamilton and Farida Shaikh observe, were increasingly convinced by the 1840s that "the British were resorting to measures aimed at suppression to advance their colonial and commercial interests." Andrew Lambert adds that "the states that resisted British demands did so for powerful reasons. All nations believed that behind the smokescreen of moral fervor and righteous indignation the British were serving their own commercial ends."[58] It could come as no surprise, then, that the Americans were unwilling to join in a British-led international system for suppression that would have—to the extent that it was successful—the result of increasing British power in the Atlantic world.

Given this complex of motivations, however, London remained determined to stamp out the trade. And thus a crisis was brewing with the United States. The Royal Navy continued to stop and "visit" American-flagged ships after the repeated failure to get American accession to a right of search agreement. In September 1841 Stevenson wrote from London to Secretary of State Daniel Webster, "Having failed in getting the American Government to unite in yielding the qualified right of Search, this Government are now disposed to exercise it under another, and more offensive form." The British government's actions seemed, to Stevenson, to be "influenced in a great measure no doubt, by the abolitionist feeling which is deep and strong here, and the mistaken opinions so generally entertained by the British public, as to the extent and influence of the same feelings, in the United States."[59]

The Webster-Ashburton Treaty and the Africa Squadron

Resolving the outstanding issues between Great Britain and the United States had become imperative. The British foreign secretary, Lord Aberdeen, sent his special emissary, Lord Ashburton, to Washington to try his hand at gaining a diplomatic solution to the set of problems, including the matter of the slave trade. Arriving in the United States in early April 1842, Ashburton began negotiations with Webster on the vexatious issues that divided the two. Ashburton knew that "any efficient right of search would, however, with difficulty be conceded." He therefore asked his American interlocutors what they would suggest "and whether America could remain in the position of refusing all remedy against crimes which they had been the most vehement to denounce, and of the existence of which they could not doubt." Webster's solution to the problem was based on the previously abjured Tucker-Paine Agreement. It was decided that the United States would deploy a force of eighty guns on the African coast and that, to the extent practicable, Royal Navy and US Navy ships would hunt in pairs. This would deny the cover of the American flag to slavers. Thus, article 8 of the Webster-Ashburton Treaty (officially the Treaty of Washington) did not address the two most troublesome issues—to wit, America's unwillingness to grant the right of search and Britain's refusal to renounce impressment. But in the agreement on joint cruising, both sides found an acceptable, and potentially workable, solution to these issues that had confounded previous diplomacy. Ashburton was led to conclude that "if this arrangement can be brought into execution by treaty, I shall consider it to be the very best fruit of this mission." He added with satisfaction that Paine was to be brought in to consult on the best means of execution of the plan.[60]

The Webster-Ashburton Treaty was signed on August 10, 1842. Despite significant opposition in the Senate by James Buchanan of Pennsylvania and Thomas Hart Benton of Missouri, the treaty was ratified on August 20. Benton, for his part, could see no point in sending an American naval squadron to the dangerous and miasmic coast of Africa "unless indeed, in excessive love of the blacks, it is deemed meritorious to destroy the whites."[61] Cass had, by this time, reappeared on the scene. His ambition for the presidency led the minister in Paris to engage in what came to be known as a war of words with Webster. Writing the secretary of state in October, Cass expressed, at some length, regret that British renunciation of the right of search had not preceded the treaty. He went on to critique the Treaty of Washington largely on these grounds, for "the mutual rights of the parties are . . . wholly untouched; their pretentions exist in full force; and what they could do prior to this arrangement they may now do." Webster's response to Cass's claims was forceful: "Inasmuch as the treaty gives no color or pretext whatever to any right of searching our ships, a declaration against such a right would have been no more suitable to this treaty than a declaration against the right of sacking our towns in time of peace, or any other outrage."[62] Cass's letters to the secretary read like "scare-mongering, electioneering broadsides."[63] Yet Webster certainly got the better of the argument. In fact, Britain did not seek to exercise the right of visit on American ships in the first decade and a half after the coming into force of the Treaty of Washington.[64]

This is not to say that the contracting parties achieved the objective of article 8 after 1842. The literature on the US Africa Squadron in the 1840s and 1850s is replete with examples of the failure of the squadron to execute its prescribed charge. Donald L. Canney concludes pithily that "the squadron was not a success," and finds "inexcusable" the fact that the naval force averaged one capture every six months over the course of its cruises.[65] By the summer of 1844, the British minister in Washington, Richard Pakenham, was providing to Secretary of State John Calhoun documentation on the participation of American vessels in the Brazilian slave trade. The British government at this time expressed the hope that "the Government of The United States will be disposed to adopt decided measures to put a stop to the abuses which have thus been brought to their knowledge, and which tend so materially to defeat the combined efforts of the 2 Governments for the prevention of the trade in slaves."[66] Having negotiated with the British a system for the more effective suppression of the trade, the Americans seemed in no great rush to implement it.

Looking at the evidence, it would be incorrect to blame the officers of the Africa Squadron themselves for the unit's shortcomings. Despite rumors to the contrary, southern officers were at least as efficient in making captures as their northern counterparts. The blame for the lackluster performance of the US Navy in suppressing the trade thus must "fall higher up than the squadron commanders."[67] From early on in its history, the squadron was hampered by a lack of zeal for suppression at the top ranks of the federal government. Abel P. Upshur, the navy secretary at the time article 8 of the Webster-Ashburton Treaty was to be implemented, was a "proslavery radical of the Calhoun stamp." Soon to be Webster's replacement at the Department of State, Upshur made it clear to the Africa Squadron's commander that suppression was only a secondary duty and that protection of American commerce was to be its primary function. Even for this function, the flotilla assembled by Upshur was meager, amounting to only four ships to police the extensive West African littoral. As Don E. Fehrenbacher forthrightly puts it, the American policy on slave trade suppression was, at this time, "essentially gestural, aimed primarily at screening American commerce from British interference."[68]

Brazil and Cuba

At a time when the Brazilian slave trade was booming, the British were understandably frustrated with American participation in the commerce, as well as with the less-than-eager policy direction emanating from Washington. In May 1847 Palmerston—back in the foreign office since the previous July—was calling the attention of the administration of President James K. Polk to the flourishing Brazilian trade in slaves. British estimates had forty-two thousand slaves entering the Empire of Brazil in 1846 alone. As Palmerston observed, the trade was "openly carried on without any attempt at hindrance on the part of the authorities." Soon the foreign secretary was to speak even more bluntly on the matter of American participation in slaving. In June he drew Pakenham's attention to "the extensive use which is made of The United States' flag, and to the frequent employment of United States' vessels, for purposes connected with the Slave Trade." Palmerston found no blame in the American naval officers, but, as has been noted, placed the blame for this situation squarely on the administration, since it was "clear that the evil complained of can only be remedied by some more active measures of prevention on the part of The United States' Government." He thus instructed Pakenham, yet again, to call the matter to the attention of the Polk administration.[69]

The administration was hardly opposed to fighting the trade to Brazil. Despite the strong proslavery predilections of the American minister to Brazil, Henry A. Wise, he proved an exceptionally vigorous campaigner against the slave trade of that nation. The Virginian in fact "distinguished himself for his tireless battle against the ongoing Atlantic slave trade and, even more, his outrage at American participation in the illegal traffic." Karp finds no contradiction in this behavior, seeing instead an ideological consistency. The desire to maintain the institution of slavery in Brazil meant working against British abolitionist intervention. This, in turn, required an end to the Brazilian slave trade, which was found to be so provocative in London: "To protect African slavery inside Brazil, the African slave trade had to be eliminated." By extension, preservation of the institution in Brazil made America's "peculiar institution" safer in the minds of its southern defenders, because it lessened the chances of British use of the trade as a wedge into abolition of slavery itself in the Western Hemisphere. As Karp observes, "The slave trade had to die, Wise insisted, so that domestic slavery could live."[70] It is no surprise that his efforts, as he perceived it, made him a pariah to Brazilian officials; or, as he put it, "obnoxious to this Govt."[71]

Still, Wise's record of action against the slave trade was not to be questioned. In June 1847 Secretary of State Buchanan told the secretary of the British mission in Washington that "it was quite impossible that any one could have carried out the spirit of [Buchanan's] instruction with greater zeal and perseverance than Mr. Wise had done; his remonstrances with the Brazilian Government had been unceasing; and that, with regard to the employment of American shipping in the conveyance of slaves to Brazil, Mr. Wise had gone to the very verge of what 'the laws of The United States would sanction, in his endeavours to prevent such employment, and to defeat the various subterfuges resorted to in order to secure it by the slave-dealers in Brazil.'"[72] Wise was unsuccessful in ending American participation in the trade, which continued in Brazil. But Brazil's domestic slave system would, in fact, outlast that of the United States by more than two decades. Wise and those who sent him could at least take solace in this.

The British would continue to protest to the Polk administration—and to the subsequent administrations of Presidents Zachary Taylor and Millard Fillmore—about the abuse of the American flag in the trade to Brazil. But this was a waning issue. The Brazilian government began to enforce anti-slave-trade laws once the nation, by the end of the 1840s, had imported as many slaves as its economy required. Now Brazilian policy shifted "from connivance to vigorous enforcement." The result was that anti-slave-trade efforts came, from this point on, to focus once again on Cuba.[73] In May 1851 the British ambassador in Madrid was able—presumably with some degree of optimism—to tell the Spanish government that Britain hoped that the Brazilian example "may be followed and with corresponding success in regulating the slave trade in Cuba and Puerto Rico."[74] It was not to be. In fact, the slave trade to Cuba underwent a resurgence in the 1850s.[75]

At the same time as the trade to Cuba was increasing, proslavery forces in the United States were making a play to acquire the island, by one means or another. The confluence of these two developments put London in a quandary. Maintaining the status quo in the Caribbean meant coming to the aid of Spain. Yet the government had no choice but to continue the pressure on Spain to live up to its treaty obligations with regard to suppression. Fortunately for successive governments in London, the Spaniards were also feeling the American pressure. Both nations were "moved to make concessions, and . . . the conciliating factor was a mutual fear of the United States." The Spanish government thus hit upon a "bold new course of action calculated to please allies and confound enemies." The plan included a slave registry, and the liberation of all slaves not on the registry by a set date. Thus, without abolishing slavery, Spain could "put an end to future purchases of contraband slaves." Britain would be placated, and its incentive for intervention in Cuba would, at the same time, be removed.[76]

While Anglo-Spanish relations were entering a period of rapprochement, the same cannot be said of Anglo-American diplomacy. The British expressed considerable frustration with the continued use of the American flag to cover the slave trade. London now found itself in quite the predicament: As Soulsby observes, "The position of the British government was indeed embarrassing, for while its cruisers succeeded in capturing many slavers whose right to American colors and papers was proved to be groundless, every mistake made provided an occasion for recrimination on the part of the United States."[77] Yet again, the British found themselves protesting the lack of American diligence in ensuring the honor of their own flag. The Earl of Clarendon, foreign secretary from February 1853 to February 1858, wrote, clearly in frustration, of the American flag being "used with impunity to cover the nefarious transactions of the slave-traders."[78] The British minister to Washington, Lord Napier, repeatedly brought the matter to the attention of Secretary of State Cass. "The demand for slaves in the Cuban market," he informed the secretary in December 1857, "is supplied by vessels constructed, purchased, and often possessed and fitted out in the ports of The United States." The number of such ships, he added, was "considerable and increasing."[79]

Cass's defense of the Buchanan administration's actions in this regard was unconvincing. As seen earlier, Cass's responses to the British could be "lengthy and disputatious" without ever addressing the situation "as frequently presented to him by the British Ministers."[80] In a long letter to the American minister in London written in February 1859, Cass laid out his position on the issue. From his perspective, the slave trade could be "annihilated" through the closure of the Cuban market. And Spanish power on the island was sufficient to achieve this end, "if seriously desired by the Spanish Government." As to Napier's request that the US government apply diplomatic pressure on Madrid by making the "necessary representations and remonstrances to the Government of Spain," Cass had no objection. The administration would do so, however, "whenever there may be reason to believe that the expression of their views by The United States would produce any favourable effect upon the action of the Spanish Government." But the British held more leverage with Madrid than did the Americans. Thus, their intervention would have "much more probability of success than could be anticipated from the representations of The United States." Once again, Cass rejected any right of search that did not emanate from belligerent claims. In any event, the value of right of visit "has been greatly overrated." Granting that all "civilized" nations had an obligation "to provide for the suppression of crimes within their jurisdiction," he nevertheless added that "a nation fully meets its responsibility when it fairly adapts its measures to the circumstances in which it is placed, and of these it must necessarily be the judge." The United States would "sternly reject" surrendering its police power to another maritime nation, even if this meant "being accused of refusing to co-operate in the effort to annihilate" the trade. Lest any of this insight be lost, Minister George M. Dallas was instructed to read the dispatch to the foreign secretary.[81] In all of Cass's verbiage, there was precious little that London could take as constructively addressing the question of how to suppress slave trade in the future.

Yet the Buchanan administration's policy toward suppression was not all obstructionism, even if it continued to be unilateralist. In fact, Buchanan "authorized a naval effort that proved to be the strongest attack on the slave trade ever launched by any administration." Fehrenbacher attributes this change to a desire to "vindicate American motives in the face of British criticism," and also, possibly, to the growing domestic troubles in the United States: the president was seeking to distance himself from proslavery extremists.[82] By the end of April 1859 the British minister to the United States, Lord Lyons, was reporting to the foreign secretary that Cass had promised two naval steamships for the Africa Squadron and three to Cuban waters. The vessels were dispatched none too early, from the perspective of the new foreign minister, Lord John

Russell, who wished Lyons to make Cass aware of the extent of the problem: "No representations made to the Spanish Government are of any avail to check the corruption and venality which prevail among their magistrates and agents, high and low, in Cuba."[83]

The British were made privy to the instructions issued by Secretary of the Navy Isaac Toucey to Africa Squadron commander William Inman. From these the British government learned that American naval ships were to "as far as possible, cruize in company" with British vessels "so that each might be in a condition to prevent abuse of the flag of its own country." But this step in the right direction came with a caveat, for although the administration sincerely desired an end to the African slave trade, "they do not regard the success of their efforts as their paramount interest nor as their particular duty. They are not prepared to sacrifice to it any of their rights as an independent nation, nor will the object in view justify the exposure of their own people to the injurious and vexatious interruptions in the prosecution of their lawful pursuits. Great caution is to be observed on this point."[84] Despite the reservations, the Buchanan offensive against the trade had significant success. Seizures of slavers rose dramatically by the end of Buchanan's term, from one a year on average to fifteen in 1860.[85]

Buchanan's willingness to work multilaterally to end the trade was, nevertheless, severely limited, as Russell found when he proposed that the Americans join with the British and other powers in London for discussions "to consider what measures should be taken to check the increase of the Slave Trade."[86] In April 1860 Cass issued a firm rejection of Russell's proposal. As he wrote Lyons, "Under any circumstances, I cannot perceive that any practical advantage would result from the proposed assemblage in London of the Diplomatic Representatives of the Powers enumerated. Besides, it is the policy of The United States to avoid participation in councils or conferences of this nature, and the President thinks it would be inexpedient upon the present occasion to depart from this policy."[87] Despite making a serious effort to interdict slavers, the Americans would continue to seek unilateral solutions to what was, in fact, an international problem.

The End of American Unilateralism

It would be left to the Republican administration of Abraham Lincoln to finally seek a solution to the problem in its multilateral context. On March 22, 1862, Secretary of State William H. Seward informed Lyons of his perceptions regarding the "inefficiency" of the American and British and patrols of the

African coast, and added that this was only exacerbated by the Union's need to withdraw "a considerable part of our own naval force from that coast to suppress a domestic insurrection." Seward sounded out Lyons on the matter: Would he be interested in negotiating on the matter of suppressing the trade? If so, Seward would submit "a Convention, upon which, if acceptable to your Government, the President would ask the advice and consent of the Senate of The United States." It would appear that the British minister was more than eager. He responded on the very same day that his government would "be prompt to agree to any stipulations giving increased efficacy to [Anglo-American] co-operation." He added that he had "no hesitation in declaring that I am ready to enter at once upon the negotiation which you do me the honour to propose to me."[88]

Matters moved quickly. By March 28, Lyons was able to send to Russell a draft treaty written by Seward. Lyons's only objection was to the limited duration of the agreement, which was set to expire in ten years. But this was a small point for the Briton, since "the Treaty proposed by Mr. Seward corresponds in every other particular to the views of Her Majesty's Government."[89] Russell soon indicated that he "entirely approve[d]" of the treaty and instructed Lyons to "sign the Treaty forthwith." By April 24, the Senate had approved the Lyons-Seward Treaty, including a limited mutual right of search, and had done so unanimously.[90] The entire matter was completed in just over a month.

The Lincoln administration had ample motive for its actions in reversing the decades-old policy of opposing the right of search. The Union was, by this time, exercising the belligerent's right to search vessels to enforce its blockade of the Confederacy. Washington thus "had good reason to soft-pedal their traditional concern about freedom of the seas." Additionally, Lincoln and Seward sought, by showing flexibility on an issue so important to the British, to decrease the likelihood of British intervention on the side of the South. If they were also motivated by a sincere desire to end the trade—as is probable— then they could hardly have taken a more salutary step: "all other remedies had been tried in vain . . . and the reciprocal right of search remained as the only possible solution of the problem."[91] That solution had finally been adopted.

The consequences of Lincoln and Seward's concession were not what Americans had feared for decades. Granting the Royal Navy the right to search American ships on the Atlantic did not, in fact, result in a new wave of impressment of American sailors. Nor was American sea power and commerce driven from the ocean by an expansionist British Empire. On the other hand, the final step required in the war against the trade had been taken; as Reginald Coupland observes, "Deprived . . . of the only flag which had protected it for thirty years, [the slave trade] was more at the mercy of British sea-power than it had ever been."[92] The Seward-Lyons Treaty was the death warrant for the Atlantic slave trade, which could not survive long in an era of Anglo-American cooperation in a move toward its extinction.

It is, however, evidence of the seriousness with which American policymakers viewed these threats from Britain that it took the most wrenching crisis in the nation's history to bring about a policy reversal. The successful suppression of the slave trade had always required international cooperation. Lincoln was able to recognize this at a time when isolating the United States from a more existential form of foreign entanglement became the dominant task of American foreign policy: he needed to do what was necessary to prevent European intervention in the American Civil War. In part, this meant giving Britain what it had long required from Washington in order to achieve one of its own most significant foreign policy goals. The successes of the Royal Navy in its suppression efforts after 1862 indicated the extent to which American policy had held the key. At long last, the goal that Americans had claimed to seek since the time of Jefferson could be accomplished. The inhuman traffic in humans across the Atlantic was now doomed.

Conclusion: Hesitant Multilateralism

Successive American administrations sought to keep US involvement in the international relations of the Atlantic world strictly limited when dealing with the suppression of the slave trade. Above all, they sought to avoid allowing the United States to get pulled into the British system of slave-trade suppression. Yet the Atlantic slave trade was inherently an international problem, encompassing as it did four continents. Washington was, thus, faced with the dilemma of conducting policy that limited the capacity of international efforts to end the trade if America wanted to maintain its unilateral stance. The slave trade therefore continued for some time, due to American reluctance to address the issue in its international context. The United States was, however, not able permanently to retain its freedom of action.

CHAPTER 5

"Only Cowards Fear and Oppose It"

Texas and Cuba

Ripe fruit falls from trees, and mighty rivers flow uninterrupted to the sea. It is what they do, and it would be a fool's errand to try to prevent them from doing so. Everyone could agree, at least, on this. But there was disagreement as to whether the expansion of the United States operated on a similar—and not entirely metaphorical—geophysical principle. References to "laws" of nature, and of history, proliferated in speeches and writings of American public officials and publicists eager to tack new lands onto the slaveholding republic during the antebellum period.

Others, both within and outside the United States, did not see America's expansionist destiny as being quite so manifest, did not view supine acceptance of the nation's expansionist urges as a prudential matter of allowing nature to take its course. Looking beyond the metaphors, one could detect the forces that drove American policymakers to make discreet decisions in favor of acquisition of new territory. One of those forces was slavery—or, more precisely, the desire to protect and expand the institution. American expansion has "been premised on the conviction that America and Americans are not tainted with evil or self-serving motives."[1] For this reason, American expansionists were often, though not *always*, reluctant to admit that slavery was a factor impelling them to seek additional territory for the nation. In fact, some of them would claim that they sought territory precisely to *rid* the nation of this divisive form of labor. That this result was to come only gradually—almost imperceptibly—was, they would add, an advantage of the plan.

These protestations aside, the cases of Texas and Cuba illustrate the extent to which slavery influenced American attempts at expansion. The desire to preserve and expand the institution was not the only factor leading to the annexation of Texas and the repeated efforts to acquire Cuba. But neither episode can be understood without taking into account the extent to which slavery motivated slaveholding statesmen and their northern allies. Put succinctly, "often those advocating national expansion also advocated the extension of slavery." Additionally, slaveholders sometimes *opposed* expansion when it would lead to the addition of nonslave territory to the Union—for example, John Calhoun's opposition to taking all of Mexico after the Mexican-American War.[2] American expansion was, in their minds, intimately linked with the health of slavery and with the domestic political power of its backers.

Slaveholders were, furthermore, well positioned, in the antebellum period, to see to slavery's health; they and their allies held "a vice-like grip on the executive branch of the U.S. national government."[3] These men successfully added Texas to the Union as a slave state. Yet the much-longed-for Cuba was beyond their grasp, try as they might to wrest it from Spain. The first would lead to war with Mexico, the second to incessant conflict with Spain, intermittent conflict with France, and the potential for armed conflict with the most powerful nation in the world, Great Britain. It was a risky business. But, from the point of view of slaveholding policymakers and their allies, it was a risk that had to be taken, if slavery were to survive in the Americas. One might as well fight the laws of nature as ask them to do otherwise.

Texas: Lone Star (Slave) State

There was for a long time a tendency to downplay the significance of slavery in the history of Texas. The Lone Star State, it was said, was "more western than southern." But, in fact, the institution of bonded labor was central to the story of the state. By the time of annexation in 1846, slavery "was as strongly established in Texas, the newest slave state, as it was in the oldest slave state in the Union." As Texas patriarch Stephen F. Austin declared in 1833, "Texas *must be* a slave country. Circumstances and unavoidable necessity compels it. It is the wish of the people there, and it is my duty to do all I can, prudently, in favor of it. I will do so." If this quote evinces something less than a passion for the institution—something of a resigned acceptance—on Austin's part, it nevertheless indicates the deep roots of slavery in the state's proverbial soil. Indeed, slavery may have been the deciding factor that led Texans to fight their war of independence against Mexico. But even here, there is nuance: slavery "was one of the differences separating Mexicans and Texians [*sic*], but it was not THE cause of the rebellion."[4]

The implication was, nevertheless, clear: if the Lone Star Republic were to join the United States, it would do so as a slave state. *When* Texas would join the Union proved to be the more vexing question. In March 1836, the Texans meeting at Washington-on-the-Brazos had declared independence from Mexico, and the interim government sought diplomatic recognition from the United States. President Andrew Jackson, however, was reluctant to move precipitously on the matter. For starters, he told the Texans delegated to negotiate with the United States government that the entity that now declared itself the government of Texas had not yet demonstrated that it was the de facto sovereign of its territory. Recognition from Washington, DC, would have to wait until the following year. Finally, on his last full day in office, Jackson announced the nomination of Louisianan Alcée La Branche as America's chargé in Texas.[5]

In the matter of Texas recognition, Jackson had acted with "uncharacteristic restraint." He did so with reason. There was the risk of war with Mexico to be considered, since that country refused to view Texas as anything other than a federal state in rebellion. Then, too, there was the issue of slavery; neither Jackson nor his immediate successor, Martin Van Buren, wanted to exacerbate the sectional differences in the nation, or divisions in the Democratic Party, over the issue of adding this newly minted slaveholding republic to the United States. Washington rebuffed Texas's request for annexation in 1837.[6] The Texans would have to wait nearly a decade.

Hope for annexationists on both sides of the Sabine River came from an unexpected source. In 1840 William Henry Harrison, a Whig, was elected to the presidency. The Whigs, unlike the Democrats, were hesitant about expansion at a time when party loyalties were still strong across sections. Proannexation Democrats thus now had "no reason to hope for anything better than the four frustrating years under Van Buren."[7] But fate would not prove kind to Whigs elected to the White House. A month into his administration, Harrison died, and Vice President John Tyler, a Virginian, was sworn into the presidency on April 6, 1841. The new president, "an ardent expansionist," found himself forsaken by his own party early that autumn.[8] This helped free him up to pursue his goal of annexation. For the expansionists, it was so far, so good.

Tyler did not, however, move immediately on annexation. The domestic situation in the United States served to slow the drive toward expansion: "antislavery feeling, together with a widespread disinclination to aggravate the slavery controversy, was impeding the extension of American sovereignty over Texas, and it continued for a time to do so." Any expansion would thus have to be presented by the administration as being in the interest of the entire nation, and not just one section of it. Additionally, Tyler had initially decided to keep on Harrison's cabinet, which included New Englander Daniel Webster as secretary of state. When Tyler broached the subject of annexation to Webster in October 1841, the secretary gave the enthusiastic president's overture a "cool reception."[9] The fruit, it would appear, was not yet ripe.

Yet patience was increasingly not seen as a virtue by annexationists, and especially not by southerners who looked at British policy toward the Southwest with increasing alarm. The fear that London sought to prevent American acquisition of Texas was borne out by the facts. But the anxiety over British plans to force abolition on an independent Texas was not. Proslavery southerners "radically overestimated the depth of Britain's commitment to antislavery action in the Gulf of Mexico." In fact, the primary foreign policy goal of the government of Prime Minister Robert Peel was "to avoid an Anglo-American clash in the region."[10] The British early on "understood that the American acquisition of Texas faced serious obstacles in the United States itself."[11] Certainly, Britain sought to convince the Texas leadership to promise abolition in exchange for Mexican recognition of their independence. But keeping Texas out of American hands took precedence.

This was, however, decidedly not the perception in Tyler's Washington. As David Pletcher has summarized the situation, "The menace of effective British intrigue for abolishing slavery among the Texan slaveholders does not seem alarming, with the perspective of time, but rumors about [the British foreign secretary, Lord] Aberdeen's devious policy lent themselves admirably to exaggeration and propaganda in 1843."[12] The year was key. Concerns had been mounting about British efforts in Texas over the course of the previous two years of Tyler's presidency. Then, in July 1843, Abel P. Upshur took the reins of the State Department, after the departure of Webster in May and the subsequent death of acting secretary Hugh S. Legaré of South Carolina. Upshur, a Virginian, had largely kept his counsel on Texas while serving as Tyler's navy secretary. Now, however, he was in the pivotal position to affect a shift in policy. His accession "brought into the State Department the driving force of slavery extremism in the South. Annexation of Texas became the passion of the Tyler Administration."[13]

In a letter dated September 28, 1843, Upshur expressed his concerns to America's minister in London, Edward Everett, noting that the "movements of Great Britain, with respect to African slavery, have at length assumed a character which demands the serious attention of this Government." The secretary had been gravely disturbed by an exchange in the House of Lords that had transpired between Lord Brougham and the Earl of Aberdeen. Brougham had expressed his hope that a British diplomatic initiative on the Texas question would produce sweeping results: "He knew that the Texian's [sic] would do much as regarded the abolition of slavery, if Mexico could be induced to recognize their independence. If, therefore, by our good offices, we could get the Mexican Government to acknowledge the independence of Texas, he would suggest a hope that it might terminate in the abolition of slavery in Texas, and ultimately in the whole of the Southern States of America." In response, Aberdeen said that the government was doing all it could to achieve "that result which was contemplated by his noble friend," and adding that "he need hardly say that no one was more anxious than himself to see the abolition of slavery in Texas."[14]

Aberdeen's response was polite, in the context of the House of Lords, yet highly inflammatory to the proslavery makers of America's foreign policy. Brougham's wish was, in fact, their worst fear: that British intervention in the Texas matter would lead to abolition in that country, thus presenting an existential threat to the institution in the neighboring American South. Aberdeen had significantly exacerbated those fears by trying to reassure his colleague, for in so doing he appeared to associate the policies of the British government with Brougham's scenario. While the foreign secretary's words were vague, they "did convey the impression that if Mexico and Texas signed a peace treaty, the abolition of slavery would be part of it."[15] Upshur, for one, was willing to entertain the most menacing reading of Aberdeen's statement and to extrapolate from there. Admitting that the foreign secretary's remarks "may perhaps admit of doubt," he nevertheless added that they might be "fairly susceptible of a more extended construction." After all, it was "quite clear that the abolition of slavery in the United States was the most important 'result' contemplated by Lord Brougham, and it is not unreasonable to suppose that it was then most prominent in the mind of Lord Aberdeen. . . . It does no violence to the rules of fair construction, to understand his language as an avowal of designs which, whether so intended or not, threaten very serious consequences to the United States." Upshur's lawyerly reading of Aberdeen's words may be questioned, since, in context, the "result" of which the latter spoke most likely referred to a Mexico-Texas armistice. But Upshur was willing to take a more expansive interpretation of the remarks. So, too, he suggested, was Tyler, who "attaches the more importance to those declarations, because they are perfectly consistent with information received from other sources, all tending to the conclusion that the policy of England, in regard to the abolition of negro slavery, is not limited to Texas alone."[16] Yet again, Britain was constructed by

American policymakers as a threat to the survival of slavery within the United States itself.

Ten days after writing the note, Upshur was back at it, instructing Everett as to the motives behind British abolitionist designs. "It is impossible to suppose," the secretary declared, "that England is actuated in this matter by a mere feeling of philanthropy." Rather, a quest for economic hegemony was at work: "Her objects undoubtedly are to revive the industry of her East and West India Colonies, to find new markets for her surplus manufactures, and to destroy, as far as possible, the rivalry and competition of the manufactures of the United States." It was, he added, "altogether probable" that abolition of slavery would achieve these results. Upshur went on to emphasize to the New Englander Everett that Britain was not, by its actions toward Texas, threatening the South alone: "The question is not sectional. Although the first and most disastrous effects of such a state of things would be felt in the slave-holding States, they would extend to and embrace important interests in every other part of the country. We must contemplate it, therefore, as a national question."[17] Indeed, this would become a mantra for slave-holding southerners: a threat to slavery in the South was, in fact, a threat to the existence of the entire nation.[18]

Aberdeen's words had come as a shock to the Tyler administration, but not as a surprise. Upshur and company had been primed for a "revelation" of this sort. Duff Green, sent to London as a special agent of the administration, had been sending back word of a British plot to end slavery in Texas.[19] On August 8, 1843, Upshur wrote to William S. Murphy, US chargé in Austin, to advise him of the perilous situation. A "citizen of Maryland then in London," in whom Upshur had full confidence, had written that the British had a plan afoot to extend a loan to the Texas government, the price of which was to be the abolition of slavery in their country. In the secretary's estimation, there seemed to be "no doubt as to the object in view, and none that the English government has offered its coöperation." Any such attempt "upon any neighboring country would necessarily be viewed by this government with very deep concern; but when it is made upon a nation whose territories join the slave-holding States of our Union, it awakens still more solemn interest. It cannot be permitted to succeed without the most strenuous efforts on our part to arrest a calamity so serious to every part of our country." Upshur was, by this point, convinced that Britain's goal was "to abolish domestic slavery throughout the entire continent and islands of America" in order to find new markets and destroy competition for its goods. This represented a grave threat to the United States: "The establishment in the very midst of our slave-holding States of an independent government forbidding the existence of slavery; and by a people born for the most part among us; reared up in our habits and speaking our language, could not fail to produce the most unhappy effects upon both parties." Texas without slavery would provide an immediate draw for runaway slaves from Arkansas and Louisiana, which in turn would bring conflict with Texas, as well as within the Union itself. "Few calamities," Upshur concluded, "could befall this country more to be deplored than the establishment of a predominant British influence and the abolition of domestic slavery in Texas."[20] Having taken Green's report as fact, it is no surprise that Tyler and his advisers responded to the Aberdeen-Brougham exchange as they did: as interpreted by Upshur, the foreign secretary's words confirmed that the danger was both real and imminent.

This raises the question of why Upshur accepted Green's summary of British policy, and acted upon it, without first seeking to verify that it had a basis in fact. The United States, after all, had a minister in London. One would assume that Everett could have provided germane commentary on the matter. The reason, according to Frederick Merk, was twofold. First, the secretary of state distrusted his envoy to Britain, confiding to a friend upon Everett's appointment by Tyler to the Court of St. James's, "The present condition of the country imperiously requires that a Southern man & a slaveholder should represent us in that court. How could a politician reared and living in lower Virginia fail to see this? And yet a Boston man is appointed, half school-master, half priest, & whole abolitionist! I see no excuse for this, it is abominable."[21] Additionally, "Upshur considered the annexation of Texas indispensable to the protection of Southern slavery, which in turn was indispensable to the South."[22] Taking Green's warnings seriously thus confirmed the correctness of the course which Upshur had wanted to pursue even before the Aberdeen-Brougham exchange. He desired to move ahead on annexation. Now, with the intelligence that the administration had received from London, there was no time to lose.

And Upshur lost no time. In October he told Texas's chargé in Washington, Isaac Van Zandt, that Tyler stood ready to support a treaty of annexation. He hastened to add that the Senate might prove to be a problem, since he could not "offer any positive assurance that the measure would be acceptable to all branches of this government." He could, however, pledge that he would present such a treaty "in the strongest manner, to the consideration of Congress." The Texan communicated Upshur's offer to Texas president Sam Houston in Austin. Van Zandt, lacking authorization from Houston, nevertheless began negotiations with Upshur on a treaty of annexation.[23]

There was, however, a problem. Although Upshur had assured Van Zandt that President Tyler was on board, this assessment appears to have been, at best, premature. For his part, Tyler was not yet convinced of the perfidious nature of Britain's Texas policy, and later recalled giving the go-ahead for treaty negotiations with the Texans in November, not October. Aberdeen was, at the time, doing what he could to cool things down in the Tyler administration. Toward the end of 1843, he wrote a dispatch to Richard Pakenham, Britain's minister in Washington, and instructed him to share its contents with Upshur. In the note he forthrightly acknowledged that Britain was eager to see Mexican recognition of Texas's independence. But he denied that London was motivated by "ambition or self-interest, beyond that interest, at least, which attaches to the general extension of our commercial dealings with other countries." As to secret plans to influence Texas, there were none: Britain had "no occult design, either with reference to any peculiar influence which we might seek to establish in Mexico or Texas, or even with reference to the slavery which now exists, and which we desire to see abolished in Texas." Freely admitting that Britain wished to see an end to slavery "throughout the world," he insisted that British methods in achieving this end were "open and undisguised." As such, in regard to Texas, "we avow that we wish to see slavery abolished there, as elsewhere, and we should rejoice if the recognition of that country by the Mexican Government should be accompanied by an engagement on the part of Texas to abolish slavery eventually, and under proper conditions, throughout the Republic. . . . [But] we shall not interfere unduly, nor with an improper assumption of authority, with either party, in order to ensure the adoption of such a course. We shall counsel, but we shall not seek to compel or unduly control either party." Aberdeen went on categorically to deny any attempt on the part of Britain to "act, directly or indirectly, in a political sense, on The United States though Texas," adding that the British "have never sought in any way to stir up disaffection or excitement of any kind in the slave-holding States of the American Union." Southerners could thus rest assured that Britain would "neither openly nor secretly resort to any measures which can tend to disturb their internal tranquility, or thereby to affect the prosperity of the American Union."[24] Aberdeen had, in his note, provided a point-by-point response to Upshur: Britain was hatching no secret plans, either for global economic domination or for undermining slavery in the American South. Yet such assurances were unlikely to have convinced the secretary of state, and thus to have changed the course of the Tyler administration's policy.

Here, however, one can only extrapolate. On February 28, 1844, in a freak accident aboard USS *Princeton*, the explosion of a bow gun killed nine of the ship's passengers. The president and other dignitaries were aboard the ship on the Potomac River for a demonstration of the new vessel and its guns. Tyler had gone belowdecks and was spared; neither Upshur nor Secretary of the Navy Thomas Walker Gilmer was as fortunate. Tyler lost two cabinet members on what had promised to be an enjoyable, if uneventful, cruise; their deaths were a personal blow to the president, but he had to move on. Above all, he needed a new secretary of state—and soon. As he wrote his daughter, "What a loss I have sustained in Upshur and Gilmer. They were truly my friends. . . . But it is all over now, and I must look for new cabinet ministers. My greatest desire will be to bring in as able men as the country can afford."[25]

Calhoun and the Annexation Debate

Apparently the most able man that the nation could provide was John C. Calhoun, who assumed the office of secretary of state on April 1, 1844. It was in some ways an odd choice, since Tyler "was not an admirer of Calhoun's." More significantly, Tyler saw in Calhoun's approach to Texas a threat to his own attempt to frame annexation as a matter that was in the interest of the all sections of the United States, not just the South. As Norma Lois Peterson observes, "Annexation required the support of the entire nation. Calhoun tended to emphasize the sectional and slavery aspect."[26] It would be wrong to say that the South Carolinian's ardor for Texas was based solely on sectional interests. The strategic interests of the broader nation also played a role in his thinking, and he viewed Texas "as a bastion of defense for the Union against the possible incursion of strong foreign powers."[27] But Tyler's concerns regarding Calhoun were, nevertheless, borne out by events. The new secretary of state could not restrain himself when it came to, as he saw it, the great benefits of the slave system as it existed in the United States. Upshur, to be fair, had also held to the "positive good" interpretation of slavery. But he had been wise enough to keep his thoughts contained to private letters.

Not so Calhoun. On April 18, 1844, the secretary penned the infamous Pakenham Letter to the British minister in Washington. The thrust of the letter should have been—and likely would have been if Upshur had written it—the Tyler administration's response to Britain's frank admission that it hoped to eradicate slavery globally. Calhoun did, in fact, begin his letter by addressing this admission. The president, he noted, regarded Britain's avowal "with deep concern." British abolitionism was all well and good when confined to British "possessions and colonies"; no nation could complain about London's policy within its own realm. But "when she goes beyond, and avows it her settled policy, and the object of her constant exertions, to abolish it throughout the world, she makes it the duty of all other countries, whose safety or prosperity may be endangered by her policy, to adopt such measures as they may deem necessary for their protection." The president evinced even "deeper concern" regarding Britain's perceived desire to see slavery eradicated in Texas and its efforts "through . . . diplomacy to accomplish it, by making abolition of slavery one of the conditions on which Mexico should acknowledge [Texas's] independence." Tyler would have to consider "what would be its effects on the prosperity and safety of The United States, should [Britain] succeed in her endeavors." Given the threat that Britain's design posed to "both the safety and prosperity of the Union," the US government was forced "to adopt in self-defence the most effectual measures to defeat it." Raising the specter of a Texas "under the influence and control of Great Britain," Calhoun foresaw that this situation would "place in the power of Great Britain the most efficient means of effecting in the neighboring States of this Union what she avows to be her desire to do in all countries where slavery exists." Thus, Calhoun informed Pakenham, Texas and the United States had concluded a treaty of annexation that would be sent to the Senate for ratification.[28]

Up to this point, Calhoun had explicated the need for annexation in terms of American national security and sovereignty. There was nothing surprising in this. But Calhoun had warmed to the topic of slavery, and now could not constrain his impulse to defend the institution on the international stage. This set him apart from Tyler, who had "never, at least publicly, attempted to justify the peculiar institution."[29] For Calhoun it was not enough to say that the United States had slavery and Britain should mind its own business. He had to tell the British why slavery was the best of all possible systems. As a result, Calhoun treated Pakenham to an eccentric disquisition on the great benefits of slavery to the slaves, as borne out by census data. He was led by his own logic to conclude that, could Great Britain "succeed in accomplishing in The United States, what she avows it to be her desire and the object of her constant exertions to effect throughout the world, so far from being wise or humane, she would involve in the greatest calamity the whole country, and especially the race which it is the avowed object of her exertions to benefit."[30] Southern slavery was a blessing for the slave. For this reason, Britain should stay out of it.

There is no scholarly consensus concerning Calhoun's reasons for penning the second part of the Pakenham Letter. If he had been hoping, however, "to provoke a *British* counterattack on both slavery and annexation," and thus to rally Americans around both the flag and the treaty, then he was to be disappointed. Pakenham's April 19 response to the secretary was a study in measured, if disappointed, diplomacy. With regard to annexation, the Briton limited himself to an expression of dismay that the Tyler administration was "assigning to the British Government some share in the responsibility of a transaction which can hardly fail to be viewed in many quarters with the most serious objection." On the matter of slavery, he refused to be baited, saying only that Britain "is not conscious of having acted in a sense to cause alarm to The United States."[31] William W. Freehling, however, is probably correct in concluding that the letter's impact on the prospects for treaty ratification was not significant. Both Whigs and some northern Democrats had come out against the treaty prior to the Pakenham Letter. Calhoun had given Tyler's opponents a talking point for their speeches against annexation; he had not altered their votes.[32]

They did, nevertheless, pounce on Calhoun's words. Senator Thomas Hart Benton of Missouri—at the time a slaveholder himself—was a strong advocate of Texas annexation. Yet he considered the Texas treaty "a wrong and criminal way of doing the right thing" and came out forcefully against it. "The difficulty now," he said, "was in the aspect that has been put upon it as a sectional, political, and slave question; as a movement of the South against the North, and of the slaveholding States for political supremacy." From what Benton could tell, the administration had been "endeavoring to pick a quarrel with England, and upon the slave question."[33] The Missourian continued on, and for some time. The upshot of his remarks was clear: the Tyler administration was using the slavery issue to sell the annexation of Texas, and, in so doing, exacerbating sectional divisions in the nation. Texas should, no doubt, join the Union. But not at this price.

Granted, not all who opposed the treaty were as explicit concerning the connection between expansion and proslavery rhetoric. There were, indeed, other reasons to oppose the Treaty of Annexation. But it was difficult to avoid the issue. Writing in the Whig organ *National Intelligencer* in April, the redoubtable Henry Clay came out against ratification. Clay did not perceive a great desire on the part of the American people to acquire Texas at this point. Nor did he relish the idea that the United States, in taking on Texas, would also be acquiring the on-and-off war simmering between that republic and Mexico. This could well result in European intervention on the side of Mexico, with Britain, France, or both now claiming that they were motivated in part by a desire "to prevent the further propagation of slavery from the United States." Like Benton, Clay also worried about the potential for the addition of new slave territory to exacerbate sectional divisions. Nothing could be "pregnant with more fatal consequences than acquiring territory for the purpose of strengthening one part against another part of the common Confederacy." Such a development "would menace the existence, if it did not certainly sow the seeds of a dissolution of the Union." As to the administration's anxiety regarding British designs on abolition in Texas, Clay was dismissive. As he noted, London had "formally and solemnly disavowed any such aims or purposes—has declared that she is desirous only of the independence of Texas—and that she has no intention to interfere in her domestic institutions." Clay puckishly added that he presumed the Tyler administration already had this information at hand.[34]

The lengthy and contentious Senate debate over the treaty is ably summarized by Merk. Supporters, and especially Robert Walker of Mississippi, played upon traditional American Anglophobia. The ratification of the treaty would, Walker claimed, recall to the British minds the results of the Battles of Yorktown and New Orleans. Virginian Whig William S. Archer saw in all this rhetoric evidence of a "fixed purpose that the English government was not to be allowed to shake off the imputation of dangerous practices or purposes in regard to slavery in Texas which had been fastened upon its forehead." When the vote was taken on June 8, the treaty went down to resounding defeat, losing by a lopsided margin of thirty-five to sixteen.[35] Tyler could count on it: he could not get to the required two-thirds majority of senators necessary to ratify.

But the cause of annexation was not to be set back for long. Nor was the Senate vote a reliable barometer of its chances. Many of the negative votes were due more to "hostility to the president and his annexationist strategy than to annexation itself."[36] Denied the nomination of the Democratic Party to run for a term in his own right under their banner, Tyler would not be refused the victory that would guarantee him a spot in the history books. Pivoting quickly, the president conceived the idea of submitting the treaty to both houses of Congress, and eventually hit upon the plan of a joint resolution, which would require only a simple majority. In the House, furthermore, Democrats held a majority after the 1842 election, thus giving additional hope to annexation's advocates. One of the eight southern Whigs who voted in favor of the resolution, Georgia's Alexander Stephens, seemed to distance himself from the Pakenham Letter in justifying his decision. "I am no defender of slavery in the abstract," he said. If annexation "were for the sole purpose of extending slavery where it does not now and would not otherwise exist, I should oppose it." But since this caveat did not apply to Texas, his vote was forthcoming.[37] Stephens was not a voice in the Whig wilderness; motivated both by "popular sentiment and a sincere concern felt for southern safety," a number Whigs in the South broke with their party's, and thus their leader's, traditional skepticism regarding expansion.[38]

On January 25, 1845, as Tyler's presidency entered its final weeks, the House passed the joint resolution by a vote of 120–98. It would take another month, but at the end of February, the Senate also approved an amended joint resolution by a vote of twenty-seven to twenty-five. On his last full day in office, Tyler was able to send the resolution to Austin.[39] Texas would formally join the Union as a state—and not as a territory—under the administration of James K.

Polk, the Tennessean who succeeded Tyler. But the outgoing president had achieved his most significant policy goal, and another slave state was added to the slaveholding republic.

Don E. Fehrenbacher begins his treatment of slavery and expansion with something of a warning for future scholars who would analyze "the influence of slavery on American expansion and expansionism in the antebellum era. The presence of such influence can scarcely be doubted, but the difficulty lies in determining its weight at each juncture and whether or not it was ever predominant." In the case of Texas, Fehrenbacher concludes that the influence was, indeed, significant: slavery "remains the heart of the matter, . . . [S]olicitude for slavery, particularly the fear of a British plot to make Texas an entering wedge for abolitionism, was primarily what inspired the aggressive annexation movement launched by the Tyler administration."[40] Matthew Karp has come to a similar conclusion, stating that bringing Texas into the Union as a slave state "was perhaps the quintessential achievement of the foreign policy of slavery."[41]

The case of Texas demonstrates the extent to which slavery was, at this time, a central element in the foreign policy thinking of America's political elite. The goal of protecting slavery in the South, and indeed adding to its realm, was a powerful determinant of the policy of those who held both southern slaves and federal power. Try as they might to portray the acquisition of the Lone Star State as being in the interest of the entire nation, expansionist policy toward the Southwest spoke, during the Tyler administration, with a southern accent.

Spain and Cuba

Cuba provides an at least equally clear case of a proslavery foreign policy. For a time it had been Washington's stated policy that the island must remain in Spain's possession. But southern slaveholders and their allies increasingly came to see Spain's most valuable colony as an alluring target for American expansion. When the institution of slavery appeared to be threatened on the island, Spain's continued dominion over Cuba became, for them, more of a menace to than a guarantee of security. Repeated attempts to acquire the island followed. Although unsuccessful, these bids for further expansion had a significant impact upon American foreign relations, involving, as they did, provocations not just of Spain but also of Britain and France. But the Democrats who held the reigns of the American federal government in the 1840s and 1850s saw their attempts at expansion as worth the risks, the threat of an abolition in Cuba being infinitely greater.

The prehistory of Cuban annexation dates back to 1810 and was connected, from the very beginning, with a desire to preserve the institution of slavery on that island. Cuban planters had, in that year, approached the American consul in Havana with a proposal for an annexationist conspiracy. Their goal was to safeguard slavery. The plot went nowhere. Nor did a similar scheme broached by a planters' agent in Washington in 1821 meet with any success. Overall, in the early decades of the nineteenth century, America sought "to let Cuba remain in the possession of Spain, to block independence movements in the island and plans to transfer it to a foreign power, while refusing to commit the United States to any future self-denial."[42] Washington was willing to bide its time during these years. Though the Americans were still quite solicitous toward the maintenance of slavery in Cuba, the threat to bonded labor did not seem acute enough to warrant drastic action at this time.

This inclination to leave things as they were was in evidence as late as 1838. In February of that year the Spanish foreign minister, Count de Ofalia, wrote to John Eaton, the American minister in Madrid, concerning the dangers that American and English abolitionist organizations posed to Spanish slaveholders in Cuba. "It is publicly notorious," Ofalia complained, "that those Societies do not actually circumscribe the propagation of their doctrines to those countries whence they originated, but they likewise extend them through the Antilles contiguous to the American continent." These agents of abolition "openly excite sedition" and were responsible for slave rebellions on the island. Eaton's response was rambling, but aimed to be reassuring. The United States wanted its citizens abroad to obey the laws of the countries in which they resided. The American government would thus never "interfere in behalf of those who shall wantonly infract those laws." While the foreign minister had not raised the issue, Eaton tried to put the Spaniard's mind at rest about the idea that "the U States desire to possess Cuba. No idea can be more rediculous [sic]." The United States wanted Cuba to remain in Spanish hands, and not to "come to the possession of some grasping, & aspiring power." The transfer of Cuba to any other power, on the other hand, would be regarded by the United States as "a departure from the subsisting friendship which now binds them to Spain" and as evidence "of intended hostility on the part of that government which should obtain it."[43] In his own bumbling way, Eaton had, in fact, articulated to Madrid the central elements of American Cuban policy as the 1830s drew to a close. Key to these was Washington's nontransfer policy with regard to Cuba: as long as the island was in Spanish hands, American interests were protected.

For Washington, one of the great attractions of Spanish rule over the economically vibrant and strategically vital island was the very weakness of Spain as an Atlantic power. Spain was neither likely to exclude American commerce from Cuba nor strong enough to use Cuba's geographic position to bottle up American sea power in the Gulf of Mexico. Yet it was a delicate balance: Spain's relative lack of power could also result in an inability to sufficiently control Cuba's internal affairs or to resist pressure from other European powers— especially Britain. The former left open the possibility of a successful insurrection on the island; the latter would put at risk American commercial and strategic interests in the Gulf. This Washington could not tolerate.

Moving toward Annexation

There was one additional threat that could emanate from the intervention in Cuban affairs of a nation more powerful than Spain. American policymakers were determined that Cuba should retain the institution of slavery. The danger that a general emancipation of Cuba's slave population would pose to slavery in the American South was taken as an article of faith, and thus as an eventuality that had to be prevented, by whatever means necessary. By the early 1840s, the "most serious threat to Cuban slavery . . . came from the imperial and abolitionist power of Great Britain."[44] The Tyler administration took the danger seriously, especially against the background of "several abortive slave uprisings on the island, including one in which a British consul was almost certainly involved."[45] In this context, annexation of Cuba to the United States became, for many, a more attractive option than the island's continued connection with Spain.

Many Cuban slaveholders likewise were driven by events in the colony to look to the same solution. According to Philip S. Foner, "It took the slave uprisings of 1842–1844 to frighten enough planters to make the annexation movement a significant force. The fear that the Spanish government would continue weak under British abolitionist pressure roused such alarm in Cuba, that a large percentage of the slave-owners looked toward junction with the slaveholding power in the United States as the only safeguard for the continuance of the institution."[46] The anxiety among the slaveholders in Cuba was, at this time, palpable. They now feared a bloody catastrophe—another Haiti, it was said—provoked by the English, by the slaves themselves, "or by a combination of the interests of both . . . The fear made them cry out [clamar hasta] for annexation to the United States."[47]

Anxiety was rife in the slaveholding republic as well; as Karp observes, "Between 1841 and 1844, the barest wisps of a rumor triggered the most frenzied reactions."[48] At the beginning of 1843, official Washington was shaken by the allegation that Britain had decided to achieve its abolitionist ends in Cuba through "the total ruin of the Island." According to word received by Webster from "a highly respectable source," British agents were now in Cuba "in great numbers, offering independence to the Creoles, on condition that they will unite with the colored people in effecting a general emancipation of the slaves, and in converting the Government into a *black Military Republic*, under British protection." The threat to slavery extended, according to Webster's information, well past the beaches of Cuba, for if "this scheme should succeed, the influence of Britain in this quarter, it is remarked, will be unlimited. . . . [S]he will, it is said, strike a death blow to the existence of slavery in the United States." The Spanish officials in Cuba, explained Webster's informant, had some knowledge of the plot, but were so "torpid" that they were unable to grasp the significance of the British policy. The informant, Webster continued, "does not hesitate to express the opinion *that the most* [sic] *of the white popula-tion of Cuba, in easy circumstances, including the Spaniards, prefer, and will always prefer, the flag of the United States to that of England.*" Madrid had been informed that the United States "never would permit the occupation of that Island by British agents or forces, upon any pretext whatsoever." The administration had, in fact, promised the Spanish government that the United States would inter-vene militarily to keep Cuba in Spanish hands. Given the alarming nature of the report from Cuba, the secretary instructed his consul in Havana promptly to investigate and report on the matter.[49]

The Tyler administration's willingness to pledge even war with Britain to preserve Spanish rule, and thus slavery, in Cuba indicates the degree to which American policymakers viewed continuation of slavery in the Caribbean as imperative to the security of the nation itself. Still, the "crisis" ended anticli-mactically. Reports from American officials in Havana and Madrid that spring helped the storm blow over. It seemed that Domingo del Monte, Webster's Cuban source, "had overstated his case." The Spanish government, for its part, felt confident in its hold on Cuba, and "gratefully refused Webster's offer of military aid."[50]

But the idea that slavery, and thus America itself, would be more secure if Spain were to cede Cuba to the United States was hardly extinguished with the end of the "black military republic" scare. After the Tyler administration gave way to that of Polk, American attempts to acquire the island would in-tensify rather than diminish. Polk's commitment to American expansion re-quires little comment, since "just as President Tyler made the annexation of Texas the principal objective of his administration, his successor Mr. Polk dreamed of imitating such conduct with respect to Cuba."[51] Dream of it he did, confiding to his diary in May 1848 that "I am decidedly in favour of purchasing Cuba & making it one of the States of [the] Union."[52] Indeed, Polk was willing to offer Spain up to $100 million for a colony that the Spaniards would not sell—at that price or any other.[53] Undaunted, Secretary of State James Buchanan—a committed expansionist himself—as late as the summer of 1848 declared to the US consul in Havana, "We believe that in the natural course of events the time is not very distant when [Cuba] will become a part of our Union by peaceful negotiation."[54] The Polk administration's attempts to convince Spain to relinquish Cuba served, however, to exacerbate relations between Madrid and Washington. The Spanish minister of state, perhaps exasperated by American importuning, remarked that his nation, "before seeing the Island of Cuba in the power [poder] of another Power, would prefer it submerged in the depths of the Ocean." Although this "very Spanish locution" accurately expressed opinion in Madrid, it "did not resolve the difficulties that were daily raised between the two countries."[55]

Relations between the two capitals improved only when the expansionistic Democrats in the Polk administration were replaced by the far less strident Whigs after the 1848 elections. Under Presidents Zachary Taylor and then Millard Fillmore, the emphasis of American diplomacy with regard to Cuba swung away from purchase and toward assurance that Spain would remain in possession of the island. At the end of May 1849 the newly installed secretary of state, Delaware's John Clayton, assured the Spanish minister in Washington that the United States wanted Spain to continue in possession of Cuba. Relations could only be improved by proclamations from—and actions by—Washington against filibusters who used American bases to launch attacks on Cuba.

The most significant of these attempts to "liberate" Cuba from Spain between 1849 and 1851 were led by Narciso López. The Venezuela native and erstwhile general in the Spanish Army sought three times in that period to lead filibustering expeditions against Cuba, assuming that the people of that island would rise up and greet his forces as liberators. These filibusters used the United States as their base of operations. Not surprisingly, the episodes brought the United States significant diplomatic difficulties, not just with Spain but also with Britain and France. Again, slavery was one—though not the only—contributor to this extended period of transatlantic crisis. Numerous southerners joined with López, seeing in his designs "a means of expanding slavery or otherwise advantaging their 'peculiar institution.'"[56] López himself called on southerners to take Cuba "while the present condition of her slaves is untouched."[57] Granted, many northerners also supported and encouraged López. Nevertheless, "slavery cast a lengthy shadow over the expeditions."[58]

Given recent history, the Taylor administration's attitude toward Spain seemed to be not only diplomatically correct "but truly friendly."[59] Yet not all was wine and roses in Spanish-American relations under the Whigs. After Taylor's untimely death, the Spaniards found President Millard Fillmore's policies to be less reassuring.[60] Fillmore and Edward Everett, now secretary of state, refused to sign on to a tripartite agreement with Britain and France that would have required the parties to renounce "now and hereafter" any desire to take possession of Cuba, and thus, for practical purposes, to end filibustering. The Whigs were not itching to take Cuba at the present, but supposed that it would eventually fall into American hands. Thus Everett would not forswear its acquisition forever. Since Spain had been the instigator of this 1852 diplomatic initiative, it could not have taken the American decision as reassuring.[61]

The Spaniards had already been worrying, and the final López expedition exacerbated that anxiety. In September 1851 Madrid had thus circulated a royal decree to its representatives abroad, addressing the sense that a potential crisis was brewing with Washington over the Cuban question. Spain wanted to maintain peaceful relations with the Americans, of course. Even so, the decree noted, "the impotence or tolerance of the [US] federal government joined to the persistence of the wanton [*desenfrenda*] and insolent democracy of the South of the Union in its desperate efforts against the Island of Cuba, can from one moment to another bring complications of such a nature as may make war inevitable, a war that by its nature, would affect, perhaps deeply, the European commercial interests."[62] The Spanish government had clearly identified the culprits in all of this: southern Democrats were pushing the annexationist agenda, and the New Yorker in the White House was, they concluded, unable or unwilling to rein them in.

The Expansionist Impulse at High Tide

The election of 1852 returned the Democrats to power, when New Hampshire's Franklin Pierce trounced the aging General Winfield Scott in the Electoral College. In what was to be their last national election, the Whigs had run on—among other planks—a proannexation platform. But it was the Democrat Pierce, "whose desire for Cuba was blatant," who would move ahead on the attempted acquisition of Cuba.[63] When this strong desire on the part of the president coincided with the fear of an end to slavery in Cuba— the "Africanization" scare—the administration plunged boldly into efforts to acquire the island before it was too late.

In his classic study of southern expansionist designs on the Caribbean in the 1850s, Robert E. May asserts that, by this time, "one can safely assert that some southerners had become possessed by a dream of Caribbean empire." He adds, "Vital to this dream of empire was the expectation that slavery would be intrinsic to its realization."[64] Karp agrees, noting that in regard to Cuba, the key issue for southerners was "the safety of Cuba's slave system."[65] The Yankee Pierce would, indeed, seek to acquire Cuba. The driving force behind this policy was southern slaveholders, and their interest in Cuba was now, more than before, determined by their interest in slavery.

The risks inherent in pursuing expansion at Spain's expense were, however, significant. Pierce was made aware of this even prior to taking office. In January 1853, the secretary of the US legation in Madrid had bumptiously written a lengthy letter to the president-elect in order to apprise him of the situation: "Spain will defend the Island of Cuba to the last effort of her power—France is her ally, and in case of War will enter the contest with her against the Government of the United States. There is no doubt that communications to this effect have taken place, and Emperor Napoleon III has guaranteed possession of Cuba to Spain with the offer of the whole power of France to sustain her against the supposed aggressive policy of the American Republic."[66] Pierce's correspondent, Horatio J. Perry, then went on to anticipate the issue that would soon lead to the Africanization scare. While his sources of intelligence are unclear, Perry confidently predicted that Spain, in a Samson-like, last-ditch effort to deny the island to the United States, would bring the walls tumbling down on Cuba. Spain, he assured Pierce, *is resolved, in the last resort—if all the ordinary resources of War should fail her—to emancipate the black population of Cuba and to give them arms.* In case of war with the United States, *this great blow of negro emancipation may be looked upon as certain,* and "its bearing upon the interior as well as exterior aspects of this question for us ought therefore to be considered."[67] Spain was, of course, well aware that an emancipated Cuba was of no attraction to the United States, whose southern policy elite would have been horrified by the prospect of taking into the republic a host of free and armed Blacks.[68] Furthermore, while Perry did not elaborate on the "interior aspects" of the question to which he alluded, it is safe to assume that he would have been understood as referring to the ruinous impact that such a development could have on the institution of slavery within the southern states. It was an ominous warning, and events would soon demonstrate that the administration took such threats very seriously.

Had Pierce been looking to provoke a crisis with Spain over Cuba, he could hardly have chosen his foreign policy team with greater diligence. New York's William L. Marcy was named secretary of state only after a Virginian had

declined the post. Marcy had not entered his new office as a rabid annexationist, and initially viewed any offer of purchase as inherently offensive to
Spain. Yet his preferred result—that Cuba "release itself or be released" from
Spanish rule to become an independent republic—was hardly more attractive to Madrid than acquisition by the United States.[69] The president sent
Buchanan to London. A northerner, like Marcy, Buchanan nevertheless had a
long history of advocating annexation and was understood to be sympathetic
to the interests of southern slaveholders. For all other relevant posts, Pierce
turned to southern slaveholders.[70] The new American minister to Paris was
Virginia's John Y. Mason, who, while serving as Polk's secretary of the navy,
had been "an ardent advocate [*partidario*] of the annexation of Cuba."[71] In
Madrid, the United States was to be represented by arch-annexationist Pierre
Soulé of Louisiana. In public life, Soulé had "stoutly defended slavery as an
economic and social system that he saw as key to southern interests."[72] The
secretary of war—should it come to that—was Mississippi's Jefferson Davis.
With the barest nod to northern sensibilities, Pierce had stacked the deck
with proslavery expansionists; he had "formed his administration for expansion."[73]

The dominance of a proslavery elite in the making of US foreign policy at
this point was impressive. One might well be struck with the confidence of
these men in their exercise of the power of the federal government and with
their intent "to advance their theoretical reflections with the material power
of the U.S. government."[74] Yet alongside confidence, these powerful men har-
bored great anxiety. Cuba provides the most salient example of this pervasive
fear. Because as these men looked at the institution that they were determined
to protect—indeed, to expand—they saw threats both at home and abroad.
The dangers faced by slavery abroad, furthermore, threatened to menace the
domestic institution of slavery. In so doing, these threats put at risk the men's
power, their region, and, in their minds, the nation itself, for America's slaveholding policymakers "could not envision a global future without the fundamental institution of African slavery."[75] National security policy must take into
account threats, opportunities, and resources. For those men making policy
in Washington during the 1850s, Cuba presented *both* threat and opportunity.
The question was whether they had at their disposal the resources necessary
to ward off the threat and take advantage of the opportunity.

Southerners were certainly conscious of the threat. In domestic terms, the
peril was to be found in Congress. The addition of new free states meant new
free state senators. As May observes, for the South "to maintain the sectional
balance of power, new slave territory would have to be acquired to counterbal-
ance free states regularly being admitted to the Union." New slave states meant

new representatives in Washington, who would "enable the South to protect the institution of slavery and 'Southern rights.'" Above all, the balance in the Senate had to be preserved.[76] Cuba thus presented an opportunity to southern policymakers and their northern allies. If added to the Union, it would certainly come in as a slave state. The fact that it might even be carved into as many as three new states, bringing the South six additional senators, made it that much more attractive. Jefferson Davis was blunt about the matter. In supporting the acquisition of Cuba later in the decade, he gave as a reason that Cuba's addition would "increase the number of slave-holding constituencies."[77]

The British government was following matters closely, and was well aware of American motivations. It was, furthermore, eager to do what could be done diplomatically to quash American expansion at Spain's expense. The British secretary of state for foreign affairs, Lord Palmerston, thus instructed his ambassador to Madrid in 1851 to "point out to the Spanish government that the great actuating motive which seems to impel the people of the Southern States of North America to repeat their attempts upon Cuba, is the desire to increase the weight and influence of the Southern States in Congress by adding another slave state to the Union. And it is evident that if the Spanish government were to take a bold and decided step, and to abolish the condition of slavery in Cuba, this actuating motive would cease to exist, and with it would cease the danger to which it gives rise." Or, as Amos Aschbach Ettinger colorfully puts it, "the slaveocracy turned with yearning eyes toward Cuba as the nearest possibility" for adding slave states to the United States.[78] Southern anxiety, as well as southern confidence, helped to determine America's policy toward Cuba during the decade before secession.

Yet the perceived menace to the slaveholders' world was not confined to the internal American political balance; slaveholders saw threats abroad as well as at home. In fact, they did not draw a distinction between foreign and domestic policies of slavery: a threat to slavery anywhere in the hemisphere was a threat everywhere, including America's southern states. As Karp notes, "The specter of freedom in the West Indies, southern elites feared, would come to haunt slavery in the United States." The very presence of large numbers of freed slaves in the region "represented an intrinsic threat to the American system of bondage."[79] Cuba thus represented both the best hope and the greatest danger. Adding it to the Union would help balance out the geographic and demographic growth of the free states. On the other side of the coin, any further threat to slavery in the Greater Antilles could only be taken as an existential threat by those who held power in Washington. Thus, "the focus of slaveholding attention in the 1850s remained Cuba."[80] The question for the Pierce administration was whether it could use the power of the US federal government, concentrated in the hands of slaveholders and their allies, to remove the threat—and to remove it through the acquisition of Cuba.

The Pierce team certainly had some reason to think that the answer to this question would be a resounding yes. As May sees it, "it is remarkable that Cuba never became United States property" in the 1840s or 1850s, despite the successive efforts of the Polk, Pierce, and Buchanan administrations.[81] The slaveholding policy elite expressed confidence that Cuba would, in good time, be theirs. Virginia senator James Mason had expressed this assurance. Who could doubt, he asked in November 1852, that "the acquisition of Cuba by The United States is a question of time only—purely a question of time? . . . [I]t is of little moment to us whether we acquire Cuba in this generation or in the next: but come to us it will, just as certain as that the world revolves upon its axis."[82] Yet the transfer of Cuba was not a matter of letting the law of nature take its course. It would have to be achieved by means of policy or not at all.

It was, of course, not achieved. Despite the concentration of power in the hands of a unified foreign policy elite sharing a clearly defined worldview, Cuba proved beyond America's grasp in the mid-nineteenth century. This was not because the Pierce administration bungled its foreign policy—although it did. And it did not fail because Soulé was shockingly unfit to conduct the necessary diplomacy—although he was. After all, Polk had failed as well. Yet the Polk administration had the advantages of competence, discipline, and the fraught Anglo-Spanish relations of the 1840s. While it is true that the Pierce administration had none of these things going for it, the most significant obstacles to American acquisition of Cuba in the 1850s were not of the administration's making. The central problem for the Pierce policy was that Spain absolutely refused to transfer Cuba to any other power, and that this refusal had the support of Britain and France. Americans, north and south, had assumed since the administration of President James Monroe that Cuba would eventually come to them. But in fact, if they wanted it, they would have to take it. Faced with the opposition of the maritime powers of Europe, the American republic lacked the power to do so.

Much has already been written about Soulé's disastrous mission to Madrid. His appointment was *incredible*—in the literal sense of the word. Rarely in the history of diplomacy could an envoy have been appointed to a nation that would have been justified in declaring him persona non grata before his arrival on its shores. An unabashed expansionist, Senator Soulé had given a lengthy speech on the floor of the Upper House in January 1853, during which, among other matters, he had suggested the possibility of armed conquest of Cuba by the United States.[83] Though it was a hugely provocative declaration, it nevertheless failed, in Pierce's mind, to disqualify Soulé for the Madrid post. Soulé's biographer, Catherine Chancerel, has stated—without citing her source, however—that southerners actually had wanted John Y. Mason sent to Madrid, because they "thought he was more likely to be active on the Cuba question" than Soulé.[84] It is hard to imagine how this would have been possible.

The choice did not go over well in Spain. The naming of the Louisiana senator as minister to Spain was met with "disgust in Madrid, as was natural." It was as if Pierce wanted to accentuate the provocatively expansionist comments in his own inaugural address by appointing to key diplomatic posts two men with the strongest ideas on annexation—namely, Mason and Soulé.[85] In fact, the Spanish government was inclined toward refusing to accept the latter's credentials. But this would have been a significant step, and would have risked a breach with the new administration in Washington. So serious was the matter that Madrid took the issue to London and Paris. The British foreign secretary responded that "Spain would certainly make a mistake in not receiving him." To fail to admit the emissary chosen by Pierce would play right into the hands of those in the United States who wanted to provoke a conflict with Spain "to justify the attempts against Cuba." He added that the French had the same concern. Having been thus advised, Madrid was in no position to refuse.[86]

Soulé's tenure in Madrid was eventful, and certainly colorful: engaging in conspiracies and fighting duels tends to get diplomats noticed. No doubt, he was a very poor choice for the job, both in terms of temperament and prudence. Yet, as has been perceptively noted, he was not an aberration. Despite the controversy and hostility which he engendered at home and abroad, Soulé "was in truth far from a peripheral outlier." Quite the contrary, the Louisianan "accurately represent[ed] antebellum expansionist thought and Democratic political culture," and as such "was merely the leading edge of a wider cross-regional Democratic expansionist push."[87] This interpretation has much to recommend it, especially when one considers that Soulé's attempts to "detach" Cuba from Spain were urged on him by a secretary of state hailing from a state that had officially abolished slavery a full half century before the Africanization scare seized official Washington. Soulé should thus be viewed as being at the center of Pierce administration policy, despite the personal excesses that might make him seem a fringe character.

The Africanization Scare

As minister to Madrid, Soulé would play a key role in the Pierce administration's response to the alleged Africanization scheme that Spain was hatching in Cuba. The causes of the scare were complex, rooted as they were in the four-cornered relations among London, Madrid, Washington, and Havana itself. Complicating matters was the pervasive Anglophobia of the mid-nineteenth-century American policy elite and the relationship that this fear bore to the issue of slavery in the Western Hemisphere. Spain had agreed in 1817 to abolish the slave trade in its possessions. But the Cuban trade in fact, as opposed to law, continued on four decades later, abetted by, among other things, an incredibly corrupt Spanish administration in Havana. Legitimately desiring an end to the trade, the government in London also feared that the continued importation of Africans into Cuba gave both incentive and pretext for American intervention in the affairs of the island. The British thus responded, throughout the 1840s and into the early 1850s, by putting diplomatic pressure on Madrid to live up to its obligations.[88]

As British frustration with Madrid's temporizing grew in the early 1850s, so, too, did the pressure on the Spanish government. By the end of January 1853, British patience was at an end. In a remarkable dispatch sent by the foreign minister, Lord Russell, to Lord Howden in Madrid, Russell speaks of the "strong feeling which prevails in this country on the subject of the Cuban Slave Trade." Cuba had signed the 1817 slave trade suppression treaty. Yet, in 1853, the "Slave Trade is flourishing in Cuba, and I have the pain of receiving the vain excuses and empty promises which are transmitted to you by the Government of Spain." This situation could not continue: As Russell explained,

> Your Lordship may be assured, that however friendly the councils of her Majesty may be to Spain; whatever may be the interest of this country not to see Cuba in the hands of any other Power than Spain; yet, in the eyes of the people of this country, the destruction of a trade which conveys the natives of Africa to become slaves in Cuba, will furnish a large compensation for such a transfer. . . . I must instruct your Lordship, therefore, to express, courteously but decidedly, the entire disbelief of Her Majesty's Government that the destruction of the African Slave Trade is beyond the power of the Government of Spain.[89]

Madrid now lacked options, other than the obvious: institute reforms in Cuba sufficient to placate the British government. By early May, Russell expressed satisfaction with the promises made by Madrid, though "there was no concrete explanation of the nature and scope of the measures that were expected."[90] In partial fulfillment of Spain's pledges, Madrid sent Juan de la Pezuela to Havana as the new captain general that September. Incorruptible and generally hostile to slavery, Pezuela was "explicitly charged . . . with suppressing the slave trade."[91] Foner provides a quite useful summary of the new captain general's policies, noting that there was "nothing actually revolutionary about these decrees, which simply sought to enforce existing treaty provisions."[92]

That the reforms were relatively moderate was, however, lost on both Cuban planters and American policymakers. On the island, Pezuela's "precipitate action" caused "genuine alarm in influential Cuban circles over the implied threat to abolish slavery."[93] This could hardly have come as surprise: Cuban slaveholders now thought themselves faced with the possibility, however remote, of complete loss of their bonded laborers, with all the consequences that this would entail. Given the fear among the island's white population of "another Haiti," general emancipation was unthinkable. The fear of looming disaster made its way quickly across the Florida Straits. On October 25, 1853, the *New York Times* was already reporting the "English scheme for the Africanization of Cuba" as an established fact, its correspondent reporting with certainty "of the union of England, France, and Spain in the scheme."[94]

Pierce administration officials shared elite Cuba's alarm and the *Times*'s certitude. From their man in Madrid they learned of the seriousness of the situation in Cuba. The Spanish choice of Pezuela as captain general "announced a settled determination on the part of the Spanish cabinet to bring matters in Cuba to a decisive crisis," wrote Soulé to Marcy. "He had been selected mostly on account of the violent prejudices he was supposed, and with truth, to entertain against us (the yankees)." Behind Pezuela, however, one saw lurking the hand of the British: "The slave trade is to be stopped. England has succeeded in forcing the Spanish government to the admission that all Africans imported into the Island since 1821 are to be considered as *libertados*, enfranchized. If the admission is acted upon rigidly, Cuba has ceased to have a slave and the dream of Lord Palmerston has become a reality. This however was effected without any formal stipulation being entered into on the part of either government. But that England holds a recognition of the state of things implied in the admission can not be the subject of doubt." Under such circumstances, Cuba "may well be considered as lost to Spain in a proximate future; and even so to the civilized world."[95]

The following January, Soulé reported to Marcy concerning a conversation that he had recently had with the Spanish minister to Washington, Ángel Calderon. The American minister took the opportunity, he declared, to let Calderon know, "frankly, that the Government of the U. States would . . . sternly and unbendingly oppose & combat any & every arrangement by which Spain with France or Spain with England or with them both & with the world in arms should attempt in the slightest degree to render the Island an injury or danger to us."[96] The impact of the Africanization scare, moreover, reached beyond the slaveholding policy elites and their northern allies. Around this same time, the *New York Times* was informing its readers of the rumored plot to introduce African laborers to the island as "apprentices," with the end goal of "the emancipation of the present slave labor in Cuba."[97] Fear for the security of slavery in America's neighborhood, exacerbated by a persistent undercurrent of Anglophobia, had precipitated a full-blown foreign policy crisis.

Buchanan took up the case with the British government itself. The American minister in London wrote to Marcy on November 1, 1853, informing him of a conversation that he had had with British foreign secretary Lord Clarendon. As Buchanan reported the conversation, he was rather forthright with Clarendon about American concerns regarding Cuba, telling him that "should a black government like that of Hayti be established there, it would endanger the peace and domestic security of a large and important portion of our people. To come then to the point:—it has been publicly stated and reiterated over and over again in the United States, that Spain, should she find it impossible to retain the Island, will emancipate the slaves upon it; and that the British Government is endeavoring to persuade her to pursue this course." Buchanan's reference to the security of a certain portion of the US population indicates the extent to which American policymakers saw the institution of slavery in the South as intrinsically linked with the continuation of slavery in Cuba. Clarendon sought to reassure, telling Buchanan that the British "certainly have no wish, very far from it, to see a Black Government established in Cuba." Aside from abolishing the slave trade to Cuba, and locating those slaves who should have by now been emancipated under Spanish law, the British "have never had any negotiation of any kind with Spain, or attempted to exercise any influence over her respecting the condition of the slaves in Cuba. We have not the most remote idea, in any event, of ever attempting to acquire Cuba for ourselves. We have, already, too many colonies,—far more than are profitable to us."[98] Although Buchanan "seemed satisfied with the assertions made by Clarendon," the same could not be said of his colleagues in Washington.[99]

The minds of Pierce and his foreign policy team moved quickly to thoughts of acquiring Cuba as the best means of forestalling Africanization. By early April 1854 the administration in Washington had resurrected Polk's policy of seeking to purchase the colony from Spain.[100] On April 3, Marcy wrote his "detach letter" to Soulé, instructing him to pursue this end. Given, he asserted, the volatile political situation in Madrid and the "troubles which may arise in the Island of Cuba from the experiment now making to introduce a new system of labor," a way might now be open to the "accomplishment of the object so much desired by the United States." The president had thus decided that Soulé was to "be furnished with full power to enter into a convention or treaty for the purchase of Cuba." Marcy added that Pierce was hopeful that the minister could "overcome the national prejudices" that had led Spain to think Cuba was a valuable possession. After all, the "natural connection of Cuba is with the United States."[101]

To that end, Soulé was authorized to offer Madrid $100 million for the island, with an extra $20–$30 million thrown in if that amount of money could make or break the deal. The time was right, given the Africanization scare: "The change of policy in Cuba, particularly in regard to supplying the demand for agricultural labor, has increased discontent and created alarm among people of that Island, and made them more averse to the continuance of Spanish rule, and more willing to come under the protection of the United States." After thus assessing the internal political situation in Cuba, Marcy gave further instructions which, in the hands of Soulé, could only prove incendiary:

> Should you, however, become convinced that Spain will not, for any consideration you are authorized to offer, entertain the proposition for a transfer of the sovereignty of Cuba to the United States, you will then direct your efforts to the next most desirable object, which is to detach the Island from the Spanish dominion and from all dependence on any European power. If Cuba were relieved from all transatlantic connection and at liberty to dispose of herself as her present interest and prospective welfare would indicate, she would undoubtedly relieve this government from all anxiety in regard to her future condition.

So that Soulé did not miss the import of his instructions, Marcy put a fine point on it, adding that any assistance the United States might "give to the people of Cuba to enable them to induce Spain to consent to their independence might be fully compensated by advantages which they would be able to secure to the United States."[102] So significant was the threat of abolition of slavery in Cuba, that Pierce—who was "as much concerned about possible emancipation as most Southerners"—was willing to aid slaveholding Cubans in an effort to "detach" the island from Spain.[103]

Not that the administration lacked reliable information that the Africanization of Cuba was being overblown. The previous year Pierce had sent a special agent, Delaware's Alexander Clayton, to Cuba to investigate the reports of, among other matters, a tripartite British-French-Spanish agreement on Africanization. When Clayton found nothing incriminating, Pierce was "unconvinced," and sent a second agent, one Charles W. Davis, who returned the information that the president, seemingly, wanted to hear.[104] Meanwhile, Marcy sought all the information he could get on the affair through more formal channels. Writing to the US acting consul in Havana on April 8, the secretary noted, "The public mind of this country has been for some time excited by rumors, currently circulated that the emancipation of all the Africans imported into Cuba since 1820, had been commenced and was steadily progressing in that Island under the supervision of the British Consul General." The State Department was "anxious to learn from an authentic source whether those rumors have any foundation or truth," and Marcy thus instructed the consul, William H. Robertson, to investigate the matter yet again.[105] The fact that Marcy asked Robertson to collect information five days *after* sending his "detach letter" to Soulé would appear to indicate two things: first, that Marcy was not yet sure that Africanization was taking place, and, second, that it did not matter very much.

Yet the Pierce team, at this point, was still undecided as to how to proceed. As May notes, "Despite Marcy's aggressive language, the administration pondered for weeks about what further action should be taken if Spain would not accept Soulé's offer." The administration's plans, Marcy told Buchanan in late May, were "unsettled."[106] It is worth noting that indecision was the word of the day in Madrid as well. Spain could not, at this time, count on the support of Britain and France to ward off threats from the United States; the Crimean War had broken out the previous October, and both powers were distinctly distracted by the so-called Eastern Question. Under these circumstances, the Spanish government considered negotiations with the United States "to try to gain time."[107] It also tried its hand at diplomacy in Paris. The Spanish ambassador to France, the Marqués de Viluma, approached the French foreign minister with a proposal for a "guarantee among the maritime Powers of Europe against all aggression on the part of the Americans against any colony that belongs to those Powers." The Frenchman, Édouard Drouyn de Lhuys, did not respond favorably; France had little to protect overseas, and had to consider how costly war with the United States would be.[108] Unfortunately, Spain had little to offer to a Paris already preoccupied with a major European war, especially after refusing the French suggestion that Spanish troops might be usefully employed in the East.[109]

Anglo-French preoccupation with Russia did, indeed, appear to offer an opportunity to the Pierce administration. The fact that London and Paris "were becoming embroiled in the Eastern war would undoubtedly help insure Spain's isolation in any conflict, and the influence of this calculation in Washington was apparent."[110] Indeed it was. John J. Seibels, American minister to Brussels, expressed this understanding of the situation well in a letter to Marcy at the end of 1854. If the administration did not take advantage of the Crimean War to secure Cuba, then "adieu to all idea of the acquisition of Cuba for a long, long time to come. So if anything can be done in this line, it ought to be done quickly."[111] One problem with acting "in this line," however, was American uncertainty about the extent of London's distraction. As Alan Dowty observes,

"The British position appeared to be one of maintaining a watchful eye on the new world and keeping the United States uncertain as to its intentions."[112] If its goal was to keep the United States guessing, Britain succeeded. Robertson, reporting from Havana in June, told Marcy of a letter from a "Spanish gentleman" that he had recently seen. The Spaniard, Robertson noted, "remarks, that the U. States will find it no easy job to take the Island as both England and France are Pledged to sustain Spain in that Event."[113] In light of such reports, the administration could not reliably count on Spanish isolation in the face of American pressure.

In fact, there was little working in Pierce's favor. War with Spain had seemed a possibility for a time, especially in light of a perceived, if overblown, insult to the American flag on the part of officials in Havana. But the so-called *Black Warrior* Affair proved a dead end.[114] Nor did Soulé's ham-handed attempts to intervene in the Spanish Revolution of July 1854 bring the desired results.[115] After the failure of the liberal revolution the following month, the US chargé in Madrid wrote Marcy to inform the secretary that "the peaceable cession of the Island of Cuba by Spain is at this time impossible," adding that Soulé's policy had proved "a complete and utter failure."[116]

Marcy believed, however, that he had one more card up his sleeve. On August 16, Marcy called on Buchanan, Mason, and Soulé to meet "at some central point" to discuss the best means of helping Soulé in his efforts to acquire Cuba.[117] The result was the infamous *Ostend Manifesto* of October 1854, a document "as belligerent as it was useless."[118] In the manifesto, the three diplomats called for the United States government to make "an immediate attempt" to purchase Cuba. The sale of Cuba to the United States, they noted, "would essentially promote the highest and best interests of the Spanish people." The sale would also be in the interest of the United States, of course, since "the Union can never enjoy repose, nor possess reliable security, as long as Cuba is not embraced within its boundaries." Thus, if Spain proved unwilling to sell, "then, by every law, human and divine, we shall be justified in wresting it from Spain if we possess the power."[119] The Ostend conspirators had thus produced a bellicose call for the United States to take the island, if Spain were not willing to part with it, and to do so even in the most threatening manner.

The manifesto may well have helped Buchanan gain southern support for his planned candidacy for the Democratic presidential nomination.[120] But it did not move administration policy any closer to its goal, and it ignited a firestorm of protest outside the slaveholding South.[121] After Ostend, any serious attempts by Pierce to gain Cuba for the United States were at an end. The passage of the Kansas-Nebraska Act, in any event, had led the administration to focus on the growing sectional rift in the United States. Under these circumstances, it seemed wise to avoid unnecessary conflicts abroad. It was not the time to provoke Spain.[122] Additionally, the passage of the act "hardened the northern Whigs' opposition to the acquisition of the island," thus creating another hurdle to annexation.[123] Then, too, the removal of Pezuela by Spain helped diffuse the fears of Africanization. His replacement, José Gutiérrez de la Concha, had already served a term as colonial governor and had hardly established a reputation for reform: he was greeted, on his arrival in Havana, as "a savior of reaction." While Concha, like Pezuela, showed himself willing to utilize Black troops in case of an invasion—a development that caused great consternation in the United States—the "crisis" was at an end.[124]

It cannot be known if Britain would have intervened militarily if the United States had sought to take Cuba by force during this period. But it was unlikely. London "would have been most reluctant" to take on a conflict with the Americans while it was still fighting the Crimean War. Thus, this situation "created an opening for Washington." But Pierce could not grasp the opportunity "because the battle over the Kansas-Nebraska bill crippled his freedom of action."[125] If this analysis is correct, then the expansionists' reach far exceeded their grasp. In pursuing expansion of slavery westward, they thwarted their best chance for American expansion to the south, and with it the addition of one or more slave states in the Caribbean. This golden opportunity would not present itself again.

Buchanan Perseveres

Pierce's successor, Ostend conspirator James Buchanan, did not give up easily on the dream of acquiring Cuba. As he proclaimed at the end of 1858, "Expansion is in the future the policy of our country, and only cowards fear and oppose it."[126] But domestic division and a surging Republican Party guaranteed that there would be a sufficient number of "cowards" to block the president's plans. His allies were not much help either. Buchanan sought to acquire from Congress funds to "facilitate the acquisition of the island of Cuba, by negotiation."[127] His point person in advocating for the bill was Senator John Slidell of Louisiana. Buchanan had sought to portray the benefits of acquiring Cuba as national, and not sectional. Yet Slidell, in advocating the proposal on January 24, 1859, used language that appeared to give the lie to Buchanan's reassurances. The senator, in his remarks, decried the "closet philanthropists of England and France," who would, in offering Spain their protection, "insist upon introducing their schemes of emancipation." As a result, "Civil and servile war would soon follow, and Cuba would present, as Hayti now does, no traces of its former prosperity, but the ruins of its once noble mansions. Its uncontrolled possession by either France or England would be less dangerous and offensive to our southern states than a pretended independent black empire or republic." Slidell had succeeded in framing the issue of purchase as a sectional matter of the preservation of slavery on the island and, by extension, in the South. In the political climate of 1859, the results were predictable. His remarks "aroused a storm of protests in the North," and became "the cause of passionate [*ardientes*] debates in Congress."[128]

Slidell's close connection with the Buchanan administration convinced Republicans that the senator's words expressed the true thinking of the White House. Senator John P. Hale of New Hampshire, a former Free Soiler, expressed his conviction that Slidell "spoke the views of Mr. Buchanan" and had done so "semi-officially." In Hale's estimation, it was clear what had transpired: "There has been a Cabinet council got together, and they recommend now a strong dose of Cuba as the only thing by which the [Democratic] party can possibly survive another presidential election. [Laughter.]"[129] New York Senator William Henry Seward proclaimed the proposal "the most atrocious act of legislation which the Senate could possibly adopt."[130] The sinister nature of the proposition was laid out by Senator James Rood Doolittle of Wisconsin: "It can only be looked upon as a proposition to put $30,000,000 into the hands of the President, to be used as secret-service money to bribe the officials of Spain to go into a treaty which, in their legislative capacity, they have absolutely and unanimously rejected."[131] On this last point, Doolittle had the advantage of being absolutely correct. Just weeks earlier, the Spanish minister in Washington had made the matter clear to Secretary of State Lewis Cass; Gabriel García Tassara had "read the remarks of the President on the acquisition of Cuba by purchase and . . . he was bound to say that no government (no administration) in Spain could ever be found to consent to the sale of the island: And lastly that any proposition to that effect, made to Spain, would not be received as one made in a friendly spirit."[132] With Spain resolutely opposed even to discussing the sale of Cuba, and the Senate refusing to appropriate funds to add a new slave state that might join the Union just in time to secede, the last attempt by southern slaveholders and their northern allies to acquire the island in the antebellum era had reached a dead end.

Conclusion: Buttressing Slavery

The important role played by slavery in America's policy toward Cuba in the antebellum period is clear. As Lester D. Langley notes, "In these years, the

American Democracy, dominated by Southerners, urged the anexation [*sic*] of Cuba in order to buttress the institution of slavery in the South."[133] Slavery was also key to the international context in which Texas joined the Union. Southern slaveholders were eager to add the twenty-eighth state, in large measure to protect and extend the institution. In both cases, American policy-makers were willing to take risks on the international stage, including the possibility of conflict with the maritime powers of Europe. They did so because the dangers of inaction seemed to them even more serious than those of aggressive expansionism. Cuba thus presented southern slaveholders with both a dream and a nightmare. Though they were especially fearful of the possibility of abolition in Cuba, slavery on that island actually outlasted slavery in their own states. In the end, the dreaded armed Blacks invading the South came not in the rags of Caribbean slaves but in the crisp blue uniforms of the Union Army.

CHAPTER 6

"Its Peculiar Moral Force"

Lincoln, Emancipation, and Colonization

Scholarship on the American Civil War has taken an internationalist turn in the twenty-first century. In 1999 Howard Jones could accurately lament that the historiography of the Civil War "seldom" mentioned "the pivotal role of foreign affairs," adding that the result of this neglect was "that few students of the war realize how integral the European response was to its outcome."[1] Today, however, the reader finds an extensive literature on the international dimension of the war. Historians have produced significant works on the Civil War and Britain;[2] on Franco-American relations during the war;[3] and on Spanish-American relations during the same period.[4] Jones himself has produced a magisterial study of both northern and southern diplomacy.[5] Scholars have begun to address the Civil War as an international, Atlantic, and even global event.[6] Additionally, an excellent work has appeared on the topic of international finance and the war,[7] while biographies of Abraham Lincoln have increasingly addressed his role in foreign relations.[8] The scholarship on the international dimensions of the war has thus grown from meager to extensive. This is as it should be. As Allan Nevins has observed, "No battle, not Gettysburg, not the Wilderness, was more important than the contest waged in the diplomatic arena and the forum of public opinion."[9]

Significantly, these works have often treated slavery as an important factor in US international relations during the war, though not always in ways that one might predict. The key to diplomatic success—and thus, in no small measure, the war itself—came down to the question of European intervention, which the South sought to bring about and the North sought to avert. In this contest, slavery would play a central role. Richmond, Virginia, aware of European hostility toward slavery, consistently sought to downplay its significance in the conflict. Washington, DC, by contrast, increasingly endeavored to cast the war as a contest between slavery and freedom, and especially so after Lincoln decided that emancipation was a vital step toward victory. Both were convinced of the potential power of the issue to influence European policy decisions, and most significantly those of Great Britain. For their part, Confederate leaders assumed "that British sympathies would initially go to the Union" because of the slavery issue. They thus sought to portray the war as a war for independence from an oppressive North.[10] Union and Confederate statesmen alike were convinced that London, and subsequently other governments, could take the step of recognizing the South only if slavery were not seen as the paramount motive for secession.

Early Steps: Downplaying Slavery

The administration of President Lincoln would thus, at first blush, appear to have had a strong motivation for stressing slavery as the cause, and emancipation as the aim, of the war. But Lincoln and his often-bumptious secretary of state, William H. Seward, were not initially able to exploit the central issue of the war for diplomatic advantage. The slaveholding border states of Delaware, Kentucky, Maryland, and Missouri had not seceded from the United States, and American success in the war, Lincoln knew, depended on retaining their loyalty. This, in turn, dictated a consistent line from the administration, emphasizing that its goal in the war was not to liberate slaves but to maintain national unity. But "Lincoln and Seward's decision to emphasize the preservation of the Union rather than the abolition of slavery" at this time "complicated . . . the conduct of diplomacy abroad."[11] Lincoln's policy on this issue was realistic, and dictated by circumstances. Yet it also denied him and his diplomatic corps use of the most effective tool at their disposal for influencing European opinion. As the American minister in Spain—the redoubtable Carl Schurz— lamented in 1861, the failure to emphasize slavery as the issue dividing the North and South had "stripped our cause of its peculiar moral force."[12] This did not mean, however, that Confederate diplomats would have an easy time of it, since "slavery may not have been the primary determinant of foreign reactions to the American Civil War, but it put Confederates on the defensive throughout the conflict."[13] America's minister to London, Charles Francis

Adams, sent a report to Seward in January 1862 that expressed just such a perception. "The pressure of the popular feeling against slavery is so great here," he wrote, "that [the Confederates'] friends feel it impossible to stem it without some such plea in extenuation as can be made out of an offer to do something for ultimate emancipation."[14] The author of *Uncle Tom's Cabin* saw things the same way. In January 1863 Harriet Beecher Stowe wrote in the *Atlantic Monthly*, "The agitation kept up by the anti-slavery portion of America, by England, and by the general sentiment of humanity in Europe, had made the situation of the slaveholding aristocracy intolerable. As one of them at the time expressed it, they felt themselves under the ban of the civilized world."[15] Although both sides in the war wished, at its beginning, to downplay the significance of the slavery issue for their own reasons, neither could evade the "peculiar moral force" that it exerted.

During the 1860 presidential campaign, Lincoln's avowed goal was that of his party—namely, to prevent the spread of slavery into new territories. Convinced that slavery contained was slavery doomed, Lincoln took an antislavery rather than an abolitionist position at this juncture. Opposition to the spread of slavery was the "lowest common denominator of Republican opinion," and Lincoln was determined to set aside all "peripheral" issues that might potentially sow division within the party.[16] His election victory that November effectively broke the power that southern slaveholders had held over the federal government during the course of the preceding decades. Previously any northerner who sought "high federal office" had to "make some kind of peace with the nation's peculiar institution."[17] As of March 1861, those days of genuflection would be at an end. Now, with the election of an Illinoisan president who clearly hoped for slavery's eventual extirpation, it was manifest that "a united North had the power to determine the nation's future."[18] The federal government would be in the hands of the Republicans, who owed no fealty to southern slaveholders, and who, minimally, wished to see slavery's slow demise.

This realignment of federal power necessarily meant that slaveholders would lose control of the apparatus of the nation's foreign policy. It was a sobering prospect: control of the "outward state" was considered by slaveholders as crucial to the vitality of the institution of bonded labor in the hemisphere.[19] In fact, Lincoln, for reasons of party unity, would appoint a significant number of the dreaded Radical Republicans "to foreign diplomatic and consular posts in the spring of 1861."[20] The reaction of southern slaveholders to this reversal of fortunes, and the threat to their social order that it entailed, was secession: if they could not control the institutions of the federal government, then they would live under a government of their own.

After secession, Lincoln long hesitated to declare that the war was fundamentally "about slavery." The need to keep the Border States in the Union, together with his misguided belief in a significant repository of Union sentiment in the slave South, led to his caution. The discretion in declaratory policy was reflected early in administration diplomacy, as Seward instructed the American minister to London, Charles Francis Adams, to avoid discussion of the slavery issue.[21] The upshot of this posturing was to be the "central political dilemma facing the president": Lincoln and Seward "now confronted the serious challenge of convincing the British and others across the Atlantic that the conflagration threatening to break out over slavery did not concern slavery at all." The president and the secretary of state did not necessarily see the problem with taking such an approach. The true cause of the war was clear to them. Thus, they assumed that the British leaders were "astute enough to recognize the obvious." The Americans did not need to articulate what they, for domestic reasons, could not state. Unfortunately, Britons tended to take Lincoln and Seward at their word. The result was that they were let off the hook. Assured by the Americans that the war was being fought over the Union, the British "no longer had to make the hard choice between upholding their moral commitment against slavery and their need to maintain connections with the Confederacy's cotton distributors."[22]

If the government of British prime minister Lord Palmerston could not believe its good fortune, there were others who did not look upon this development with glee. British abolitionists could be forgiven if they found Lincoln's initial justification of the war frustrating. After all, if the goal was to bring the southern states back into the Union without ending slavery, then there was no point in getting mixed up in the matter.[23] Even the staunchly antislavery Duke of Argyll, the Lord Privy Seal in Palmerston's cabinet, saw restoration of the Union as problematic. In Argyll's view, the "breakup of the Union would remove US protection from the evil institution and permit the world's progressive opinion to exert its remedial influence on the wayward Americans. . . . *Both* Union and Confederacy were responsible for impeding the advance of civilization."[24] From this perspective, the preservation of the Union might actually *impede* the course of abolition. Were Lincoln to proclaim emancipation as his administration's goal, then the Union's integrity could instead have been viewed abroad as key to achieving abolition. But force of circumstance prevented the president from issuing such a pronouncement in 1861. Thus, the British people in general, though "violently opposed to slavery," did not make the connection between Union and emancipation.[25]

In fact, many among Britain's governing class also failed to make this linkage. The fault for this lied in part, no doubt, with the administration itself, as the British foreign secretary, Lord Russell noted in the fall of 1861. Lincoln and Seward were, however, "puzzled when Europeans seemed unable or unwilling to acknowledge the seemingly obvious reality that the morality and fate of slavery constituted the fundamental differences between the North and South."[26] But the president had "erroneously assumed that the British and other Europeans would automatically understand that slavery lay at the root of the American conflict."[27] What appeared so obvious to the statesmen in Washington was, apparently, lost in translation as it crossed the Atlantic. Lincoln's declaratory policy only "muddied the diplomatic waters."[28]

A dynamic similar to that in Britain prevailed across the English Channel. Those French who were most friendly toward the Union found themselves in a predicament. Although they saw in the North the "embodiment of the abolitionist force that had spread even to the remotest corners of France," Lincoln was giving them nothing to work with. In fact, "for an intolerable period, the [French] liberals had to face the dilemma of attributing to the North an ideal which the president steadily refused to acknowledge." As the liberal Republican journalist Auguste Nefftzer summarized the situation, Lincoln's "vacillation" on the slavery issue was a factor that "stopped the American conflict from becoming the cause of our civilization. . . . What should we hate if not slavery?"[29] Lincoln's denial that the American crisis was fundamentally about freedom versus slavery must, indeed, have come as a surprise to the French, who had been told by a majority of their newspapers that this was in fact the issue that had provoked southern secession. As a progovernment newspaper wrote on January 10, 1861, the conflict was the result of the burgeoning division between the South's growing attachment to slavery and the North's increasing abolitionist sentiment, and, "from these two opposed movements is born the present situation in the United States." The South was rebelling in order to protect "that dear 'peculiar institution.'" It was slavery that was "the principal cause of the catastrophe."[30]

Lincoln's reticence on slavery was no doubt a boon to the European diplomacy of the Richmond government. Yet the president's early caution in articulating the fundamental issue at stake in the newborn war did not mitigate French hostility toward slavery. An unofficial representative of the Richmond administration summarized the situation in an undated memorandum, and it was bleak indeed. The Louisianan Paul Pecquet du Bellet lamented the propaganda successes of Union representatives in Paris and urged that a pro-Confederate newspaper be founded in Paris to counter local "friends of the North." The message of the pro-Union forces in the French capital was a potent one. "Slavery was proclaimed a national crime which ought to be extirpated from Confederate soil if it were to cost the blood of every white

Southerner; the old principle of the red Republicans was exhumed: *'Perisse une nation plutot qu'un principle'* [*sic*; "Perish a nation rather than a principle," a reference to a similar quote from Maximilien Robespierre]." These assertions, "printed and circulated every day without refutation" had become *"political axioms"* among the French. By the time Richmond got around to sending representatives to Paris to "correct the evil, it was too deeply rooted in the mind of the french people to admit of radical cure." In fact, "so intense had the hatred of the people become for that institution" that French emperor Napoleon III *"dared not manifest his well known sympathy for the South* much less continue *to give them aid and comfort."*[31] Du Bellet must surely have thought French antislavery sentiment virulent if it were enough to daunt the emperor himself.

The Struggle over Foreign Intervention

The issue of European opinion regarding the Civil War was integral to the diplomacy of both the North and the South. Lincoln and Seward sought, at all costs, to forestall European—and especially British—diplomatic intervention in the conflict; this was, in fact, the central component of their diplomacy. The survival of the Union depended upon their success at preventing British recognition of Richmond: with "the precarious balance of the war on the battlefield, such a decision by London virtually assured calamity for the Union."[32] The president and the secretary of state viewed Britain as the key to the game, believing as they did that that no other European nation would intervene in the American crisis if London remained aloof. French policy was nevertheless a significant, if secondary, concern, particularly due to the unpredictable and adventurous nature of Napoleon III.

Eventually, southern slavery came to play a greater role in Washington's foreign policy with regard to Europe. The administration sought to use the South's oppressive labor system to gain diplomatic leverage. Given the broadly spread public hostility to slavery in both Britain and France, this approach offered real possibilities: the British government "faced a voting public steeped in antislavery sentiment" and would thus have to tread very carefully when evaluating the benefits of intervention. The French government, while less beholden to voters, could not ignore the powerful abolitionist sentiment of the vast majority of its population. Nor, to its frustration, could it tame the French opposition press, which "urged France not to cooperate with a Republic that maintained such an 'anachronistic practice'" as slavery.[33] To Europeans in general, "the true voice of the United States was the North, however hesitant it might have been to assume the moral responsibility thrust upon it by the world."[34] Lincoln's initial reluctance to address forthrightly the fundamental issue of the war no doubt frustrated his French sympathizers, who "had to face the dilemma of attributing to the North an ideal which the president steadily refused to acknowledge."[35] Yet the fact that the Confederacy was built upon the cornerstone of inhuman racial exploitation gave Union diplomats an advantage in the contest with the South.

Southerners were thus motivated to downplay the significance of slavery as an issue in the war, just as they ironically maintained, for domestic consumption, that the war was fundamentally about liberty. Confederate policymakers and diplomats—direct heirs to the foreign policy of slavery elucidated by historian Matthew Karp—faced the unenviable task of trying to convince Europeans that the bedrock of their economy and social order had been irrelevant to secession and that the war was actually a struggle to vindicate the fundamental principles on which the United States had been founded. It was an uphill task. Nor was it made easier by the often poor quality of the diplomats whom Confederate president Jefferson Davis had dispatched to make this improbable case.[36]

The Confederates had two advantages going for them in the diplomatic sphere. Their foremost mistake was in gravely overrating one of them—namely, the power of cotton. The other, Lincoln's reticence on the slavery question, they sought to exploit for all it was worth—though with limited results. In deploying both they aimed minimally at gaining formal recognition from European states. The maximum goal was European military intervention in the war on the side of the South. In between stood the possibility of a united European diplomatic intervention. Though ostensibly aimed at bringing an end to a bloody and economically disruptive war, European mediation would almost certainly have resulted in achievement of southern independence. Richmond's most valuable source of leverage in this endeavor was to be cotton: the Europeans needed it to keep their factories and economies running and their workers employed. "White gold" was to be their trump card on the Atlantic world stage.

The thought that this precious commodity, and access to it, would move diplomatic mountains for the South was not, on its face, ridiculous. By the year of Lincoln's election to the White House, over four million Britons "owed their livelihood to the cotton mills," and the vast majority of the cotton which kept those mills running came from the South.[37] French industry was more diversified, yet imported an even higher percentage of its cotton from the US South. Indeed, nearly all of France's cotton came from the United States prior to the war.[38] It was not much of a stretch to assume that the disruption of the flow of cotton to Europe would impel governments there to intervene in order to end the war and restore the regular flow of the commodity across the ocean. Indeed, "by every economic measure, King Cotton Diplomacy should have won British recognition of southern independence."[39]

Where southerners erred was in overconfidently assuming that economics would be the determining factor in European, and especially British, decisions regarding intervention in American affairs. Foreign governments had to weigh economic interests against other considerations. The most significant of these by far was the danger that *any* sort of intervention would mean war with a rapidly arming United States. Seward had made at least one point crystal clear: recognition of the South would be viewed as a hostile act by the federal government. In the end, "the risk of war with the United States was always greater than the benefits gained from supporting Confederate independence."[40] Additionally, the clumsy way in which Richmond attempted to play the cotton card did nothing to ingratiate the Confederate government with its British and French counterparts. Davis's decision to exercise diplomatic leverage through an informal, self-imposed embargo of cotton exports was difficult to explain to Europeans. After all, his own government sought to present the Union blockade of southern ports as an illegal "paper blockade" due to its initially porous nature. It was thus difficult to explain why the cotton could not get through to European ports. The Confederates' "arrogant assumption that King Cotton would bring the world to heel was not soon forgotten abroad."[41] Confederate secretary of state Judah P. Benjamin may indeed have been "obsessed with enticing France and Britain into the war," but the methods by which he and his colleagues pursued King Cotton Diplomacy only made that goal more remote than it already had been.[42]

The second arrow in the Confederate diplomatic quiver was Lincoln's own assertion, often repeated, that the Union was fighting for the sole purpose of keeping the nation whole; his administration was not seeking to eradicate slavery where it already existed. The reassurances had started early. Lincoln was uncharacteristically taciturn during the Secession Winter that separated his election from his inauguration, but he was not silent. Using his Illinois colleague, Senator Lyman Trumbull, as a surrogate spokesman, the president-elect penned a speech that was soon attributed by the press to him. Through Trumbull, Lincoln told the nation that when the Republicans assumed power "each and all of the States will be left in as complete control of their affairs respectively, and at as perfect liberty to choose, and employ, their own means of protecting their property, and preserving peace and order within their respective limits, as they have ever been under any administration."[43] His administration would be no more of a threat to slavery—where it currently existed—than Buchanan's had been.

Lincoln amplified this assertion on March 4, 1861. In his inaugural address, the newly sworn-in president sought to convince southern leaders that his administration would pose no threat to slavery where it already existed. Attempting to appeal in part to the eight slave states that had not yet seceded, Lincoln proclaimed that "he had neither the power nor inclination to interfere with slavery where it existed." Three days later, the new president took a step in the direction of protecting the right to slavery. On that day he sent to the states a proposed constitutional amendment that would permanently preclude federal interference with the South's institution.[44] Lincoln was thus seeking to portray himself as anything but the "Black Abolitionist" whom the southerners claimed to fear. The issue at stake, he repeatedly indicated, was between union and disunion, not slavery and abolition.

European Responses and Interests

Many in Europe took Lincoln's words and actions at this decisive point, and in the year that followed, at face value. Southern representatives in European capitals, moreover, were advancing a similar argument—namely, that this was a war over independence and not human bondage. As a result, "the arguments of Southern emissaries gained in force as the Northern case weakened."[45] Both sides "ironically found agreement on the most emotional issue that divided them: slavery itself. In a move that astounded observers thousands of miles away in Europe, Lincoln echoed the Confederacy's cry that slavery had nothing to do with the American crisis." Thus, "slavery retreated from center stage to assume a public status barely secondary in nature. The Confederacy sought diplomatic recognition from England and other nonslaveholding nations and predictably tried to remove slavery from the international picture. The Lincoln administration surprised Europeans by likewise dismissing the importance of slavery."[46] The governments in both London and Paris "acted primarily upon . . . ideological, economic, and geopolitical considerations," and had their own interests to advance.[47] But Lincoln had provided them—and particularly Palmerston—with greater flexibility in pursuing these ends: domestic pressure stemming from hostility to slavery was largely neutralized as long as both sides in the war claimed that this was a nonissue.

Lincoln had also given an unmerited gift to Confederate representatives in Europe, who would not constantly be faced with the need to defend the South's slave system to those who had already eradicated the institution in their overseas possessions. Still, Richmond's representatives in European capitals perceived themselves as fighting an uphill battle. True, the Confederate emissary in Paris, John Slidell, was granted access to leaders in the French government in a manner that Seward could only interpret as unfriendly. Yet Slidell remained convinced "that at the highest level slavery thwarted his efforts at recognition and weakened his position."[48] There was apparently some truth to Slidell's perception, since throughout the Civil War, the French foreign office was always under the direction of a minister who opposed slavery: initially Édouard Thouvenel, and, following his resignation in October 1862, Édouard Drouyn de Lhuys. Yet as French historian Stève Sainlaude asserts, the slavery issue was never a significant determinant of Thouvenel's or Drouyn's opposition to recognition of the Confederacy.[49] For his part, the emperor was "more tolerant" of slavery than were his foreign ministers. In the end, the slavery issue simply was not a major factor in the considerations of the French government when it came to recognition, and it "treated slavery as a marginal issue that could on no account steer or determine its diplomacy."[50]

Napoleon had reasons for wanting to intervene in America, but they had nothing to do with slavery. Of particular interest to him was Mexico. The ambitious emperor had visions of attaining a new empire in the Western Hemisphere, and the key to this was America's neighbor to the south. A united and powerful America would, of course, never allow France to dominate Mexico; war with the United States would have been a far more likely result than supine acquiescence on the part of the US government. The Civil War, however, gave him—in his view—a golden opportunity. With the Americans divided, weakened, and the Union now geographically cut off from Mexico, they would be in a poor position to thwart Napoleon's designs in Latin America. Indeed, he hoped that southern independence would result in the emergence of a buffer state that would separate French-dominated Mexico from the United States, making American intervention that much more difficult. Additionally, if France were to intervene diplomatically in the Civil War in such a way as to help the South gain independence, Napoleon assumed he could then rely on a friendly Richmond government. In fact, "with the support of the South, the Mexican empire would have been consolidated and perpetuated [perennisé]." Southern diplomats, sensing an opportunity, sought to use the Mexico issue as leverage to gain recognition from Paris.[51]

Seeking recognition from some European power, Davis's government also sought to cultivate Spain. Franco-Confederate diplomacy was "purely tactical."[52] On the other hand, Richmond perceived that it might find kindred spirits in Madrid. Alone among the powers of Europe, Spain was a slaveholding empire with a presence in the New World; indeed, its most valuable possession, Cuba, still relied extensively on bonded labor to sustain its economy. To southern policymakers, this commonality with the South appeared to present an opportunity. Judah Benjamin's predecessor as secretary of state, R. M. T. Hunter, wrote in August 1861 that "of all the great powers of Europe Spain alone is interested through her colonies in the same social system which pervades the Confederate States."[53] In fact, the Confederates were "enchanted with the idea of an alliance with Spain."[54] Lincoln's first minister to Madrid, the fiery German immigrant and staunch abolitionist Carl Schurz, believed that Spain was ripe fruit for southern picking. Repeatedly during his brief foray into diplomacy, Schurz informed Washington that Spanish recognition of the Confederacy was just around the corner.[55] Yet, here again, Richmond was to suffer disappointment. Madrid was willing to act on recognition, but only if Britain or France did so as well; all the more so since the Spanish feared European intervention on the side of the Confederacy would provoke Russian entry on the side of the Union.[56] But since Paris would not act at this point in the war without London, Britain remained at the center of the diplomatic struggle between the Union and the Confederacy.

Palmerston's policy toward intervention thus became the key issue for Lincoln and Seward's diplomacy. In this, slavery initially played a rather minor role—one that would only increase by stages. For reasons mentioned previously, Lincoln and Seward kept the slavery issue muted in their foreign policy, assuming that Europeans would comprehend the fundamental issue at stake in the war, and becoming perplexed when they did not. The Lincoln administration's relations with Britain were, furthermore, not improved in the early days of the war by the secretary of state's reputation for inveterate Anglophobia. As a senator from New York, Seward had indeed engaged in significant baiting of John Bull, sometimes blatantly for his own political benefit, as when he "stirred up Irish-American animosities toward Britain in order to win votes." Likewise, his perennial interest in US acquisition of Canada was not likely to go over well with the British.[57] Seward, moreover, was convinced that this hostility toward Britain was reciprocal, that Britain sought to use the opportunity presented by secession to weaken a growing strategic and commercial rival. He thus presumed general British animosity toward the North after the onset of war.

Seward was wrong. The fact was that Britons were deeply divided over the North-South struggle. The debate over the American Civil War was, in reality, of such broad interest to British society that "no other agitation in the period, not the movements in support of Polish or Hungarian independence or Italian unification, engaged the public interest so extensively as did the debate over the war in America."[58] On the nonelite level, there was nothing like a consensus in favor of the Confederacy. Nor did pro-South sentiments reign among elite policymakers: "Rarely ones to be swayed by passions, [Foreign Secretary John] Russell, Palmerston and other leading British statesmen viewed the Civil War in a detached and pragmatic manner. Though they recognized the virtues of the causes of both sides and the international opportunities presented by the conflict, they were more compelled to stay at arm's length from both the Union and Confederacy and to maintain a policy of neutrality."[59] As Palmerston wrote in May 1861 with regard to diplomatic intervention, "there would . . . be great difficulty in suggesting any basis of arrangement to which both parties could agree, and which it would not be repugnant to English feelings and principles to propose. We could not well mix ourselves up with the acknowledgement of slavery."[60] The fact that the American minister to London, Charles Francis Adams, "saw a southern supporter in every Briton" says more about American perceptions than British opinions.[61] A desire to see the United States weakened as a challenger in the international arena, or a wish that an expansionistic upstart republic would get its comeuppance, did not translate into anything like a predilection for intervention in the American crisis.

If the British were in no mood to go to war, the same cannot be said of Seward. Infamously, the secretary submitted a "bizarre" memorandum to Lincoln on April 1, 1861, urging the president to provoke a crisis with France and Spain over the former's reconquest of Santo Domingo. As if two European enemies were not enough, he urged the new president to "seek explanations from Great Britain and Russia." If, furthermore, Spain and France did not provide satisfaction, the president should then "convene Congress and declare war against them."[62] Seward submitted his memorandum on April Fool's Day. But the implications of his proposal were quite serious, even if his goal was unclear. Joseph A. Fry concludes that Seward "sought a 'foreign crisis' rather than a foreign war," being too well apprised of the realities of international politics to seek to take on all comers.[63] Characteristically circumspect, Lincoln quashed the idea. The new president nonetheless found Seward's transatlantic reputation for belligerence useful. The administration sought to signal consistently and forcefully to London and Paris that recognition of the Confederacy would result in war with the Union, and to emphasize that America would be a formidable foe.[64] Seward eagerly took on the task using "his Anglophobic reputation to cultivate the image of a madman willing to go to war to prevent foreign recognition of the Confederacy."[65] The extent to which the administration's brinkmanship was successful, or even useful, is open to debate. Both Howard Jones and Dean B. Mahin believe that it was, the latter asserting that, "on the whole, the strategy was successful." Duncan Andrew

Campbell, by way of contrast, suggests that the belligerent approach was superfluous: "The British government . . . was always convinced of the need to tread warily when it came to American affairs in general . . . and the Civil War in particular."[66] D. P. Crook insightfully observes that Seward's blustering diplomacy was directed not just at London and Paris but also at Richmond. His goal, thus, was not to provoke a transatlantic war, but to "demoralize the rebels by depriving them of the hope of foreign intervention or sympathy."[67] Davis's government was as aware as Lincoln's of the stakes of foreign recognition—hence, the prospect of diplomatic isolation was always to be feared.

The *Trent* Affair

The greatest threat of a third Anglo-American war during the period came about not because of Seward's threats but because of an event that the administration could not have foreseen. The *Trent* Affair began on November 8, 1861, when an American naval vessel stopped and boarded the British steamer *Trent* in the waters between the Bahamas and Cuba. The boarding party removed two Confederate diplomats—James Mason and John Slidell—who had been dispatched by Davis to Europe. The American sailors asserted that, as the "embodiment of dispatches," the diplomats were contraband of war. Britons in and out of the Palmerston government responded to the seizure of the emissaries with fury, interpreting the action as a direct attack on the honor of the British nation. The risk of war between the two nations was real until Lincoln wisely decided the following month to release Mason and Slidell.[68] American capitulation to this British demand forestalled, at least for the time, British intervention in the Civil War: "British officials and their public received Lincoln and Seward's decision with great relief, for they too recognized the calamitous consequences of an Anglo-American war."[69] British utilitarian philosopher John Stuart Mill put well the dilemma that had faced the British people during the crisis. Mill, who would later proclaim that slavery was an "unmitigated abhorrence," had no desire to see his nation intervene on the side of the slaveholding South: "It would have been a war in alliance with, and, to practical purposes, in defense and propagation of slavery."[70] In fact there was "in most Englishmen a very decided aversion to adopt a position of open alliance with slaveholders."[71] What Britons labeled the "*Trent* outrage" had, nevertheless, "done incalculable damage to the British public's views of the United States." Additionally, the affair had sown division between American and British abolitionists, the latter already expressing concern that their internationalist movement was becoming tainted with nationalist passions.[72]

The settling of the *Trent* dispute to the satisfaction of Britain did not, however, end the possibility of British intervention in the Civil War. While armed intervention by Britain now was less likely, the Lincoln administration continued to seek to preclude diplomatic intervention by either the British, the French, or both. Lincoln's insistence throughout 1861 that the war was about preserving the Union did not help matters. According to one insightful analysis of the situation, "Southern separation, to the French as well as to the British, became an acceptable solution to the American crisis. As the focus of interest in the war turned from questions regarding the morality of slavery to those of an economic or political nature, a new danger developed: the increased chances of a foreign involvement that could benefit only the South."[73] The declared policy of the administration—preserving the Union—gave Lincoln and Seward no added diplomatic leverage to forestall this eventuality.

Lincoln Seeks to Forestall Intervention

Lincoln was, nevertheless, quite conscious of the international ramifications of his policy toward slavery. In 1862 the government in Washington undertook a series of actions that helped to prepare the way for the Emancipation Proclamation that would come in September. Congress ended slavery in the District of Columbia, and the president proposed a plan of compensated emancipation to the Border States. Such measures—aside from being the right thing to do—helped Lincoln to placate the radicals within his party. But Lincoln was also aware of the effects of his actions on European opinion. Schurz recalled Lincoln telling him early in the year that "I cannot imagine that any European power would dare to recognize and aid the Southern Confederacy if it becomes clear that the Confederacy stands for slavery and the Union for freedom."[74] While not the sole motivation for the president's actions, the connection between foreign relations and slavery was very much on his mind as he took these significant steps toward a broader emancipation.

Some other decisions that Lincoln made at this time were, moreover, clearly taken with his mind firmly focused on Europe. The most significant of these was the signing of a slave trade suppression treaty with Britain. The Royal Navy would, under the new agreement, be allowed to stop and search US-flagged ships. Britain could now take the last step necessary for the effective suppression of the trade. Given the charged history of this issue in Anglo-American relations, the decision made by Lincoln and Seward to reverse a half century of policy indicates the seriousness with which they approached the issue of British intervention and the degree to which they believed slavery to be a complicating factor in transatlantic relations. Also significant was the American recognition, at long last, of the Black-ruled nations of Haiti and Liberia. The decision resulted in the first Black diplomats being sent as ministers representing their countries in Washington, a controversial development that Lincoln, however, found altogether acceptable.[75] These steps were welcomed by radicals in the United States, as well as by antislavery advocates abroad. The London *Times*, for its part, hailed the compensated emancipation act as "the greatest day" in US history since the signing of the Declaration of Independence; "the day of this century which will be honored throughout all time."[76]

American diplomats abroad, convinced of the force of antislavery sentiment among the European people, had urged Lincoln for some time to clarify what issue—what principle—was truly at stake. From St. Petersburg, Lincoln's minister, Cassius Marcellus Clay, went so far as to encourage the president to declare the slaves emancipated. Clay was personally invested in the cause; a Kentucky landowner who had become an abolitionist while at Yale College and subsequently freed his inherited slaves, he was to serve twice as minister to St. Petersburg.[77] It was Clay's conviction that only by proclaiming the slaves free could Lincoln forestall European recognition of the Confederacy. Lincoln heard precisely the same message from his envoy in Vienna. John Motley had traveled to London, Paris, and Berlin and had come away with the impression that, in the words of Russian historian R. F. Ivanov, "emancipation of the slaves was one of the most important decisions which might stop the European powers from recognizing the rebellious Confederacy." Or, as Motley wrote Seward, emancipation "would strike the sword from England's hands."[78] This was, in fact, the consensus among American diplomats by September 1862; a month after Lincoln issued his Preliminary Emancipation Proclamation, Seward wrote American minister to London Charles Francis Adams, telling him that "all our representatives abroad . . . have long and earnestly urged an earlier adoption of such measure as the President has at last accepted."[79] As the British chargé in Washington, William Stuart, saw it, one of Lincoln's motivations for issuing the proclamation was to "render intervention impossible."[80] Lincoln may well have assumed that his actions had made foreign intervention significantly less likely, if not impossible.

The opposite was, however, the case. One of the ironies of Civil War international relations was that the preliminary proclamation actually *increased* Anglo-French interest in intervening to stop the war. As Jones observes, "Despite Lincoln's high hopes, the Union victory at Antietam had combined with his preliminary Emancipation Proclamation to encourage, rather than undermine, intervention. . . . Contrary to the traditional story, the battle of Antietam and the Emancipation Proclamation did not stop the British movement toward intervention; rather, they only slowed down a process that once again had gotten underway."[81] The proclamation "further eroded the Confederacy's chances for diplomatic recognition—though at first it seemed to have the contrary effect." Indeed, the Union's foes in London portrayed the proclamation "not as a genuine antislavery act but as a cynical attempt to deflect European opinion or as a desperate effort to encourage a slave insurrection."[82]

It was this latter matter—the danger of a "servile insurrection"—that the Union's foes in the British government and press now stressed. Fear of a "race war" in the United States had influenced British thinking on intervention prior to September 1862. Memories of British experiences in Haiti still influenced statesmen in London.[83] Lincoln's policy of progressively allowing African Americans, including former slaves, into the Union military had only added to these fears. To many, such an act was unconscionable: "Arms in the hands of slaves violated the rules of civilized warfare, threatening wholesale slave revolt and descent into barbarism."[84] Rare were the voices, like that of British liberal Richard Cobden, who would say a good word about arming African Americans. Indeed, Cobden wrote Sumner in January 1864, "I hope to see a hundred thousand coloured men under arms before midsummer. Nothing will tend so much to raise the Africans in the social scale as to put muskets in their hands and drill them as soldiers."[85] Of course, Cobden wrote these words a year after the Emancipation Proclamation went into effect, and thus after experience had demonstrated that a massive slave revolt was a chimerical monster. Much more common at the time was the opinion of British chargé Stuart, who called the proclamation "cold, vindictive, and entirely political," bringing with it, as it did, the prospect of a slave revolt.[86] For its part, the London *Times*—never friendly toward the Lincoln administration—declared that Lincoln's goal in issuing his proclamation was to incite the slaves to "murder the families of their masters."[87] This was strong stuff. Yet the matter can be overstated. As Campbell indicates, the British press was not unanimous in condemning Lincoln's decision. The influential *Economist*, for its part, sought to tamp down the fears of slave insurrection, the editors declaring that "we do not anticipate any such consequences, nor do we believe that Mr Lincoln designed nor desired them."[88] The overall picture is, however, one of a "generally negative reception accorded to the proclamation in Europe."[89]

Russian Opinion

The salient exception to this rule among the powers of Europe was the nation that had consistently thrown its considerable diplomatic weight against

European intervention in the war. Russia was, at that time, in the process of liberating its own serfs, a step that Tsar Alexander II had initiated in 1861. This major transformation in Russian society was likely on the minds of Russian liberal intellectuals as they sought to address the causes and consequences of emancipation in the United States. In assessing Lincoln's decision, they proved to be both aware of, and sardonic toward, the response of their counterparts in more liberal nations of Europe. There was some irony in this. In a now famous quote from an 1855 letter to his closest friend, Joshua Speed, Lincoln had held up tsarist Russia as the incarnation of oppression; as a place "where despotism can be taken pure, and without the base allow of hypocrasy [sic]."[90] Yet the tsar's government had played a role in scuttling a great power intervention that would almost certainly have meant independence for the Confederacy. Now, once Lincoln proclaimed the permanent emancipation of slaves in rebel territory, editors at major Russian periodicals jumped to support his decision, and to lambaste his European critics.

No sooner had word of Lincoln's proclamation reached Russia than the *Sankt-Peterburgskie Vedomosti* newspaper in Russia's capital began the drumbeat in its favor. On January 12 the editors wrote a lengthy editorial on the subject. It was a tour de force of advocacy and analysis. The editors began by observing that "Lincoln's proclamation of the emancipation of the slaves in the southern states has aroused against itself, as one would expect, a variety of denunciations [*obvinenii*] and reproaches, more or less pathetic, more or less passionate, but in essence rather unanimous and, in our opinion, equally unjust." Critics, the Russians noted, attacked Lincoln for issuing the proclamation due to interest and not principle; "not a conviction, but a necessity." The president's detractors added that Lincoln's action was cynical, since "he retains slavery where he could destroy it, and destroys it where it is not at all in his power; that the destruction of slavery, as it is expressed in the [London] *Times*, serves as nothing more than punishment for insurrection—saving it as a reward for loyalty to the Union." But such assessments of Lincoln's motives—whether accurate or not—missed the mark: "It is not so important for us what motivations guided Lincoln, in what degree his emancipationist tendencies are sincere and unselfish; the act of emancipation itself is important to us; it is considered separately, independently from those reasons for which it took place. From an unclean source can come a clean, salutary [*blagotvornoe*] thing, and a deed caused by necessity may be at the same time as just as is possible. What could one say about the historian who would condemn the Magna Carta because it was given by the despicable King John . . . ?" Granted, Lincoln had never been an abolitionist and, in the first year of his administration, he had not acted in the interest of emancipation. But Lincoln was also surrounded by advisers and friends, "on whom the *Times* practically calls down the curse of God, many of whom have long been committed to the cause of emancipation." Therefore, it was "impossible to say that [the Proclamation] was inspired exclusively by calculation."[91]

Certainly, the editors continued, it would have been better for the federal government, and for its "honor," had the "war against the South adopted, at the very beginning, the character of a war against slavery." But the abolitionists were too weak, while the desire to bring the South back to the Union as well as racial prejudice were both too strong. But "time and circumstances changed the situation, and Lincoln's merit consists in that he decided to take advantage of circumstances. We see nothing heroic about this, but even less can we pronounce it shameful." And here one saw the hypocrisy of London outlets like the *Times* and the *Morning Post*. They would not stop describing the Emancipation as a "clear, blatant, traitorous . . . violation of the Constitution." Yet in the same breath, "they reproach Lincoln for the fact that he did not commit violations ten times more blatant and flagrant!" They could not have it both ways. As to the constitutionality of the proclamation, the Russian editors had no doubt: the Constitution provided that the central government was forbidden from touching the "local institutions of the individual states—and slavery, as is known, naturally is numbered among these local institutions." But the rebellious states had declared that the Constitution no longer applied to them. Hence, they had "naturally also lost the rights which this constitution ensured them; accordingly, liberation of the slaves in rebel states may be carried out without any violation of the Constitution."[92] In making this case, it should be noted, *Vedomosti* was advancing an analysis that—though comporting with Lincoln's thinking[93]—was not open to the president: Lincoln had to maintain that the southern states were still governed by the Constitution, since they had never legally left the Union.

On the other hand, the Border States had remained under the Constitution. Therefore, the president and Congress had, in regard to them, "only those rights which are vested in the central authority in a peaceful and ordinary time. The federal government can, nay should, make every effort to persuade them to voluntarily liberate the blacks; but forcing them into this is not right until the Constitution is changed." Lincoln had, in fact, shown "the determination to take all possible measures for the amicable abolition of slavery in the Border States." To demand more would "obviously be an injustice—and we are sure that the *Times* itself knows this very well." Besides, the Russian editors hoped that "the same force of things which led Lincoln to the proclamation of January 1 will lead the Border States to voluntary emancipation of their blacks, and in this, in our opinion, lies one of the best aspects of [Lincoln's] proclamation."[94]

But were the proclamation's harshest critics correct in saying that it would lead to spontaneous and sanguinary slave insurrections? Numerous European news outlets had said that it would, and "next follows eloquent phrases about innocent women and children, about torrents of blood, every drop of which is put upon Lincoln's head, and so on." Again, those critics were trying to have it both ways. They portrayed the Emancipation Proclamation as a "dead letter" that accomplished nothing; "not worth the pen with which Lincoln signed it." Yet for them it was also the mighty document which would set off "thunder and the bowels of the earth will open." Such contradictory arguments were not worth refuting, "bearing witness only to what kind of blindness defenders of the South come." Given the slaves' history of subjugation and their awareness of the power of slaveholders, the editors believed that the prospect of organized slave uprisings was quite remote. But did Lincoln's allowance in the proclamation for slaves to act in self-defense encourage the enslaved to "revolt everywhere where they can be supported by the Federal troops"? The *Times* said that it would, but the editors of *Vedomosti* heartily disagreed. In fact, slaves were likely to turn to violence only when "the slaveholders will threaten their lives, when resistance will be the lesser of two evils" between which they were forced to choose. If, furthermore, slaves were to rise up in the presence of Union troops, those troops would, of course, constrain the revolt "within certain limits and restrain it from those excesses which one could fear from the fury of the slaves." The editors, in any event, preferred candor "to the *Times*'s hypocrisy." They evinced no greater admiration for French newspapers that likewise denounced the Emancipation Proclamation on spurious grounds.[95]

Following up in early April, the newspaper reviewed the steps taken by Lincoln prior to the issuance of the Emancipation Proclamation, and in particular the plan for compensated emancipation in the Border States and the ending of slavery in the nation's capital. This latter had, the editors noted, been "accomplished peacefully and calmly: no riots occurred, contrary to the predictions—and perhaps the hopes—of the defenders of slavery." From the Russians' perspective, "one of the most important consequences of the January 1 proclamation is the inclusion of blacks in the Federal military." Black soldiers had now fought engagements, and fought with surprising courage. Indeed, they "feel all the American people are watching them." The editors also pointed to Lincoln's reception of diplomats from Haiti and Liberia; a development that had been "unthinkable two years ago." And facts had now proved, "beyond doubt," the "idea, so fervently denied by defenders of the South, that blacks are fit for freedom, and deserve it." The experience that had been gained of Black federal soldiers in combat in the South, furthermore, "attests that the danger of the massacre of slaveholders, and other horrors of slave war, belong to the phantoms created by the imagination of the *Times* and newspapers of its ilk."[96] Many European newspapers had declared that disaster would befall southern whites when slaves were liberated. But even a couple months of experience proved to the satisfaction of *Vedomosti* that this was all a febrile dream.

The newspaper, furthermore, was not a lone voice crying out in the St. Petersburg wilderness. Joining it in support of Lincoln's proclamation was the monthly *Sovremennik*. Founded by Aleksander Pushkin, the journal had recently been a leading advocate for the liberation of the Russian serfs.[97] In an extended treatment of recent developments in the American Civil War, *Sovremennik*'s editors ruminated on the meaning of emancipation of America's slaves and, in doing so, found much fault with their journalistic counterparts in Britain. As they saw it, the preliminary Emancipation Proclamation had "made a terrible storm, and reproaches poured down on Lincoln from various sides."[98] *Sovremennik*'s editors had seen this sort of treatment of the Union's civilian and military leadership before from the British and French press: "All that is done in the North—everything was subjected to the most biased, unfair criticism"; not so, however, "about their separatist friends."[99] Not that the journal was itself a partisan cheerleader for the North: responding to Lincoln's annual message to Congress of December, 1862, the editors confessed that "in general, we did not understand the need to restore the Union before reading Lincoln's message, and do not understand it now." For them, the salient issue was not Union, but slavery.[100] On this, they found the *Times*'s hypocrisy worthy of their withering sarcasm: "The same *Times*, which is always so eloquently talking about gradual progress, about the danger of all leaps and all violent upheavals, about legality and things of that sort, before getting carried away by friendship with the South . . . started very wittily to laugh at the cowardice of Mr. Lincoln, his excessive slowness [*medlitel'nost*], caution and so forth. It must be that this venerable newspaper wishes that he acted as energetically as possible to cut the Gordian Knot."[101] The Russians found the *Morning Herald*'s coverage of Lincoln's address to be at least as worthy of ridicule. The London newspaper simply called attention to Lincoln's "weakness," Seward's "shamelessness," Secretary of the Treasury Salmon P. Chase's "lack of talent," and the "vainglory [*khvastlivost*]" of Secretary of War Edwin Stanton. The *Morning Post* also came in for criticism, based on its "prophecies" that Lincoln was going to go back on his proclamation.[102] This was not a glowing record for the London papers.

The official southern response to the preliminary Emancipation Proclamation proved no more satisfying to the editors of *Sovremennik*. With good reason, the Russians castigated General Robert E. Lee's announcement that he would shoot all captured Union officers if the proclamation went into effect and ridiculed Davis's subsequent "restrictions" on his commander in chief's declared policy. Davis, it seemed, was "studying" limiting the executions to officers who had served under General Benjamin Butler—"a novel restriction!"—as well as those who aided or commanded armed Blacks. As for those Blacks, Davis announced that they would be returned to their respective states, to be dealt with "according to the laws. For those of our readers who would like to know what 'according to the laws' means, we can add that by law of the individual states the insurgent slaves can be burned alive or whipped to death." The Russians then went on to chastise the British and French "governments, the press, and the upper classes," which lacked the moral fiber of the "noble lower classes" that had rallied to support liberation of their fellow disenfranchised laborers.[103] As to the British press's response when Lincoln announced the permanent manumission of the slaves on January 1, *Sovremennik* once again, and at length, criticized the duplicity of the British newspapers, urging them to be honest in the future: "Frankness is always better than a lie."[104] As these Russians saw it, the proverbial die had now been cast: slavery was going to be eradicated in the United States, even if Lincoln were to try to go back on the Emancipation Proclamation, as British papers suggested he might. Of course, many innocent whites might well die as the result of the slave insurgency that the British press professed to fear. But "still more likely to die also are blacks, even more innocent. But it has come to the point that there is no other solution (except for the project to postpone this issue until the next century)."[105] It was quite obvious to the editors in St. Petersburg that this was a ridiculous idea. Although the Russian minister in Washington, for his part, reported home the opinions of congressional Democrats, who claimed that the arming of large numbers of Blacks was "humiliating for the country," such a reading of world opinion did not apply to these journalists in Russia.[106]

Indeed, the criticism of Western newspapers by Russian intellectuals reveals a great rift between the elites of Britain and France, on one side, and those of America's closest great power "friend," on the other. It has been well established that Russian policymakers were hostile to the possibility of Anglo-French intervention in the American Civil War, and that they were so for reasons of national interest. But numerous Russian journalists—not always friendly to the tsar's regime—also displayed a marked hostility to prevalent Anglo-French opinions on the broad range of issues associated with slavery, race, and the war. Their arguments were, furthermore, based on ideology and principle, rarely addressing Russia's national interests. The schism between western European opinion on emancipation and that of Russia thus warrants a close study. This has yet to be undertaken.[107]

Emancipation and Colonization

This is not to say that emancipation ended the threat of European intervention entirely. Two misconceptions regarding the international history of American emancipation have been challenged by scholars. The first of these is that the Emancipation Proclamation effectively ended any chance of European intervention in the American crisis. Although a French plan for mediation arose in 1863, its significance was easy to dismiss. As *Sovremennik*'s editors opined, "we do not attach any importance to the new mediation attempt made again by France (this time alone)."[108] It was easy enough to believe that France would make no serious attempt at intervention without Britain and that the Emancipation Proclamation had made impossible any British diplomatic initiative that would benefit the slaveholding South. Yet Napoleon III's postemancipation initiative was quite serious, and was taken to be so by the Lincoln administration.[109]

A second misconception is that Lincoln gave up on the idea of colonization after issuing the Emancipation Proclamation. Scholarship has called this interpretation into question. Robert E. May, Michael J. Douma, and Phillip W. Magness and Sebastian N. Page have all found evidence of continued administration interest in colonization after the promulgation of the Emancipation Proclamation.[110] The significance of these discoveries has aroused scholarly debate.[111] Any discussion of slavery and Lincoln and Seward's foreign relations must, nevertheless, address at least briefly the diplomacy connected with these colonization proposals.

It is generally known that Lincoln explored two attempts at colonization in 1862: one at Chiriqí, in what is now Panama, and the other the ill-fated Île á Vache (or Cow Island) experiment. The first was opposed by London and within Latin America, and it failed to materialize.[112] The second attempt actually settled some 450 African Americans on an island near Haiti; the colony "proved a disaster from the outset," with the surviving settlers being rescued by the US Navy in 1864.[113] The president and his administration bore some responsibility for this debacle, since they had been lackadaisical with regard to the contract and "remiss" in oversight of the effort.[114] Lincoln's early experiments with colonization bore no fruit and did not seem to presage future success. Yet the president and his administration would at least explore two more possibilities before giving up on the idea.[115]

British Honduras was, at the time, in need of laborers. Lincoln proved willing to consider sending African Americans to the colony to meet this need. He appears, in so doing, to have been motivated in part by a belief that "the British colonies would provide stronger protections for the rights of the freedmen than would the postwar South."[116] But attempts to negotiate an agreement proved frustrating to the British. On November 22, 1862, Foreign Secretary Lord Russell wrote to Lord Lyons, Britain's minister in Washington, to ask for "observations . . . upon a plan for the introduction of free Negroes from this country into British Honduras." According to Lyons, "the uncertain position of some of the principle Members of the Cabinet has retarded for some time my obtaining information with regard to the views of the Government." Finally, on December 25, he was able to discuss the matter with the secretary of state. The result, however, "was not very encouraging." Seward, who was not himself positively disposed toward colonization, "seemed to think that the Cabinet would be unwilling or unable to come to a decision at the present moment with regard to any definite scheme, and that it would be undesirable to press the subject until after the close of the session of Congress" on March 4.[117] Seward was likely concerned about opposition to colonization from Republicans in Congress. For his part, Charles Sumner, chairman of the Senate Foreign Relations Committee, opposed colonization but held off on confrontation over the issue at the time in order to "avoid a difference with the Presdt. [sic]."[118] Seward could not, however, count on such forbearance indefinitely.

Nor could Seward reassure Lyons regarding Lincoln's own policy team: "The opinions of Members of the Cabinet were, [Seward] said, so various and at the same time so indefinite on this question of emigration, that it would be impossible for him to bring them to an agreement, unless he had some plain written statement to produce as a basis of the discussion." Seward thus encouraged the British to draw up a paper stating their views. Even if they did so, however, he did not give Lyons much reason for hope:

> Many, he said, might, and indeed the President himself, be inclined to the opinion that the most desirable thing for both races was to separate them, and to reserve North America exclusively for the whites. On the other hand, the more ardent members of the emancipation party strongly objected to the removal of the Negroes. Nor was this feeling confined to the emancipation party. There existed in many quarters a strong opposition to sending away the coloured people at all and a special dislike of transferring them to the British of French colonies. It was asked whether it was wise to deprive the country of so much muscle and sinew, whether it was prudent to add to the strength of nations which might not be always friends of the United States.

Of particular concern to many was the need for Black labor and Black soldiers during a time of war. As Seward noted, "many excellent coloured regiments have been formed." In summing up, he discouraged optimism: "Looking at matters practically, he certainly did regard it as extremely doubtful whether an emigration on a great scale would ever take place. The appearance was that neither whites nor blacks would be in favour of it."[119]

The government in London had its own concerns. As Lyons confided to Russell, "it is obviously necessary to take care that no arrangement be made likely to embarrass the imperial government, either in its relations with the United States or in its neutral position with regard to the two belligerents."[120] Of particular importance was to avoid coming to any sort of agreement with Washington that might suggest an attenuation of British neutrality. Russell was especially concerned that Britain not be seen as accepting "contrabands" into its colonies, which would inevitably cause diplomatic troubles with Richmond. "We must not expose ourselves to charges of kidnapping," he declared.[121] With such hurdles to overcome on both sides of the Atlantic, it is no wonder that the Honduras project proved to be a nonstarter.

More serious was the possibility that freed African Americans would be sent to the Dutch colony of Suriname as laborers. In the 1850s Dutch advocates for slaves were demanding an end to the "abhorrent system of coercion" [*verfoeide dwangstelsel*] in the colonies of the Netherlands.[122] While "a good number of ministers were already in favor of abolition," there were hurdles to be cleared. One was the issue of compensation for the owners. Additionally, there was "the idea that those who lived in slavery should be prepared for their freedom."[123] Then there arose the central question of finding workers once the slaves were freed. After the emancipation of the slaves in July 1863, "the Surinamese planter class grew desperate for new sources of labor."[124] In anticipation of this development, the Dutch colonial minister had raised the possibility of importing African Americans to fill the need. As he noted, the US government had, "under President Monroe already seen the necessity of sending the bulk of free Negroes and others away, with the consequence that on the west coast of Africa the Negro Republic of Liberia was founded." He added that "if the Negroes from the United States can be received as emigrants with equal freedom and protection under the Dutch laws in Suriname, and advantages of this extensive and fertile land offered to them under the provisions of the Government established there, they could enter into contracts for, say, five years, with planters, and all of this would be fit to encourage an emigration to Suriname."[125] The Dutch minister of foreign affairs, Paul Thérèse van der Maesen de Sombreff, acted within days on his colleague's suggestion. On July 1 he wrote to the Dutch minister in the United States, asking him to take the first steps toward negotiations with the Americans on "an emigration of Negroes from the United States to the Dutch Colony." By July 19 the minister,

Theodorus Marinus Roest van Limburg, had approached Seward.[126] The Dutch officials were clearly wasting no time in pursuing this possible source of cheap labor for Suriname.

As with the British, Seward sought to tamp down on Dutch optimism. "I have to state," he wrote Roest van Limburg, "that it is believed the demand for laborers of that class in the military and naval service of the United States alone is sufficient to outweigh any inducement to their emigration abroad likely to be offered by foreign countries." He did, however, refer the Dutchman to the secretary of the interior, Caleb Smith, since he "has been charged with that business" on behalf of the administration.[127] The minister followed up on the suggestion that September, with a request that he be informed of the terms on which the administration would enter into an agreement with The Hague "concerning an emigration of free negroes to Surinam." It would appear that Roest van Limburg was by this time under no illusions about the long-term prospects of any negotiation, writing to van der Maesen de Sombreff on September 25 that not a single senator was likely to support an emigration treaty.[128] The administration nevertheless moved ahead. At the end of October the American minister in The Hague, James Shepherd Pike, informed van der Maesen de Sombreff that the United States was "ready to enter into negociations [sic] upon the subject" of African American emigration. One of the "general principles" guiding the discussions was, he added, that "all emigration of persons of African derivation to take place under the stipulations of the treaty, shall be perpetually free and voluntary."[129]

With this principle established, negotiations could begin. But Roest van Limburg remained skeptical of the enterprise. He was, at the time, relying in part on the advice of his father-in-law, former secretary of state Lewis Cass. Cass told the minister that "in the U.S. there is a sort of divide in the attempts to reach an agreement on emigration, which sooner or later will lead to unpleasant complications" in the government. In addition, he added, the Blacks sought by the Dutch were "very unfit" for the intended goal.[130] A convention was, nevertheless, signed in November 1863. Yet it was never submitted to the Senate for ratification. Seward did not believe that the treaty could be ratified by the Senate. As he told Pike, "the American people have advanced to a new position in regard to slavery, and the African class since the President in obedience to their prevailing wishes accepted the policy of colonization. Now not only their labor, but their military service is also appreciated and accepted."[131] Seward was being overly generous to Lincoln, whose interest in colonization had, after all, antedated his presidency. But as to Senate sentiment, Seward was representing the situation accurately: growing anticolonization sentiment in Congress had led the administration to withhold the treaty from Senate consideration.[132] Even within Lincoln's own cabinet, there was nothing like unanimity on the wisdom of African American emigration. Secretary of War Edwin M. Stanton, in particular, wanted to utilize freedmen in the Union Army and did what he could to hinder the project.[133] Meanwhile, the chief American negotiator for the convention, Pike, believed that the principle behind the treaty was a "vicious" one, and privately confessed in April 1864 that he hoped it would not be ratified.[134] With such opposition, both legislative and executive, the scheme never had a chance. The Dutch still hoped as late as 1866 that at least some African Americans would arrive in Suriname, but executive enthusiasm for emigration appears to have been spent.[135]

Conspicuous by its absence during this episode was the hand of the president. According to Allen C. Guelzo, this lack of evidence "is the most telling measure of Lincoln's interest in colonization." He adds that had the president "in any energetic way been determined to cram colonization down the emancipated black's throats, then the new national energies that the Civil War put into his hands as president would have allowed very little to stand in his way."[136] As it was, internal administration infighting and opposition from legislators like Sumner were enough to derail the most developed of emigration schemes. Lincoln may have flirted with colonization after emancipation, but the relationship never came close to consummation.

American slavery forced the United States to act in the international sphere in ways that it otherwise would not have, and to interact with the Atlantic world in a more dynamic way than its leaders might have preferred. Yet in the case of colonization, one administration after another managed to maintain a rather low international profile and to keep American commitments limited. They did so, furthermore, in spite of the fact that many influential policymakers, presidents included, were advocates of Black emigration. Colonization plans had been no mere velleity on the part of these players, who, for a variety of reasons, saw exporting America's free Black population as a key to solving the issues raised by slavery. But the drive was not strong enough to lead policymakers to, say, risk conflict with Britain on the west coast of Africa, let alone to jeopardize federal unity during the Civil War. Other considerations, foreign and domestic, always took priority over removing African Americans from the nation.

Conclusion: Lincoln, Seward, and the Powers

With regard to the Lincoln administration's top foreign policy priority, the president and the secretary of state met with success: the powers of Europe did not intervene diplomatically in the American Civil War, let alone militarily. There was a constellation of reasons for this, including lack of unity between London and Paris; Russian hostility toward European meddling in American affairs; and, above all, fear of provoking war with the Union. The British and French had priorities of their own, and these did not, in the end, align with intervention in America's crisis. Slavery, then, was not the primary determinant of transatlantic relations during the war. Southern slavery, however, gave the Union diplomatic leverage from the beginning; the Confederates were always at a disadvantage, especially with Britain. Furthermore, the North's leverage increased after September 1862. The preliminary Emancipation Proclamation clarified the core issue that divided North and South. With this issue now manifest in Union diplomacy, British intervention on the side of the South was next to unthinkable.

Thus, in the final analysis, slavery proved to be less an advantage that the United States could actively exploit in its diplomacy than it was a disadvantage the Confederacy could not overcome in its own. Whether Lincoln and Seward chose to press the issue or, as early on in the war, to downplay it, the South always labored diplomatically under the weight of its "peculiar institution." From the British laborer to the French foreign minister, the hostility of most Europeans toward southern slavery was a hurdle that Jefferson Davis's exterior policy would have to overcome if foreign intervention were to be achieved. Richmond never overcame it. Lincoln's was the first—and thus the only—administration to focus on restricting and then ending slavery rather than protecting or expanding it. Yet the edge that it gained from this internationally was less a result of its own skillful diplomacy than it was an unforced error on the side of its adversary in Richmond. But in a duel in which foreign intervention, or its prevention, was the salient issue, this was sufficient.

Epilogue
American Foreign Relations Unchained

Slavery had both impelled and enticed the United States to engage the wider Atlantic world. The nation was forced to deal with Great Britain and Spain in order to avoid legitimation of slave escape. Washington, DC, could not avoid diplomacy, and eventually cooperation, with London in order to combat the slave trade effectively. The desire to export African Americans compelled the republic to engage itself with sub-Saharan Africa, and brought it into negotiations with London, The Hague, and Latin America. And Lincoln and Seward found themselves obliged to deal with France and Britain as they worked to keep the American Civil War a completely domestic matter. These were connections that were unavoidable if the nation were to pursue important goals. But there was also a positive desire on the part of the nation to reach out and make connections with the world, and slavery played an important role in this as well. Expansionists were well aware of the value of new slave territory—and not, incidentally, new proslavery Senators—to the institution of slavery. They thus pursued this policy—sometimes successfully, sometimes not. Over the course of its entire early history, slavery had brought the United States into significantly greater contact with the Atlantic world than would have been the case absent the institution.

The international relations that emerged cannot be understood merely by looking at the prejudices, interests, and assumptions of a certain set of US policymakers. Rather, the international context significantly conditioned the

American policies that emerged from a complex set of Atlantic interrelations. Slavery was one of a number of issues that shaped these relations and interactions, and it would be a mistake to attribute too much causative effect to the institution. Issues of security, commerce, and imperial rivalries all played a significant role in the development of Atlantic international relations in the period beginning with the age of Atlantic revolutions and lasting until the end of the American Civil War. Having acknowledged this, it is nevertheless crucial to recognize that slavery was one of the major determinants of these relations.

This was particularly true in the case of the United States. Slavery was defined by policymakers and laypeople alike as central to US interactions with four continents—whether for good or bad. America's security, prosperity, and geographical and political reach were all connected, in one way or another, with bonded labor. It is no surprise, then, that Americans looked on, and conducted, their relations with the world with a conviction that slavery was central to the nation's international role. For some Americans, this meant the active preservation of slavery in the Western Hemisphere, while for others it meant the final eradication of the evil of the trade in human beings. For some, seemingly paradoxically, it meant both.

This last point indicates what one might call the "messiness" of the connection between slavery and America's foreign relations. Even slaveholders like Thomas Jefferson and James Madison proved willing, at one point, to aid the self-liberated Blacks of Haiti. On the other hand, Abraham Lincoln's complicated relationship with slavery played out in his policy of seeking to encourage emigration of freed slaves even after emancipation. And the redoubtable John Quincy Adams himself, though famous for his later opposition to slavery, used the power of the federal government to gain compensation for slaves carried away from American masters. In addition, though resolutely hostile to the slave trade, he refused to utilize that same government's power in the only way that would have ended the international commerce in humans.[1]

This untidy relationship of American foreign relations and slavery does not mean that the "slaveholding republic" was not generally committed to advancing the cause of slavery in the nation and, indeed, the hemisphere. Rather, it is an indication of the extent to which Washington had—and still has—to make policy in a complicated international environment. Don E. Fehrenbacher notes that the proslavery thrust of America's foreign relations benefited "from the inertial tendencies of government and more specifically from a good deal of incremental decision making that was perfunctory, unreflective, and more often than not in southern hands."[2] This is all true. Yet it is also the case that America's external relations with regard to slavery were conditioned, influenced, and constrained by the actions of other actors in the Atlantic sphere. In this sense, even the southerners who ran American foreign policy were never in a position to fully control the issues that confronted American policymakers. The world itself was too messy for that.

Yet one significant issue had, in fact, been cleanly resolved. Slavery was ended in the United States. Thus, one of the most important determinants of US foreign relations since the founding of the nation vanished in the wake of the horrific Civil War. No longer would the matter of slavery push and pull the nation into international affairs. During the Gilded Age, Americans found themselves "absorbed in domestic problems and less concerned with external threats than at any time in their nation's history." Given the circumstances in which the United States now found itself, "world events naturally receded in the scale of national priorities."[3] The legend of a nation drawing into isolation after the Civil War is merely a legend, as the United States engaged the world in new and often active ways in the three decades prior to the Spanish-American War. America would certainly engage in foreign intervention, and economic and territorial expansion, in these years. But slavery had ceased to be a factor that helped to determine the perception of threats and opportunities for America abroad.

Rarely has a major, long-term element driving US foreign policy disappeared so quickly and completely. One thinks of the collapse of the Soviet Union and the end of the Cold War. There are few other examples. If Washington policymakers were indeed more focused on domestic than foreign issues after 1865—if they were required to give international affairs less of their time and attention—then one reason for this was that slavery was not continually, persistently, compelling them to deal with the wider Atlantic world. It had done so since the founding. For nine decades, slavery had been one of the primary driving forces in American external relations. American foreign policymakers in the post–Civil War years would be able to look to other long-term goals, like hemispheric security and commercial expansion, and newer aims, such as extracontinental expansion, without the ever-present need to secure chattel slavery. This change could not help but introduce a degree of flexibility of action that would otherwise have been absent. Up to this point, the perceived need to protect and expand a reprehensible institution had both driven and constrained America's external policy. Nine decades of this particular messiness was long enough. A new era of American foreign relations could begin. The chains had finally fallen.

Yet the years of slavery's influence on American foreign relations would cast a somber shadow over post–Civil War foreign relations. The long years of racism toward African Americans would not end with emancipation. And this proclivity of race to shape America's external policy was to continue. As America took on territories abroad in the coming decades, the nonwhite peoples in those lands found that they were denied the rights that had been extended to, for instance, white Texans. The fact that American policies toward nonwhite insular peoples echoed those pursued toward nonwhites on the North American continent was not coincidental.[4] Americans had a history that would not disappear with slavery.

After the abolition of slavery in the United States, race continued to be a significant factor in American foreign relations, although the issue became more diffuse. As Michael Hunt has perceptively argued, various nonwhite peoples were increasingly classified according to a "hierarchy of race." Although the image of these peoples was neither static nor consistent, those of African descent, more than any other group, "served as the anvil on which Americans forged this notion of racial hierarchy and the attendant color-conscious view of the world."[5] The tendency to view the world in terms of distinct and stratified races easily permeated the barrier between centuries, and served to influence US foreign relations into the 1900s. Americans had "fixed race at the center of their world view."[6] This predisposition to think in terms of race would continue to shape significantly American policy toward what would eventually be termed the Third World. Definitions of race helped to justify, and thus facilitate, American intervention in Latin America, conquest of the Philippines, and exclusion of East Asian immigrants.[7] It is inconceivable that race would have played this role in American exterior policy without the "anvil" of slavery shaping American thinking.

The persistence of racial biases in shaping US foreign relations was on full display in 1919, when world leaders met to negotiate the Treaty of Versailles which put a formal end to the war with Germany. Representing the United States was President Woodrow Wilson, as thoroughgoing a racist as ever occupied the Oval Office. He famously admitted at one point that "I have very little ease with coloured people or they with me. Why is it?"[8] The answer comes easy to the student of his administration. That the president who would segregate the federal workforce should ask such a question is itself surprising. But this very ignorance speaks to the pervasiveness of such racism in American thinking. Wilson was like the proverbial fish that did not know that it swam in water.

Wilson's racism was not confined to African Americans. Indeed, he distributed it widely. One of the most egregious examples of its impact on his foreign policy occurred in Paris. The issue concerned a proposal advanced by the Japanese delegation to add an amendment to the "religious liberty" clause of the Covenant of the League of Nations. This amendment bound signatories not to, as Margaret MacMillan summarizes it, "discriminate against anyone within their jurisdiction on the basis of creed, religion, or belief."[9] The Japanese proposed to add, "The equality of nations being a basic principle of the League of Nations, the High Contracting Parties agree to accord, as soon as possible, to all alien nationals of States members of the League equal and just treatment in every respect, making no distinction, either in law of in fact, on the account of their race or nationality."[10] The amendment quickly gained the support of almost all delegations. But there were holdouts, including Britain and Poland. Joining this unlikely combination was the United States. Wilson simply could not imagine opening the borders of the United States or its possessions "to Japanese or other Asian immigrants." As the leading historian of Wilson's diplomacy has noted, Wilson had drawn "a global color line. His liberal ideals, although ostensibly universal, were exclusive in practice. The full benefits of Wilsonianism were available only for white nations of the West."[11] Thus, even after a vote was taken on the amendment, and it was passed, Wilson tabled the measure.[12] He had refused "to let even the principle of racial equality stand."[13] Resentful of this development, the Japanese delegation nevertheless withdrew the amendment.[14] But significant damage had been done to relations between Tokyo and Washington, and was one factor that, in the following two decades, led Japan to take an increasingly confrontational stance with the Western powers.[15]

As with American policies prior to abolition, race had been a significant determinant of American decisions in this episode. Granted, it was, in 1919—as in the pre-1865 period—one of a number of factors shaping foreign policy choices. At Paris, bald racism had been accompanied by the related issue of preservation of empire; after all, Britain and its imperial delegations had joined the United States in strenuously opposing a declaration of equality. What would such a proclamation have meant in, for example, Australia?[16] Broader issues of race did not serve by themselves to determine American policymakers' decisions. Rather, they became enmeshed with considerations of matters such as security, trade, and expansion.

Similarly, slavery had never been the only factor guiding any of Washington's major foreign relations decisions prior to 1865. Instead, issues regarding slavery—its preservation, its expansion, and finally its eradication—had interacted with other interests to shape those decisions. It had, however, been as central a determinant as those other interests. Slavery was, at last, extirpated in 1865. Its legacy for American foreign relations, however, did not end with the Thirteenth Amendment. To understand America's diplomatic history, one must understand the impact and legacy of slavery on America's relations with the world.

ACKNOWLEDGMENTS

President John F. Kennedy quipped after the Bay of Pigs fiasco that "victory has 100 fathers and defeat is an orphan." If this book meets with somewhat more success than that operation, then it is testimony to all of its "parents." I am pleased to be able to acknowledge the help that they have given me over the course of the five years during which I wrote this book.

David F. Schmitz read nearly every word of the manuscript of this book in draft form and made extensive comments. I cannot overstate my debt of gratitude to him. Authors often say that their book would have been better if they had taken all of their colleagues' suggestions. In this case, this book is better because I *have* taken all of David's suggestions. The Reverend Wilson D. Miscamble, CSC, provided me with his invariably sagacious guidance on too many matters to detail here, and helped keep me focused on the end result. Thomas A. Schwartz was an early and consistent enthusiast for this project, and was always ready with helpful advice. David, Bill, and Tom are true friends.

My editor at Cornell University Press, Michael McGandy, has been everything that an author could hope for: insightful, frank, and meticulous. A fellow early riser, Michael may be the only editor who responds in real time to emails sent at 5:00 a.m. I am deeply indebted to him. I also owe a debt of gratitude to the readers whom Michael lined up to review earlier drafts of the manuscript. Robert E. May and the anonymous second reader were of inestimable assistance in improving this book. Having reviewed manuscripts, I know that this is often viewed as a "thankless" task. That is not, strictly speaking, literally true in this case: these scholars do indeed have my sincere thanks.

The research for *Chained to History* was necessarily polyglot, and I am no great linguist. Fortunately for me, my dear friend Maureen G. Dawson, Donald LaSalle, and Erin Moira Lemrow were always available to provide guidance on my translations of obscure two-hundred-year-old French words and phrases. Leonor Wangensteen provided similar guidance with "out-of-date" Spanish. And I am indebted to my friend and George Washington University colleague Muriel Atkin for allowing me to run mid-nineteenth-century Russian obscurities by her in the departmental lunchroom. I wish her all the best in her well-earned retirement, but I will miss our lunches. Michael Douma of Georgetown University generously shared his transcriptions and translations of Dutch governmental documents with me, for which I am tremendously grateful. None of these scholars, however, bears responsibility for any errors in translation; these are mine alone.

On the personal front, my sister Eileen Schopen and her family have provided me with constant support over the course of the years. Thank you Eileen, Keith, Drew, Tom, Hannah, and Jenna. Our parents died when we were still young, and never knew about my academic endeavors. But I suspect that Ward and Marie Alice Brady would have been proud to hold this book in their hands. Mom and Dad never gave me brothers, so I had to find them for myself. Marc Dubey, Michael Knock, and Sidney Stein have been a source of incredible support and encouragement. I am truly fortunate to call them friends. Since they are all far away from Washington, I am indeed blessed to have Julius Blackwell and Robert Scott here *in loco fratres*. Duane Jundt has been a friend since the start of my days in graduate school. I would have ended my studies early, after a family tragedy, had he not convinced me to continue. Kathy Hardman kept me going during the "Mar-Main days" with her love of books and tolerance of eccentricities. Dan Berger has been my close friend longer than anyone else, which shows good judgment on both of our parts. In South Bend, Indiana, I especially valued the friendship of John Deak and Dan Graff. I still do. I have valued the friendship of Jeanne Petit and Anita Specht since grad school. Thank you, my friends.

Friends and colleagues in the Department of History at the George Washington University (GW) deserve special thanks. I never imagined that any academic department could be so collegial. Thanks go especially to Denver Brunsman, who befriended me early on, and who gave me feedback and encouragement on the early chapters of this book. In addition to his valued friendship, I owe Trevor Jackson thanks for suggesting this book's subtitle. Abigail Agresta has been the best "next door neighbor" that one could ask for. And she never complains when I play Beethoven much louder than is fitting for a man my age. The late Leo Ribuffo made my transition to GW go more smoothly than it otherwise could have. I valued his advice on matters great and small. Put simply, I miss him. Perhaps the department would survive without Michael Weeks and Sam Nohra, but I would not want to be there to clean up the mess. I am pleased to be able to thank Thomas Long for both his mentorship and his friendship. Finally, my students have been, over the years, one of my greatest sources of inspiration.

Every day of my life, I am thankful for my children, William, Matthew, and Lydia Grace.

I owe my greatest debt to my partner in life; Monica has been research assistant, librarian, cheerleader, and therapist as I have worked on this project, and she has been so much more. Words fail me. It is to her that this book is dedicated. After five years, she can finally say "Es ist für mich!"

Notes

Introduction

1. James E. Lewis Jr., *John Quincy Adams: Policymaker for the Union* (Wilmington, DE: Scholarly Resources Inc., 2001), 106. On the background of the Congress of Panama, and Bolívar's apprehension regarding US participation, see Germán A. de la Reza, "The Formative Platform of the Congress of Panama (1810–1826): The Pan-American Conjecture Revisited," *Revista Brasileira de Política Internacional* 56, no. 1 (2013): esp. 15–16. See also Samuel Flagg Bemis, *John Quincy Adams and the Foundations of American Foreign Policy* (New York: Alfred A. Knopf, 1965), 549.

2. James Traub, *John Quincy Adams: Militant Spirit* (New York: Basic Books, 2016), 345.

3. Mary W. M. Hargreaves, *The Presidency of John Quincy Adams* (Lawrence: University Press of Kansas, 1985), 150.

4. Lewis, *John Quincy Adams: Policymaker for the Union*, 107.

5. George C. Herring, *From Colony to Superpower: U.S. Foreign Relations since 1776* (New York: Oxford University Press, 2008), 162–163. On opposition in Congress to American participation at Panama, see Bemis, *John Quincy Adams and the Foundations of American Foreign Policy*, 552–553.

6. Traub, *John Quincy Adams: Militant Spirit*, 346. See also Hargreaves, *The Presidency of John Quincy Adams*, 151–152; and William Earl Weeks, *The New Cambridge History of American Foreign Relations*, vol. 1, *Dimensions of the Early American Empire, 1754–1865* (New York: Cambridge University Press, 2013), 205.

7. Herring, *From Colony to Superpower*, 163; Hargreaves, *The Presidency of John Quincy Adams*, 152. And see especially Charles N. Edel, *Nation Builder: John Quincy Adams and the Grand Strategy of the Republic* (Cambridge, MA: Harvard University Press, 2014), 222–223.

8. David Walker Howe, *What Hath God Wrought: The Transformation of America, 1815–1848* (New York: Oxford University Press, 2007), 257; Hargreaves, *The Presidency of John Quincy Adams*, 157–158. On the US Congress and the Congress of Panama, see Jeffrey J. Malanson, "The Congressional Debate over U.S. Participation in the Congress of Panama, 1825–1826: Washington's Farewell Address, Monroe's Doctrine, and the Fundamental Principles of U.S. Foreign Policy," *Diplomatic History* 30, no. 5 (2006): 813–838.

9. Jorge Pacheco Quintero, *El Congreso anfictiónico de Panamá y la política internacional de los Estados Unidos* (Bogota: Editorial Kelly, 1971), 5 (author's translation). See also Salvador Rivera, "Diplomats, Idealists, and Technocrats: The Long Quest for Latin American Integration" (PhD diss., University at Albany, State University of New York, 2003), 31–32; Germán A. de la Reza, *El Congreso de Panamá de 1826 y otros ensayos de*

integración latinoamericana en el siglo XIX (Mexico City: Ediciones y Gráficos Eón, 2006), 29; and Caitlin Fitz, *Our Sister Republics: The United States in an Age of American Revolutions* (New York: Liveright, 2016), 226.

10. Bemis, *John Quincy Adams and the Foundations of American Foreign Policy*, 561.

11. Matthew Karp, *This Vast Southern Empire: Slaveholders at the Helm of American Foreign Policy* (Cambridge, MA: Harvard University Press, 2016).

12. Michael Zeuske, *Sklaverei: Eine Menschheitsgeschichte von der Steinzeit bis Heute* (Stuttgart: Reclam, 2018), 15 (author's translation).

13. On this assertion of rights, and Britain's response, see, e.g., the brief treatment in Andrew Preston, *Sword of the Spirit, Shield of Faith: Religion in American War and Diplomacy* (New York: Alfred K. Knopf, 2012), 110–111.

14. On America's early unilateralism, see especially Walter A. McDougall, *Promised Land, Crusader State: The American Encounter with the World since 1776* (New York: Houghton Mifflin, 1997), 39–56.

1. "Things Odious or Immoral"

1. James Oakes, *The Scorpion's Sting: Antislavery and the Coming of the Civil War* (New York: W. W. Norton, 2014), 109. For the full text of article 7 of the Treaty of Paris, see Richard B. Morris, *The Peacemakers: The Great Powers and American Independence* (New York: Harper and Row, 1965), 464.

2. Morris, *The Peacemakers*, 535n156.

3. Woody Holton, "'Rebel against Rebel': Enslaved Virginians and the Coming of the American Revolution," *Virginia Magazine of History and Biography* 105, no. 2 (1997): 161; Lord Dunmore, "Proclamation," in George Livermore, *An Historical Research Respecting the Opinions of the Founders of the Republic on Negroes as Slaves, as Citizens, and as Soldiers* (Boston: John Wilson and Son, 1862), 135. See also Robert G. Parkinson, *The Common Cause: Creating Race and Nation in the American Revolution* (Chapel Hill: University of North Carolina Press, 2016), 153–154.

4. Declaration of the Virginia General Convention, December 13, 1775, in Livermore, *An Historical Research*, 138–139.

5. Washington to Joseph Reed, December 15, 1775, in Livermore, *An Historical Research*, 139.

6. Hamilton to Jay, March 14, 1779, in Livermore, *An Historical Research*, 170.

7. See Oakes, *The Scorpion's Sting*, 105–106; and Simon Schama, *Rough Crossings: Britain, the Slaves, and the American Revolution* (New York: HarperCollins, 2006), 100.

8. Oakes, *The Scorpion's Sting*, 106; Maya Jasanoff, *Liberty's Exiles: American Loyalists in the Revolutionary World* (New York: Alfred A. Knopf, 2011), 49.

9. Washington, quoted in Oakes, *The Scorpion's Sting*, 111. See also "Letters of George Washington Bearing on the Negro," *The Journal of Negro History* 2, no. 4 (October 1917): 415.

10. "The Substance of the Conference between General Washington and Sir Guy Carleton at an Interview at Orange Town, May 6, 1783," George Washington Papers, Library of Congress (emphasis in the original).

11. "The Substance of the Conference."

12. Oakes, *The Scorpion's Sting*, 112–113.

13. See Oakes, *The Scorpion's Sting*, 113.

14. John Jay, "Office of Foreign Affairs," October 13, 1786, in *Journals of the Continental Congress 34v. (1774–1789)* (hereafter *JCC*) 31:863–864 (emphasis in the original).

15. Jay, "Office of Foreign Affairs," in *JCC* 1:863, 864–865 (emphasis in the original).

16. Jay, "Office of Foreign Affairs," in *JCC* 31:865.

17. For a discussion of Jay and slavery, see Walter Stahr, *John Jay: Founding Father* (New York: Hambledon and London, 2005), 236–239.

18. Jay, "Office of Foreign Affairs," in *JCC* 31:865 (emphasis in the original).

19. Jay, "Office of Foreign Affairs," in *JCC* 31:866.

20. Oakes, *The Scorpion's Sting*, 115.

21. Jay to Randolph, September 13, 1794, in *American State Papers: Foreign Affairs, 38 v.* (hereafter *ASP: FA*) 1:485, 486.

22. Randolph to Jay, December 3, 1794, in *ASP: FA* 1:509.

23. Randolph to Jay, December 15, 1794, in *ASP: FA* 1:510.

24. Oakes, *The Scorpion's Sting*, 116–117.

25. Jay to Randolph, February 6, 1795, in *ASP: FA* 1:518.

26. Randolph to Jay, December 3, 1795, in *ASP: FA* 1:510.

27. On the vitriolic partisan battle over the treaty, see Sean Wilentz, *The Rise of American Democracy: Jefferson to Lincoln* (New York: W. W. Norton, 2005), 67–68.

28. *Annals of Congress, House of Representatives,* 4th Congress, 1st Session (1796), 1004, 1005, 1006.

29. *Annals of Congress,* 4th Congress, 2nd Session (1796), 1027–1028.

30. *Annals of Congress,* 4th Congress, 2nd Session (1796), 1018.

31. Camillus [Alexander Hamilton], *A Defence of the Treaty of Amity, Commerce, and Navigation* (New York: Francis Childs, 1795), 12. For Hamilton's remarks on the treaty, drafted for Washington on July 9–11, 1795, at Washington's request, see "Remarks on the Treaty of Amity Commerce and Navigation lately made between the United States and Great Britain," in *The Papers of Alexander Hamilton*, vol. 18, ed. Harold C. Syrett (New York: Columbia University Press, 1973), esp. 415–418.

32. Camillus, *A Defence of the Treaty*, 15 (emphasis in the original).

33. Camillus, *A Defence of the Treaty*, 15 (emphasis in the original).

34. Camillus, *A Defence of the Treaty*, 16 (emphasis in the original).

35. Oakes, *The Scorpion's Sting*, 120, 122.

36. Oakes, *The Scorpion's Sting*, 132.

37. Jasper M. Trautsch, "The Causes of the War of 1812: 200 Years of Debate," *Journal of Military History* 77, no. 1 (2013): 291. See also Nathaniel Millett, *The Maroons of Prospect Bluff and Their Quest for Freedom in the Atlantic World* (Gainesville: University Press of Florida, 2013), 14.

38. See Gene Allen Smith, *The Slaves Gamble: Choosing Sides in the War of 1812* (New York: Palgrave Macmillan, 2013).

39. Oakes, *The Scorpion's Sting*, 133.

40. Monroe to Adams, May 11, 1815, in *American State Papers: Foreign Relations, 38 v. (1789–1838)* (hereafter *ASP: FR*) 4:106; Monroe to Baker, April 1, 1815, in *ASP: FR* 4:106.

41. Baker to Monroe, April 3, 1815, in *ASP: FR* 4:107–108.

42. American Commissioners to Clavelle, February 23, 1815, in *ASP: FR* 4:108–109.

43. Bayly to Clavelle, April 13, 1815, in *ASP: FR* 4:109; Clavelle to Bayly, April 15, 1815, in *ASP: FR* 4:109.

44. Extract of a letter, Spalding to Monroe, May 1815, in *ASP: FR* 4:113.

45. Spalding to Griffith, May 22, 1815, in *ASP: FR* 4:114.

46. Griffith to Spalding, May 23, 1815, in *ASP: FR* 4:115.

47. Adams to Castlereagh, August 9, 1815, in *ASP: FR* 4:115–116.

48. Adams to Monroe, August 22, 1815, in *ASP: FR* 4:117.

49. Adams to Monroe, August 22, 1815, in *ASP: FR* 4:117.

50. Adams to Castlereagh, September 5, 1815, in *ASP: FR* 4:118; Adams to Monroe, September 21, 1815, in *ASP: FR* 4:118.

51. Monroe to Adams, November 16, 1815, in *ASP: FR* 4:121.

52. Monroe to Adams, November 20, 1815, in *ASP: FR* 4:121.

53. Adams summary of conversation with Castlereagh, in Adams to Monroe, February 8, 1816, in *ASP: FR* 4:121. For Bathurst's letter, see Bathurst to Adams, October 24, 1815, in *ASP: FR* 4:119–121.

54. Monroe to Adams, May 21, 1816, and Adams to Castlereagh, September 17, 1816, in *British and Foreign State Papers 71 v. (1812–1814 to 1959–1960)* (hereafter *BFSP*), 4:320; John Bew, *Castlereagh: A Life* (New York: Oxford University Press, 2012), 423 (and regarding Castlereagh's exhausting schedule in the spring and summer of 1816, see 422–423).

55. Castlereagh to Adams, September 28, 1816, in *BFSP* 4:320–321.

56. See Harold Edward Bergquist Jr., "Russian-American Relations, 1820–1830: The Diplomacy of Henry Middleton, American Minister at St. Petersburg" (PhD diss., Boston University, 1970), 62; and Norman E. Saul, *Distant Friends: The United States and Russia, 1763–1867* (Lawrence: University Press of Kansas, 1991), 93.

57. Bergquist, "Russian-American Relations," 62; Saul, *Distant Friends*, 93–94.

58. Adams's instructions to Middleton are treated extensively in Bergquist, "Russian-American Relations"; see esp. 84–102.

59. Harold Edward Bergquist Jr., "Henry Middleton and the Arbitrament of the Anglo-American Slave Controversy by Tsar Alexander I," *South Carolina Historical Magazine* 82, no. 1 (1981): 21.

60. Adams to Middleton, July 5, 1820, Diplomatic Instructions of the Department of State (hereafter DI: DS), 1801–1906, All Countries, vol. 99 (February 10, 1820–July 15, 1823), no. 77, roll 4, p. 27, National Archives, College Park, MD.

61. Adams to Middleton, July 5, 1820, DI: DS, vol. 99, no. 77, roll 4, p. 28 (emphasis in the original).

62. Adams to Middleton, July 5, 1820, DI: DS, vol. 99, no. 77, roll 4, p. 29.

63. Adams to Middleton, July 5, 1820, DI: DS, vol. 99, no. 77, roll 4, p. 30 (emphasis in the original).

64. Adams to Middleton, September 15, 1820, DI: DS, vol. 99, no. 77, roll 4, p. 47.

65. Adams to Middleton, November 4, 1820, DI: DS, vol. 99, no. 77, roll 4, p. 59 (emphasis in the original).

66. Middleton to Adams, August 28, 1820, Diplomatic Despatches, Russia (hereafter DD: R), record group 59, microcopy 35, vol. 8, roll 8, National Archives, College Park, MD.

67. Middleton to Adams, September 15, 1820, DD: R, record group 59, microcopy 35, vol. 8, roll 8.

68. Middleton to Adams, September 15, 1820. For the formal joint statement on the last of these points, see DD: R, record group 59, microcopy 35, vol. 8, roll 8, document (F).

69. Middleton to Adams, September 15, 1820. A copy of the *projet* can be found appended to the letter as document (E).

70. Middleton to Adams, June 20, 1821, DD: R, record group 59, microcopy 35, vol. 8, roll 8. (All dates regarding the tsar's activity in this period given NS.) On Alexander's foreign policy during this period, and Kapodistrias's departure from the foreign ministry, see Barbara Jelavich, *St. Petersburg to Moscow: Tsarist and Soviet Foreign Policy, 1814–1974* (Bloomington: Indiana University Press, 1974), 51.

71. Middleton to Nesselrode, June 21, 1821, DD: R, record group 59, microcopy 35, vol. 8, roll 8.

72. Bergquist, "Henry Middleton," 29.

73. Convention Signed at St. Petersburg, July 12, 1822, in *BFSP* 11:773.

74. Bergquist, "Russian-American Relations," 163; N. N. Bolkhovitinov, *Doktrina Monro: Proiskhozhdenie i Kharakter* (Moscow: Institut Mezhdunarodnykh Otnoshenii, 1959), 204n321.

75. Bergquist, "Russian-American Relations," 185.

76. Charles Webster, *The Foreign Policy of Castlereagh, 1815–1822: Britain and the European Alliance* (London: G. Bell and Sons, 1963), 445; Oakes, *The Scorpion's Sting*, 141–142.

77. Bergquist, "Russian-American Relations," 167.

78. Oakes, *The Scorpion's Sting*, 142.

79. Bergquist, "Russian-American Relations," 188–189.

80. Bemis, *John Quincy Adams*, 293.

81. On American fears during the War of 1812, see Adam Rothman, *Slave Country: American Expansion and the Origins of the Deep South* (Cambridge, MA: Harvard University Press, 2005), 140–141.

82. On the arming of escaped slaves by Great Britain, see Frank Lawrence Owsley Jr. and Gene A. Smith, *Filibusters and Expansionists: Jeffersonian Manifest Destiny, 1800–1821* (Tuscaloosa: University of Alabama Press, 1997), 103–104. On the fear of a slave uprising like Haiti's, see 105.

83. Crawford to Jackson, March 15, 1816, in *Letter from the Secretary of War Transmitting [. . .] Information Relating to the Destruction of the Negro Fort in East Florida* (1819), 5.

84. Jackson to the Governor of Pensacola, April 23, 1816, in *Letter from the Secretary of War*, 8. On the "national self-defense" rationale for attacking Blacks in Florida, see Deborah A. Rosen, *Border Law: The First Seminole War and American Nationhood* (Cambridge, MA: Harvard University Press, 2015), 158.

85. Jackson to Maj. Gen. E. P. Gaines, April 8, 1816, in *Letter from the Secretary of War*, 10–11.

86. Patterson to the Secretary of the Navy, August 15, 1816, in *Letter from the Secretary of the Navy [. . .] Transmitting [. . .] Documents Relating to the Destruction of the Negro Fort in East Florida* (1819), 13–14.

87. William Earl Weeks, *John Quincy Adams and American Global Empire* (Lexington: University Press of Kentucky, 1992), 107. On escaped slaves in Florida after the Battle of Negro Fort, see Aline Helg, *Slave No More: Self-Liberation before Abolitionism in the Americas*, trans. Lara Vergnaud (Chapel Hill: University of North Carolina Press, 2019), 223.

88. On the continued flight of slaves to Florida after the Adams-Onís Treaty, see Larry Eugene Rivers, *Slavery in Florida: Territorial Days to Emancipation* (Gainesville: University Press of Florida, 2000), 199.

89. Millett, *The Maroons*, 247.

90. Matthew J. Clavin, *The Battle of Negro Fort: The Rise and Fall of a Fugitive Slave Community* (New York: New York University Press, 2019), 158.

2. "'Tis Ill to Fear"

1. Alyssa Goldstein Sepinwall, "The Specter of Saint-Domingue: American and French Reactions to the Haitian Revolution," in *The World of the Haitian Revolution*, ed. David Patrick Geggus and Norman Fiering (Bloomington: Indiana University Press, 2009), 319.

2. Michael Zeuske, *Sklavereien, Emanzipationen und atlantische Weltgeschichte. Essays über Mikrogechichten, Sklaven, Globalisierung und Rassismus* (Leipzig: Leipziger Universitätsverlag, 2002), 174–175 (author's translation); Don E. Fehrenbacher, *The Slaveholding Republic: An Account of the United States Government's Relations to Slavery* (New York: Oxford University Press, 2001); Yves Auguste, "Jefferson et Haïti (1804–1810)," *Revue D'Histoire Diplomatique* 86, no. 4 (1972): 333 (author's translation).

3. See, e.g., Caitlin Fitz, *Our Sister Republics: The United States in an Age of American Revolutions* (New York: W. W. Norton, 2016), 2–3, 205.

4. Sidney Mintz, *Three Ancient Colonies: Caribbean Themes and Variations* (Cambridge, MA: Harvard, 2010), 94 (emphasis in the original).

5. See, e.g., Edward B. Rugemer, *Slave Law and the Politics of Resistance in the Early Atlantic World* (Cambridge, MA: Harvard University Press, 2018), 214.

6. Zeuske, *Sklavereien*, 183; Laurent Dubois, *Avengers of the New World: The Story of the Haitian Revolution* (Cambridge, MA: Belknap, 2004), 1. On slave resistance in Saint-Domingue prior to the revolution, see especially Philippe Girard, *Toussaint Louverture: A Revolutionary Life* (New York: Basic Books, 2016), chap. 4. On the universality of the enslaved Dominguans' claims, see especially Jean-Pierre Le Glaunec, *L'armée indigène: Le défaite de Napoléon en Haïti* (n.p. [Port-au-Prince?]: Éditions de l'Université d'État d'Haïti, 2014), 46–47. See also Ashli White, *Encountering Revolution: Haiti and the Making of the Early Republic* (Baltimore: Johns Hopkins University Press, 2010) 2–3.

7. Dubois, *Avengers*, 94. See also Ada Ferrer, "Cuba en la sombra de Haití: Noticias, sociedad, y esclavitud," in Dolores González-Ripoll, Consuelo Naranjo, Ada Ferrer, Gloria García, and Josef Opatrný, *El rumor de Haití en Cuba: Temor, raza y rebeldía, 1789–1844* (Madrid: Consejo Superior de Investigaciones Científicas, 2004), 179 (author's translation). For information on the opening stages of the rebellion, see Thomas O. Ott, *The Haitian Revolution, 1789–1804* (Knoxville: University of Tennessee Press, 1973), 47–51.

8. Timothy M. Matthewson, "George Washington's Policy toward the Haitian Revolution," *Diplomatic History* 3, no. 3 (1979): 322. For statistics on trade, see Donald R. Hickey, "American Responses to the Slave Revolt in Haiti, 1791–1806," *Journal of the Early Republic* 2, no. 4 (1982): 363.

9. Pinckney to Washington, September 20, 1791, quoted in Matthewson, "George Washington's Policy," 324.

10. Washington to Ternant, September 24, 1791, in *The Papers of George Washington: Presidential Series*, vol. 9 (Charlottesville: University of Virginia Press, 1956–1987), 15; Ternant to Washington, September 24, 1791, in *The Papers of George Washington*

9:16; Timothy M. Matthewson, *A Proslavery Foreign Policy: Haitian-American Relations during the Early Republic* (Westport, CT: Praeger, 2003), 25.

11. Jefferson to William Short, November 24, 1791, in *The Papers of Thomas Jefferson*, 45 vols., vol. 22 (Charlottesville: University of Virginia Press, 1950), 330; Rayford Logan, *The Diplomatic Relations of the United States with Haiti, 1776–1891* (Chapel Hill: University of North Carolina Press, 1941), 36; Ternant to Count de Montmorin, September 28, 1791, in Frederick Jackson Turner, ed., *Correspondence of the French Ministers to the United States: Annual Report of the American Historical Association for 1903* (Washington, DC: Government Publishing Office, 1904), 47 (author's translation). See also Gordon S. Brown, *Toussaint's Clause: The Founding Fathers and the Haitian Revolution* (Jackson: University Press of Mississippi, 2005), 54.

12. Ternant to Hamilton, September 21, 1791, in *The Papers of Alexander Hamilton*, 27 vols., vol. 9 (New York: Columbia University Press, 1961–1979), 219; Hamilton to Ternant, September 21, 1791, in *The Papers of Alexander Hamilton* 9:220; Hamilton to Washington, September 22, 1791, in *The Papers of Alexander Hamilton* 9:225; Washington to Hamilton, September 24, 1791, in *The Papers of Alexander Hamilton* 9:238. See also Ternant to Montmorin, September 28, 1791, in Turner, *Correspondence of the French Ministers*, 48–49.

13. Jefferson to William Short, January 5, 1792, in *The Papers of Thomas Jefferson* 23:26; Jefferson to Washington, January 4, 1792, in *The Papers of Thomas Jefferson* 23:24; Logan, *Diplomatic Relations*, 39; Joseph Fauchet, quoted in Logan, *Diplomatic Relations*, 44.

14. Ott, *The Haitian Revolution*, 55; Ternant to Lessart, March 26, 1792, in Turner, *Correspondence of the French Ministers*, 101. On US aid to France, see Hickey, "American Responses," 364.

15. Hamilton to Washington, November 19, 1792, in *The Papers of Alexander Hamilton* 13:169–170.

16. Hamilton to Washington, November 19, 1792, in *The Papers of Alexander Hamilton* 13:169, 170, 171, 173 (emphasis in the original). On events in France, see Georges Lefebvre, *The French Revolution* (London: Routledge Classics, 2001), especially 230–232; and William Doyle, *The Oxford History of the French Revolution* (Oxford: Oxford University Press, 1990), chap. 8.

17. Ott, *The Haitian Revolution*, 57 (and see, generally, 56–57); Dubois, *Avengers*, 128.

18. Girard, *Toussaint Louverture*, 138 (and see, generally, 134–138); Dubois, *Avengers*, 154–164.

19. Matthewson, *A Proslavery Foreign Policy*, 48; White, *Encountering Revolution*, 124, 126. On southerners' fears of slave rebellion spreading to the United States, see especially Joseph A. Fry, *Dixie Looks Abroad: The South and U.S. Foreign Relations, 1789–1973* (Baton Rouge: Louisiana State University Press, 2002), 27–28.

20. See, e.g., Ott, *The Haitian Revolution*, 53; Matthewson, *A Proslavery Foreign Policy*, 22, 32; and Dubois, *Avengers*, 304.

21. Dubois, *Avengers*, 225; Arthur Scherr, *Thomas Jefferson's Haitian Policy: Myths and Realities* (Lanham, MD: Lexington Books, 2011), 34 (see also 61).

22. David Patrick Geggus, *Slavery, War, and Revolution: The British Occupation of Saint Domingue, 1793–1798* (Oxford: Oxford University Press, 1982), 79, 87; Ott, *The Haitian Revolution*, 76.

23. Morris to Jefferson, February 13, 1793, in *The Papers of Thomas Jefferson* 25:189, all spelling in the original.

24. Lawrence S. Kaplan, *Alexander Hamilton: Ambivalent Anglophile* (Wilmington, DE: Scholarly Resources, 2002), 119. A useful analysis of Jay's Treaty, and especially Hamilton's key role in the framing and ratification of the pact, can be found in Kaplan, *Alexander Hamilton*, 117–121, 125–130. On the benefits of the treaty for American trade and security, see Samuel Flagg Bemis, *Jay's Treaty: A Study in Commerce and Diplomacy* (New Haven, CT: Yale University Press, 1962), 371–373.

25. See Geggus, *Slavery, War, and Revolution*, 140–141, 153–154; and Charles Callan Tansill, *The United States and Santo Domingo, 1798–1873: A Chapter in Caribbean Diplomacy* (Baltimore: Johns Hopkins University Press, 1938), 19.

26. See Geggus, *Slavery, War, and Revolution*, chap. 13.

27. Geggus, *Slavery, War, and Revolution*, 116. On Toussaint's volte-face, see Girard, *Toussaint Louverture*, 141–145.

28. Philippe R. Girard, "Black Talleyrand: Toussaint Louverture's Diplomacy, 1798–1802," *William and Mary Quarterly*, 3rd ser., 66, no. 1 (2009): 93.

29. Girard, "Black Talleyrand," 91. For a brief but useful summary of the context of Toussaint's demarche to Adams, see Franklin Jameson, ed., "Letters of Toussaint Louverture and Edward Stevens, 1798–1800," *American Historical Review* 16, no. 1 (1910): 64–65.

30. Toussaint to Adams, November 6, 1798, in Jameson, "Letters of Toussaint Louverture and Edward Stevens," 66–67.

31. Logan, *Diplomatic Relations*, 73. On Toussaint's choice of Bunel and the controversy that ensued, see especially Girard, *Toussaint Louverture*, 178. For an excellent and readable treatment of the early days of the Adams administration's flirtations with Dominguan independence, see Ronald Angelo Johnson, *Diplomacy in Black and White: John Adams, Toussaint Louverture, and Their Atlantic World Alliance* (Athens: University of Georgia Press, 2014), 23–29.

32. Pickering to Jacob Mayer, November 30, 1798, Timothy Pickering Papers, reel 9, 671, Massachusetts Historical Society, Boston; Gerard H. Clarfield, *Timothy Pickering and American Diplomacy, 1795–1800* (Columbia: University of Missouri Press, 1969), 148.

33. King to Pickering, December 7, 1798, in *The Life and Correspondence of Rufus King*, 6 vols., vol. 2 (New York: G. P. Putnam, 1894–1900), 477 (emphasis in the original); King to Pickering, July 14, 1798, in *The Life and Correspondence of Rufus King*, 368–369 (emphasis in the original).

34. Girard, *Toussaint Louverture*, 175; Tansill, *The United States and Santo Domingo*, 67. A translation of the agreement, from which the quotes herein are taken, can be found in Logan, *Diplomatic Relations*, 65–66.

35. Johnson, *Diplomacy in Black and White*, 83–84.

36. Brown, *Toussaint's Clause*, 133; Pickering to King, March 12, 1799, Thomas Pickering Papers, reel 10, 476; Pickering to King, November 7, 1799, Thomas Pickering Papers, reel 12, 315A; Pickering to John Quincy Adams, April 24, 1799, Thomas Pickering Papers, reel 10, 632A; Pickering to King, March 12, 1799, quoted in Hickey, "American Responses," 365. On John Quincy Adams's support for independence, see, e.g., Logan, *Diplomatic Relations*, 89.

37. Adams to Pickering, July 2, 1799, in *Naval Documents Related to the Quasi-War Between the United States and France*, 7 vols., vol. 3 (Washington, DC: Government Printing Office, 1935–38), 453.

38. Adams to Pickering, July 2, 1799, in *Naval Documents* 3:453; Adams to Stoddard, June 7, 1799, in *Naval Documents* 3:312–313. See also Scherr, *Thomas Jefferson's Haitian Policy*, 79.

39. Pickering to Stevens, April 20, 1799, in *Naval Documents* 3:70, 71, 72.

40. Toussaint's Clause, quoted in Brown, *Toussaint's Clause*, 138.

41. Albert Gallatin, quoted in Brown, *Toussaint's Clause*, 141. On the clause's career in Congress, see especially Brown, *Toussaint's Clause*, 138–143.

42. Arthur Scherr, *John Adams, Slavery, and Race: Ideas, Politics, and Diplomacy in an Age of Crisis* (Santa Barbara, CA: Praeger, 2018), 47.

43. Stevens to Pickering, May 3, 1799, in Jameson, "Letters of Toussaint Louverture and Edward Stevens," 67; Stevens to Pickering, June 24, 1799, Jameson, "Letters of Toussaint Louverture and Edward Stevens," 77; Johnson, *Diplomacy in Black and White*, 96.

44. Brown, *Toussaint's Clause*, 157; Stevens to Pickering, June 23, 1799, in Jameson, "Letters of Toussaint Louverture and Edward Stevens," 74; convention quoted in Johnson, *Diplomacy in Black and White*, 99; Tansill, *The United States and Santo Domingo*, 70; for Adams's proclamation of June 26, 1799, See *Naval Documents* 3:408–409.

45. Stevens to Pickering, *Naval Documents* 3:389, 390, 391, 392.

46. Tansill, *The United States and Santo Domingo*, 74 (and, for an early treatment of this episode, see 73–74).

47. Wolcott to Adams, November 18, 1799, in *Naval Documents* 3:418; Pickering to King, March 12, 1799, Thomas Pickering Papers, reel 10, 476.

48. Logan, *The United States and Santo Domingo*, 112; Marshall to Toussaint, November 26, 1800, in *The Papers of John Marshall*, 12 vols., vol. 6 (Chapel Hill: University of North Carolina Press, 1974–2006), 22.

49. Dubois, *Avengers*, 225; Johnson, *Diplomacy in Black and White*, 164.

50. Scherr, *Thomas Jefferson's Haitian Policy*, 161; Matthewson, *A Proslavery Foreign Policy*, 97.

51. Jefferson to Madison, February 5, 1799, in *Papers of Thomas Jefferson* 31:9–10 (lowercasing in the original).

52. Edward Thornton, quoted in Tansill, *The United States and Santo Domingo*, 78.

53. Lear to Madison, July 17, 1801, *The Papers of James Madison: Secretary of State Series*, 9 Vols. (Charlottesville: University of Virginia Press, 1962–), 427.

54. Lear to Madison, July 17, 1801, *The Papers of James Madison: Secretary of State Series*, 9 Vols., vol. 1 (Charlottesville: University of Virginia Press, 1962–), 427–428.

55. See, e.g., Matthewson, *A Proslavery Foreign Policy*, 101–102.

56. The summary herein is based on Ott, *Haitian Revolution*, 139–141 (quote on 140).

57. Girard, *Toussaint Louverture*, 230–231.

58. Pichon conversation with Jefferson, July 19, 1801, quoted in Tansill, *United States and Santo Domingo*, 81. On the Jefferson-Pichon discussion generally, see Tansill, *United States and Santo Domingo*, 80–81; and Matthewson, *A Proslavery Foreign Policy*, 100.

59. Scherr, *Thomas Jefferson's Haitian Policy*, 166–167.

60. Madison to Lear, January 8, 1802, in *The Papers of James Madison* 2:373–374.

61. Tansill, *The United States and Santo Domingo*, 85. On the Gabriel Rebellion and Jefferson's policy toward Saint-Domingue, see especially Matthewson, *A Proslavery Foreign Policy*, 101–102.

62. Thomas Jefferson, quoted in Francis D. Cogliano, *Emperor of Liberty: Thomas Jefferson's Foreign Policy* (New Haven, CT: Yale University Press, 2014), 189.

63. Coxe to Madison, ca. November 28, 1801, in *The Papers of James Madison* 2:281, 282, 283 (emphasis in the original); Madison to Livingston, September 28, 1801, in *The Papers of James Madison* 2:144.

64. Ott, *The Haitian Revolution*, 144; Philippe R. Girard, *The Slaves Who Defeated Napoleon: Toussaint Louverture and the Haitian War of Independence, 1801–1804* (Tuscaloosa: University of Alabama Press, 2011), 63. On Toussaint's preparations for war in late 1801 to early 1802, see especially Dubois, *Avengers*, 262.

65. Ott, *The Haitian Revolution*, 144–145.

66. King to Madison, October 31, 1801, in *The Papers of James Madison* 2:214; summary of Lear to Madison, February 12, 1802, in *The Papers of James Madison* 2:463 (emphasis in the original). On Madison's fears that the Leclerc expedition was destined for Louisiana, see, e.g., Logan, *Diplomatic Relations*, 135.

67. Matthewson, *A Proslavery Foreign Policy*, 105.

68. Leclerc to the Minister of the Marine (Denis Decrès), February 9, 1802, in Charles Victor Emmanuel Leclerc, *Lettres du Général Leclerc: Commandant en chef de l'armée de Saint Domingue en 1802*, ed. Paul Roussier (Paris: Société de L'Histoire des Colonies Françaises, 1937), 82; Pichon to Madison, March 17, 1802, in *The Papers of James Madison* 3:41–42.

69. Ott, *The Haitian Revolution*, 170. On French death and disease statistics, see Girard, *Toussaint Louverture*, 242.

70. Dubois, *Avengers*, 298.

71. On the durability of this fear, see Edward B. Rugemer, "Slave Rebels and Abolitionists: The Black Atlantic and the Coming of the Civil War," *Journal of the Civil War Era* 2, no. 2 (2012): 194.

72. Manuel Barcia, "From Revolution to Recognition: Haiti's Place in the Post-1804 Atlantic World," *American Historical Review* 125, no. 3 (2020): 901.

73. Herbert S. Klein and Ben Vinson III, *Historia Minima de la Esclavitud en América Latina y in el Caribe* (Mexico City: El Colegio de Mexico, 2013), 295 (author's translation).

3. "Separate from Foreign Alliances"

1. Brenda E. Stevenson, *What Is Slavery?* (Cambridge: Polity, 2015), 40. For contemporaneous comparisons of various slave systems, see, e.g., Roland T. Ely, *Cuando reinaba su majestad el azucar: Estudio histórico-sociológico de una tragedia latinoamericana* (Buenos Aires: Editorial Sudamericana, 1963), 473–487.

2. For a brief treatment of the Middle Passage, see Egon Flaig, *Weltgeschichte der Sklaverei*, rev. ed. (Munich: Verlag C. H. Beck, 2018), 176–178.

3. Francis D. Cogliano, *Thomas Jefferson: Reputation and Legacy* (Charlottesville: University of Virginia Press, 2006), 200.

4. Brian Schoen, *The Fragile Fabric of Union: Cotton, Federal Politics, and the Global Origins of the Civil War* (Baltimore: Johns Hopkins University Press, 2009), 68.

5. See, e.g., Edward B. Rugemer, "The Southern Response to British Abolitionism: The Maturation of Proslavery Apologetics," *Journal of Southern History* 50, no. 2 (2004): 227.

6. See Steven Deyle, "The Irony of Liberty: Origins of the Domestic Slave Trade," *Journal of the Early Republic* 12, no. 1 (1992): 43–46; Peter Kolchin, *American Slavery, 1619–1877* (New York: Hill and Wang, 2003), 96; and Steven Deyle, *Carry Me Back: The Domestic Slave Trade in American Life* (New York: Oxford University Press, 2005), 21–22. For background on the issue, see Lacy K. Ford, *Deliver Us from Evil: The Slavery Question in the Old South* (New York: Oxford University Press, 2009), esp. 27–30.

7. *Abridgment of the Debates of Congress*, 16 Vols., vol. 3 (New York: D. Appleton, 1857) (hereafter *ADC*), 131.

8. *ADC* 3:142.

9. Matthew E. Mason, "Slavery Overshadowed: Congress Debates Prohibiting the Atlantic Slave Trade to the United States," *Journal of the Early Republic* 20, no. 1 (2000): 63.

10. Don E. Fehrenbacher, *The Slaveholding Republic: An Account of the United States Government's Relations to Slavery* (New York: Oxford University Press, 2001), 136–137.

11. On this last point, see Hugh G. Soulsby, *The Right of Search and the Slave Trade in Anglo-American Relations, 1814–1862* (Baltimore: Johns Hopkins University Press, 1933), 10–11.

12. R[eginald] Coupland, *The British Anti-Slavery Movement* (London: Thornton Butterworth, 1933), 153.

13. Coupland, *The British Anti-Slavery Movement*, 153; Paul Michael Kielstra, *The Politics of Slave Trade Suppression in Britain and France, 1814–1848: Diplomacy, Morality and Economics* (New York: St. Martin's, 2000), 6.

14. Jeremy Black, "Suppressing the Slave Trade," in *British Abolitionism and the Question of Moral Progress in History*, ed. Donald A. Yerxa (Columbia: University of South Carolina Press, 2012), 29.

15. Harold Nicolson, *The Congress of Vienna: A Study in Allied Unity, 1812–1822* (New York: Harcourt, Brace, Jovanovich, 1974), 211; Kielstra, *The Politics of Slave Trade Suppression*, 52.

16. See Flaig, *Weltgeschichte der Sklaverei*, 206–207.

17. Coupland, *The British Anti-Slavery Movement*, 160 (emphasis in the original); Kielstra, *The Politics of Slave Trade Suppression*, 61–62.

18. Gaston Martin, *Histoire de l'Esclavage dans les Colonies Françaises* (Paris: Presses Universitaires de France, 1948), 254 (author's translation).

19. Denver Brunsman, *The Evil Necessity: British Naval Impressment in the Eighteenth-Century Atlantic World* (Charlottesville: University of Virginia Press, 2013), 248. See also Bradford Perkins, *Prologue to War: England and the United States, 1805–1812* (Berkeley: University of California Press, 1968), 428.

20. "Message of the President of the United States, on the Opening of Congress," December 3, 1816, in *BFSP* 4:13.

21. *ADC* 6:11.

22. *ADC* 6:12.

23. John Quincy Adams, *Memoirs of John Quincy Adams: Comprising Portions of His Diary from 1795 to 1848*, vol. 5, ed. Charles Francis Adams (Philadelphia: J. B. Lippincott, 1874–77), 182.

24. Adams, *Memoirs* 5:182.

25. John Quincy Adams, *Memoirs of John Quincy Adams: Comprising Portions of His Diary from 1795 to 1848*, 12 vols., ed. Charles Francis Adams, vol. 5 (Philadelphia: J. B. Lippincott, 1874–77), 182–183.

26. Adams, *Memoirs* 5:183.

27. Canning to Castlereagh, October 3, 1820, quoted in Soulsby, *The Right of Search*, 22.

28. Soulsby, *The Right of Search*, 24; Castlereagh to Canning, August 7, 1820, in *BFSP* 8:393.

29. Adams, *Memoirs* 5:214; Canning to Castlereagh, December 30, 1820, in *BFSP* 8:395; Canning to Adams, December 20, 1820, in *BFSP* 8:396.

30. Adams to Canning, December 30, 1820, in *BFSP* 8:397, 399.

31. Adams, *Memoirs* 5:222.

32. Castlereagh to Lords Comm'rs. of the Admiralty, March 13, 1821, in *BFSP* 8:399; Adams, *Memoirs* 5:225–226.

33. Canning to Adams, June 1, 1821, in *BFSP* 9:78–79.

34. Adams to Canning, August 15, 1821, in *BFSP* 9:82 (and see, generally, 80–83).

35. Donald L. Canney, *Africa Squadron: The U.S. Navy and the Slave Trade, 1842–1861* (Washington, DC: Potomac Books, 2006), 7. See also Judd Scott Harmon, "Suppress and Protect: The United States Navy, the African Slave Trade, and Maritime Commerce, 1798–1862" (PhD diss., College of William and Mary, 1977), 67–69.

36. Adams to Canning, August 20, 1821, in *BFSP* 9:83; Instructions to American Ships of War, in *BFSP* 9:83.

37. Adams, *Memoirs* 5:448–449.

38. Soulsby, *The Right of Search*, 25; Castlereagh to Canning, April 15, 1822, in *BFSP* 10:246–247.

39. Memorandum of Conversation, Castlereagh and Rush, April 1822, in *BFSP* 10:247–248.

40. Canning to Castlereagh, May 8, 1822, in *BFSP* 10:248; Soulsby, *The Right of Search*, 25–26.

41. Canning to Castlereagh, July 16, 1822, in *BFSP* 10:252.

42. George Canning to Stratford Canning, October 11, 1822, in *BFSP* 10:254–255.

43. Adams, *Memoirs* 6:84; Soulsby, *The Right of Search*, 23.

44. Stratford Canning to George Canning, January 1, 1823, in *BFSP* 10:256.

45. *ADC* 7:456; Fehrenbacher, *The Slaveholding Republic*, 159. See also Christopher Lloyd, *The Navy and the Slave Trade: The Suppression of the African Slave Trade in the Nineteenth Century* (London: Longmans, Green, 1949), xi.

46. Harmon, "Suppress and Protect," 72–73.

47. Harmon, "Suppress and Protect," 74; James E. Lewis Jr., *John Quincy Adams: Policymaker for the Union* (Wilmington, DE: Scholarly Resources, 2001), 83.

48. Adams, *Memoirs* 6:361–362, 366.

49. Adams, *Memoirs* 6:329. See also Fehrenbacher, *The Slaveholding Republic*, 160.

50. Fehrenbacher, *The Slaveholding Republic*, 161; Soulsby, *The Right of Search*, 37–38.

51. Adams, *Memoirs* 6:37.

52. Thomas Jefferson, "Notes on the State of Virginia," in *Thomas Jefferson: Writings*, ed. Merrill D. Peterson (New York: Library of America, 1984), 264.

53. See P. J. Staudenraus, *The African Colonization Movement, 1816–1865* (New York: Columbia University Press, 1961), 2–3.

54. Eric Burin, *Slavery and the Peculiar Solution: A History of the American Colonization Society* (Gainesville: University Press of Florida, 2005), 10.

55. See, e.g., David Brion Davis, *The Problem of Slavery in the Age of Emancipation* (New York: Alfred A. Knopf, 2014), 83.

56. Burin, *Slavery and the Peculiar Solution*, 12.

57. See, e.g., Staudenraus, *The African Colonization Movement*, 8–9.

58. Lawrence C. Howard, *American Involvement in Africa South of the Sahara, 1800–1860* (New York: Garland, 1988), 163.

59. Burin, *Slavery and the Peculiar Solution*, 14.

60. Slave Trade Act, quoted in Charles Henry Huberich, *The Political and Legislative History of Liberia*, vol. 1 (New York: Central Book, 1947), 68.

61. Burin, *Slavery and the Peculiar Solution*, 14.

62. Adams, *Memoirs* 4:293.

63. Adams, *Memoirs* 4:293–294.

64. Staudenraus, *The African Colonization Movement*, 53.

65. Staudenraus, *The African Colonization Movement*, 55; Huberich, *The Political and Legislative History of Liberia*, 68–69.

66. Huberich, *The Political and Legislative History of Liberia*, 69.

67. Staudenraus, *The African Colonization Movement*, 56.

68. Monroe's Special Message to Congress, December 17, 1819, quoted in Huberich, *The Political and Legislative History of Liberia*, 70–71.

69. Howard, *American Involvement*, 187–188.

70. Thompson to Bacon, January 17, 1820, in *Correspondence of the Secretary of the Navy Relating to African Colonization 1819–1844*, 2 rolls (hereafter *CSNAC*), National Archives and Records Administration, Record Group 45, M205. On Thompson's instructions to Bacon, see Howard, *American Involvement*, 189–190.

71. Howard, *American Involvement*, 190–191.

72. Bacon to Thompson, March 20, 1820, quoted in Huberich, *The Political and Legislative History of Liberia*, 90.

73. See, e.g., Howard, *American Involvement*, 192.

74. Davis, *The Problem of Slavery*, 110.

75. Howard, *American Involvement*, 195–196.

76. Thompson to Winn, December 1, 1820, in *CSNAC*.

77. Winn to Thompson, April 19, 1821, quoted in Huberich, *The Political and Legislative History of Liberia*, 162.

78. Howard, *American Involvement*, 197.

79. Huberich, *The Political and Legislative History of Liberia*, 183–184.

80. Huberich, *The Political and Legislative History of Liberia*, 213.

81. See, e.g., Ayers to Southard, March 15, 1824, in *CSNAC*.

82. Howard, *American Involvement*, 212.

83. David F. Ericson, *Slavery in the American Republic: Developing the Federal Government, 1791–1861* (Lawrence: University Press of Kansas, 2011), 53.

84. Huberich, *The Political and Legislative History of Liberia*, 258.

85. Nicholas P. Wood, "The Missouri Crisis and the 'Changed Object' of the American Colonization Society," in *New Directions in the Study of American Recolonization*, ed. Beverly C. Tomek and Matthew J. Hetrick (Gainesville: University Press of Florida, 2017), 146–147.

86. Howard, *American Involvement*, 216–217.

87. Staudenraus, *The African Colonization Movement*, 92–93.

88. Staudenraus, *The African Colonization Movement*, 94–95, 97. For the new consti-tution, see "Documents Relating to the United States and Liberia," *American Journal of International Law* 4, no. 3, supplement: official documents (1910): 193–198.

89. See, e.g., Southard to Ashmun, January 26, 1825, *CSNAC*.

90. Staudenraus, *The African Colonization Movement*, 174–175.

91. Report of the Fourth Auditor of the Treasury Department to the Secretary of the Navy, August 1830, quoted in Huberich, *The Political and Legislative History of Liberia*, 623, 627 (emphasis in the original).

92. Report of the Fourth Auditor, quoted in Huberich, *The Political and Legislative History of Liberia*, 621.

93. Howard, *American Involvement*, 230; Staudenraus, *The African Colonization Movement*, 178. See also Penelope Campbell, *Maryland in Africa: The Maryland State Coloni-zation Society, 1831–1857* (Urbana: University of Illinois Press, 1971), 10.

94. Burin, *Slavery and the Peculiar Solution*, 22.

95. Pennsylvania Colonization Society, *Report of the Board of Managers of the Penn-sylvania Colonization Society* (Philadelphia: T. Kite, 1830), 3.

96. On this, see especially Edlie L. Wong, *Neither Fugitive nor Free: Atlantic Slavery, Freedom Suits, and the Legal Culture of Travel* (New York: New York University Press, 2009), 184.

97. See Alan F. January, "The First Nullification: The Negro Seamen Acts Contro-versy in South Carolina, 1822–1860" (PhD diss., University of Iowa, 1976), 106n24.

98. January, "The First Nullification," 84, 88.

99. Carol Wilson, *Freedom at Risk: The Kidnapping of Free Blacks in America, 1780–1865* (Lexington: University Press of Kentucky, 2009), 59.

100. Philip M. Hamer, "Great Britain, the United States, and the Negro Seamen Acts, 1822–1848," *Journal of Southern History* 1, no. 1 (1935): 3.

101. South Carolina legislature, "A Bill to prohibit the bringing of slaves into this state for sale, barter, or exchange and the better regulation and government of free Negroes and persons of color and for other purposes," quoted in January, "The First Nullification," 60.

102. Hamer, "Great Britain, the United States, and the Negro Seamen Acts," 4. See also Michael Schoeppner, "Navigating the Dangerous Atlantic: Racial Quarantines, Black Sailors and United States Constitutionalism" (PhD diss., University of Florida, 2010), 59.

103. Hamer, "Great Britain, the United States, and the Negro Seamen Acts," 4.

104. Alan F. January, "The South Carolina Association: An Agency for Race Control in Antebellum Charleston," *South Carolina Historical Magazine* 78, no. 3 (1977): 195. See also Michael A. Schoeppner, *Moral Contagion: Black Atlantic Sailors, Citizenship, and Diplo-macy in Antebellum America* (New York: Cambridge University Press, 2019), 38.

105. Michael Schoeppner, "Peculiar Quarantines: The Seamen Acts and Regula-tory Authority in the Antebellum South," *Law and History Review* 31, no. 3 (2013): 564, 566. On the legal difficulties presented by the contagion analogy, see Schoeppner, *Moral Contagion*, 45.

106. Hamer, "Great Britain, the United States, and the Negro Seamen Acts," 8.

107. Schoeppner, "Navigating the Dangerous Atlantic," 77.

108. Hamer, "Great Britain, the United States, and the Negro Seamen Acts," 8.

109. The treatment of the diplomatic back-and-forth during these years in Hamer, "Great Britain, the United States, and the Negro Seamen Acts," is detailed and comprehensive.

110. Philip M. Hamer, "British Consuls and the Negro Seamen Acts, 1850–1860," *Journal of Southern History* 1, no. 2 (1935): 138–139.

111. Hamer, "British Consuls," 140–141.

112. Hamer, "British Consuls," 151.

113. Michael Schoeppner, "Legal Redress for Transatlantic Black Maritime Laborers in the Antebellum United States: A Case Study," *World History Bulletin* 29, no. 1 (2013): 20.

114. Larry Eugene Rivers, *Rebels and Runaways: Slave Resistance in Nineteenth-Century Florida* (Urbana: University of Illinois Press, 2013), 79.

115. Irvin D. S. Winsboro and Joe Knetsch, "Florida Slaves, the 'Saltwater Railroad' to the Bahamas, and Anglo-American Diplomacy," *Journal of Southern History* 79, no. 1 (2013): 51.

116. Winsboro and Knetsch, "Florida Slaves," 54; Aberdeen to Edward Everett, April 18, 1842, in *BFSP* 31:701. See also *Niles National Register*, August 12, 1843, 374.

117. Winsboro and Knetsch, "Florida Slaves," 56.

118. Arthur T. Downey, *The Creole Affair: The Slave Rebellion That Led the U.S. and Great Britain to the Brink of War* (Lanham, MD: Rowman and Littlefield, 2014).

119. On the *Amistad* episode, see especially Howard Jones, *Mutiny on the Amistad: The Saga of a Slave Revolt and Its Impact on American Abolition, Law, and Diplomacy*, rev. ed. (New York: Oxford University Press, 1988).

120. Everett to Aberdeen, March 1, 1842, in *BFSP* 31:646. For a thorough treatment of the episode and its consequences, see especially Edward D. Jervey and C. Harold Huber, "The *Creole* Affair," *Journal of Negro History* 65, no. 3 (1980): 196–211.

121. Christopher J. Leahy, *President without a Party: The Life of John Tyler* (Baton Rouge: Louisiana State University Press, 2020), 259. On the "Hidden Atlantic," see Michael Zeuske and Orlando García Martínez, "'La Amistad' de Cuba: Ramón Ferrer, contraband de esclavos, captividad y modernidad atlántica," *Caribbean Studies* 37, no. 1 (2009), 148; and Dorothea Fischer-Hornung, "The Hidden Atlantic: Michael Zeuske Reflects on His Recent Research," *Atlantic Studies* 15, no. 1 (2018): 137.

122. Matthew Mason, *Apostle of Union: A Political Biography of Edward Everett* (Chapel Hill: University of North Carolina Press, 2016), 126.

123. Winsboro and Knetsch, "Florida Slaves," 61; Mason, *Apostle of Union*, 134.

124. Everett to Aberdeen, March 1, 1842, in *BFSP* 31:679–680.

125. Everett to Aberdeen, March 1, 1842, in *BFSP* 31:680, 683.

126. Everett to Aberdeen, March 1, 1842, in *BFSP* 31:684–685.

127. Mason, *Apostle of Union*, 141, 142.

128. Aberdeen to Everett, April 18, 1842, in *Great Britain. Parliament. House of Lords. Sessional Papers*, session 1843, vol. 16, 196.

129. Leahy, *President without a Party*, 260–261; Winsboro and Knetsch, "Florida Slaves," 63.

130. See Jervey and Huber, "The *Creole* Affair," 207–208. See also Wilbur Devereux Jones, "The Influence of Slavery on the Webster-Ashburton Negotiations," *Journal of Southern History* 22, no. 1 (1956): 52–53; and Winsboro and Knetsch, "Florida Slaves," 60.

4. "Fully Meets Its Responsibility"

1. On Nat Turner's Rebellion and its significance, see. e.g., Edward B. Rugemer, *Slave Law and the Politics of Resistance in the Early Atlantic World* (Cambridge, MA: Harvard University Press, 2018), 297–298; William W. Freehling, *The Road to Disunion: Secessionists at Bay, 1776–1854* (New York: Oxford University Press, 1990), 178–181; and especially Lacy K. Ford, *Deliver Us from Evil: The Slavery Question in the Old South* (New York: Oxford University Press, 2009), 361–389.

2. See Eric Burin, *Slavery and the Peculiar Solution: A History of the American Colonization Society* (Gainesville: University Press of Florida, 2005), 24; and Lawrence C. Howard, *American Involvement in Africa South of the Sahara, 1800–1860* (New York: Garland, 1988), 231.

3. Howard, *American Involvement*, 233.

4. See Penelope Campbell, *Maryland in Africa: The Maryland State Colonization Society, 1831–1857* (Urbana: University of Illinois Press, 1971), 235–237.

5. Howard, *American Involvement*, 235–237.

6. Report of the Committee of Commerce on African Colonization, 27th Congress, 3rd Session, House of Representatives Report No. 283 (February 28, 1843), in "Documents Relating to the United States and Liberia," *American Journal of International Law* 4, no. 3, supplement: official documents (1910): 203.

7. Report of the Committee of Commerce on African Colonization, 205.

8. Report of the Committee of Commerce on African Colonization, 205–206.

9. Fox to Upshur, August 9, 1843, in "Documents Relating to the United States and Liberia," 211–212.

10. Upshur to Fox, September 25, 1843, in "Documents Relating to the United States and Liberia," 214.

11. Report of the House Committee on Foreign Affairs, 28th Congress, 1st Session, House of Representatives Report 469 (May 4, 1844), quoted in Charles Henry Huberich, *The Political and Legislative History of Liberia*, vol. 1 (New York: Central Book, 1947), 270.

12. Statement of the Board of Managers, Massachusetts Colonization Society, quoted in Huberich, *The Political and Legislative History of Liberia*, 1:272–273.

13. See, e.g., Howard, *American Involvement*, 258.

14. George W. Brown, *The Economic History of Liberia* (Washington, DC: Associated, 1941), 130.

15. Ronald P. Falkner, "The United States and Liberia," *American Journal of International Law* 4, no. 3 (1910): 536.

16. Howard, *American Involvement*, 261.

17. On this point, see especially Falkner, "The United States and Liberia," 539.

18. See "Extract from Report of R. R. Gurley to the Secretary of State," February 15, 1850, in "Documents Relating to the United States and Liberia," 215–217.

19. See Eric Foner, *The Fiery Trial: Abraham Lincoln and American Slavery* (New York: W. W. Norton, 2010), 125–127.

20. Adams to Canning, June 24, 1823, in *BFSP* 11:419.

21. Kenneth Morgan, *Slavery and the British Empire: From Africa to America* (New York: Oxford University Press, 2007), 169, 171.

22. Richard Huzzey, *Freedom Burning: Anti-Slavery and Empire in Victorian Britain* (Ithaca, NY: Cornell University Press, 2012), 41, 51–52.

23. John Quincy Adams, quoted in James E. Lewis Jr., *John Quincy Adams: Policymaker for the Union* (Wilmington, DE: Scholarly Resources, 2001), 90.

24. Hugh G. Soulsby, *The Right of Search and the Slave Trade in Anglo-American Relations, 1814–1862* (Baltimore: Johns Hopkins University Press, 1933), 41.

25. Vaughn to Palmerston, March 28, 1831, in *BFSP* 19:591–593.

26. Vaughn to Palmerston, December 12, 1833, in *BFSP* 23:135–136.

27. Soulsby, *The Right of Search*, 44–45.

28. Vaughn to Palmerston, December 12, 1833.

29. Vaughn to McLane, December 10, 1833, in *BFSP* 23:137. See also Vaughn to McLane, December 25, 1833, in *BFSP* 23:138.

30. McLane to Vaughn, March 24, 1834, in *BFSP* 23:139–140.

31. Palmerston to Vaughn, July 7, 1834, in *BFSP* 23:140–141.

32. Forsyth to Vaughn, October 4, 1834, in *BFSP* 23:146, 147.

33. Jeremy Black, *The Atlantic Slave Trade in World History* (New York: Routledge, 2015), 122.

34. Herbert S. Klein, *The Atlantic Slave Trade* (Cambridge: Cambridge University Press, 2010), 192.

35. Bishop Don Félix Varela, "Memoria que demuestra la necesidad de extinguir la esclavitud de los negros en la isla Cuba," quoted in Eduardo Torres-Cuevas and Eusebio Reyes, *Esclavitud y sociedad: Notas y documentos para la historia de la esclavitud negra en Cuba* (Havana: Editorial de Ciencias Sociales, 1986), 149 (author's translation).

36. Mario Hernández y Sánchez-Barba, "David Turnbull y el problem de la esclavitud en Cuba," *Anuario de estudios Americanos* 14 (1957): 272 (author's translation).

37. Philip S. Foner, *A History of Cuba and Its Relations with the United States*, vol. 1, *1492–1845: From the Conquest of Cuba to La Escalera* (New York: International, 1962), 202–203; Hernández y Sánchez-Barba, "David Turnbull," 273.

38. Foner, *A History of Cuba* 1:205.

39. Matthew Karp, *This Vast Southern Empire: Slaveholders at the Helm of American Foreign Policy* (Cambridge, MA: Harvard University Press, 2018), 63.

40. Arthur F. Corwin, *Spain and the Abolition of Slavery in Cuba, 1817–1886* (Austin: University of Texas Press, 1967), 71.

41. Corwin, *Spain and the Abolition of Slavery*, 70.

42. Palmerston to Stevenson, December 14, 1836, in *BFSP* 25:348–349; Stevenson to Palmerston, December 19, 1836, in *BFSP* 25:349.

43. Don E. Fehrenbacher, *The Slaveholding Republic: An Account of the United States Government's Relations to Slavery* (New York: Oxford University Press, 2001), 164.

44. Palmerston to Fox, April 16, 1839, in *BFSP* 27:758.

45. Palmerston to Fox, July 2, 1839, in *BFSP* 28:912.

46. Fehrenbacher, *The Slaveholding Republic*, 164–165; Stevenson to Palmerston, February 7, 1840, in *BFSP* 28:937.

47. Fox to Forsyth, October 29, 1839, in *BFSP* 28:923–924.

48. Stevenson to Palmerston, February 5, 1840, in *BFSP* 28:933.

49. Forsyth to Fox, February 12, 1840, in *BFSP* 28:942.

50. Soulsby, *The Right of Search*, 51.

51. Stevenson to Palmerston, November 13, 1840, in *BFSP* 29:644, 645; Palmerston to Stevenson, November 19, 1840, in *BFSP* 29:646.

52. Christopher Lloyd, *The Navy and the Slave Trade: The Suppression of the African Slave Trade in the Nineteenth Century* (London: Longmans, Green, 1949), 53; Mark C. Hunter, *Policing the Seas: Anglo-American Relations and the Equatorial Atlantic, 1819–1865* (St. John's, NL: International Maritime Economic History Association, 2008), 128–129.

53. Fehrenbacher, *The Slaveholding Republic*, 166.

54. Soulsby, *The Right of Search*, 107–108.

55. An American [Lewis Cass], *An Examination of the Question, Now in Discussion between the American and British Governments Concerning the Right of Search* (Detroit: n.p., January 1842), 7–8, 13, 21, 77; Willard Carl Klunder, *Lewis Cass and the Politics of Moderation* (Kent, OH: Kent State University Press, 1996), 106.

56. An Englishman [Sir William Gore Ouseley], *Reply to an "American's Examination"* (London: n.p., April 1842), 7–9.

57. Fehrenbacher, *The Slaveholding Republic*, 167–168; Karp, *This Vast Southern Empire*, 26–27.

58. Keith Hamilton and Farida Shaikh, "Introduction," in *Slavery, Diplomacy, and Empire: Britain and the Suppression of the Slave Trade, 1807–1975*, ed. Keith Hamilton and Patrick Salmon (Portland, OR: Sussex Academic, 2009), 10; Andrew Lambert, "Slavery, Free Trade and Naval Strategy, 1840–1860," in Hamilton and Salmon, eds., *Slavery, Diplomacy, and Empire*, 66.

59. Stevenson to Webster, September 18, 1841, in Daniel Webster, *The Papers of Daniel Webster: Diplomatic Papers*, vol. 1, *1841–1843*, ed. Kenneth E. Shewmaker, Kenneth R. Stevens, and Anita McGurn (Hanover, NH: Dartmouth College Press, 1983), 122–123.

60. Ashburton to Aberdeen, April 25, 1842, in *BFSP* 31:708–709; Donald L. Canney, *Africa Squadron: The U.S. Navy and the Slave Trade, 1842–1861* (Washington, DC: Potomac Books, 2006), 31; Fehrenbacher, *The Slaveholding Republic*, 169.

61. Thomas Hart Benton, quoted in Earl E. McNeilly, "The United States Navy and the Suppression of the West African Slave Trade, 1819–1862" (PhD diss., Case Western Reserve University, 1973), 128.

62. Cass to Webster, October 3, 1842, in Webster, *The Papers of Daniel Webster* 1:717–721; Webster to Cass, December 20, 1842, quoted in Soulsby, *The Right of Search*, 113.

63. Soulsby, *The Right of Search*, 114.

64. Soulsby, *The Right of Search*, 118.

65. Canney, *Africa Squadron*, 222–223. See also Gerald Horne, *The Deepest South: The United States, Brazil, and the African Slave Trade* (New York: New York University Press, 2007), 139–142.

66. Pakenham to Calhoun, August 5, 1844, in *BFSP* 33:657.

67. Canney, *Africa Squadron*, 224. Fehrenbacher, *The Slaveholding Republic*, 176, makes this point.

68. Fehrenbacher, *The Slaveholding Republic*, 173, 174.

69. Palmerston to Pakenham, May 13, 1847, in *BFSP* 36:738; Palmerston to Pakenham, June 22, 1847, in *BFSP* 36:738–739.

70. Karp, *This Vast Southern Empire*, 73, 75, 80.

71. Henry A. Wise, quoted in Karp, *This Vast Southern Empire*, 74. For a thorough treatment of Wise and the Brazilian slave trade, see Horne, *The Deepest South*, 67–84.

72. John F. Crampton to Palmerston, June 13, 1847, in *BFSP* 36:740.

73. Fehrenbacher, *The Slaveholding Republic*, 180.

74. Henry Bulwer quoted in Corwin, *Spain and the Abolition of Slavery*, 97.

75. Fehrenbacher, *The Slaveholding Republic*, 183.

76. Corwin, *Spain and the Abolition of Slavery*, 112–113.

77. Soulsby, *The Right of Search*, 140.

78. Clarendon to Napier, September 26, 1857, in *BFSP* 48:1236.

79. Napier to Cass, December 24, 1857, in *BFSP* 48:1244.

80. Soulsby, *The Right of Search*, 140.

81. Cass to Dallas, February 23, 1859, in *BFSP* 49:1119, 1120, 1121.

82. Fehrenbacher, *The Slaveholding Republic*, 187.

83. Lyons to the Earl of Malmsbury, April 30, 1859, in *BFSP* 50:971; Russell to Lyons, in *BFSP* 50:972.

84. Toucey to Inman, in *BFSP* 50:976.

85. Fehrenbacher, *The Slaveholding Republic*, 187.

86. Lyons to Russell, April 5, 1860, in *BFSP* 51:1078–1079.

87. Cass to Lyons, April 8, 1860, in *BFSP* 51:1081.

88. Seward to Lyons, March 22, 1862, in *BFSP* 53:1425; Lyons to Seward, March 22, 1862, in *BFSP* 53:1426.

89. Lyons to Russell, March 28, 1862, in *BFSP* 53:1427; Lyons to Russell, March 31, 1863, in *BFSP* 53:1427–1428.

90. Russell to Lyons, April 17, 1862, in *BFSP* 53:1429; Lyons to Russell, April 25, 1862, in *BFSP* 53:1430.

91. Fehrenbacher, *The Slaveholding Republic*, 189; Howard Jones, *Blue and Gray Diplomacy: A History of Union and Confederate Foreign Relations* (Chapel Hill: University of North Carolina Press, 2010), 122; Soulsby, *The Right of Search*, 175. See also Warren S. Howard, *American Slavers and the Federal Law, 1837–1862* (Berkeley: University of California Press, 1963), 60–61.

92. R[eginald] Coupland, *The British Anti-Slavery Movement* (London: Thornton Butterworth, 1933), 187.

5. "Only Cowards Fear and Oppose It"

1. Walter Nugent, *Habits of Empire: A History of American Expansion* (New York: Alfred A. Knopf, 2008), xvi.

2. Daniel Walker Howe, *What Hath God Wrought: The Transformation of America, 1815–1848* (New York: Oxford University Press, 2007), 705. On slaveholders and the "all-Mexico" movement, see Nugent, *Habits of Empire*, 208.

3. Matthew Karp, *This Vast Southern Empire: Slaveholders at the Helm of American Foreign Policy* (Cambridge, MA: Harvard University Press, 2018), 4.

4. Randolph B. Campbell, *An Empire for Slavery: The Peculiar Institution in Texas, 1821–1865* (Baton Rouge: Louisiana State University Press, 1989), 2–3; Randolph B. Campbell, *Gone to Texas: A History of the Lone Star State* (New York: Oxford University Press, 2003), 132 (capitalization in the original). See also Lester D. Langley, "Slavery, Reform, and American Policy, 1823–1878," *Revista de Historia de América* 65–66 (1968): 71.

5. Campbell, *Gone to Texas*, 162–164.

6. Don E. Fehrenbacher, *The Slaveholding Republic: An Account of the United States Government's Relations to Slavery* (New York: Oxford University Press, 2001), 119.

7. Fehrenbacher, *The Slaveholding Republic*, 120. See also Thomas R. Hietala, *Manifest Design: Anxious Aggrandizement in Late Jacksonian America* (Ithaca, NY: Cornell University Press, 1985), 6.

8. Fehrenbacher, *The Slaveholding Republic*, 120. On Tyler's alienation from the Whig Party, see Norma Lois Peterson, *The Presidencies of William Henry Harrison and John Tyler* (Lawrence: University Press of Kansas, 1989), 89–90.

9. Fehrenbacher, *The Slaveholding Republic*, 120; Peterson, *The Presidencies*, 176.

10. Karp, *This Vast Southern Empire*, 86–87.

11. Lelia M. Roeckell, "Bonds over Bondage: British Opposition to American Annexation of Texas," *Journal of the Early Republic* 19, no. 2 (1999): 262.

12. David M. Pletcher, *The Diplomacy of Annexation: Texas, Oregon, and the Mexican War* (Columbia: University of Missouri Press, 1973), 122.

13. Frederick Merk, *Slavery and the Annexation of Texas* (New York: Alfred A. Knopf, 1972), x.

14. Upshur to Everett, September 28, 1843, in *Diplomatic Correspondence of the United States: Inter-American Affairs, 1831–1860*, ed. William R. Manning, 12 vols., vol. 7 (Washington, DC: Carnegie Endowment for International Peace, 1932–1939) (hereafter *DCUS*), 6, 7, 8.

15. John Niven, *John Calhoun and the Price of Union: A Biography* (Baton Rouge: Louisiana State University Press, 1988), 272.

16. Upshur to Everett, September 28, 1843, in *DCUS* 7:9.

17. Upshur to Everett, September 28, 1843, in *DCUS* 7:11–12.

18. See, e.g., Hietala, *Manifest Design*, 22.

19. See Merk, *Slavery and the Annexation of Texas*, 11.

20. Upshur to William S. Murphy, August 8, 1843, in *DCUS* 12:49.

21. Upshur to N. Beverley Tucker, August 7, 1841, quoted in Merk, *Slavery and the Annexation of Texas*, 18 (and see generally 17).

22. Merk, *Slavery and the Annexation of Texas*, 17.

23. Upshur to Van Zandt, October, 1843, quoted in *The Letters and Times of the Tylers*, vol. 2, ed. Lyon G. Tyler (New York: Da Capo Press, 1970), 284. See also Campbell, *Gone to Texas*, 183; and Peterson, *The Presidencies*, 193.

24. Aberdeen to Pakenham, December 26, 1843, in *BFSP* 33:232–233. The discussion of Tyler's stance at this time relies on Peterson, *The Presidencies*, 191–193.

25. Tyler to Mary Tyler-Jones, in Tyler, *Letters* 2:289.

26. Peterson, *The Presidencies*, 205.

27. Niven, *John Calhoun and the Price of Union*, 269.

28. Calhoun to Pakenham, April 18, 1844, in *BFSP* 33: 237–238.

29. Peterson, *The Presidencies*, 205.

30. Calhoun to Pakenham, April 18, 1844, in *BFSP* 33:238, 239, 240.

31. Sydney Nathans, "The Southern Connection: Slaveholders and Antebellum Expansion," *Reviews in American History* 1, no. 3 (1973): 394 (emphasis in the original); Pakenham to Calhoun, April 19, 1844, in *BFSP* 33:241. See also Christopher J. Leahy, *President without a Party: The Life of John Tyler* (Baton Rouge: Louisiana State University Press, 2020), 329–330.

32. William W. Freehling, *The Road to Disunion*, vol. 1, *Secessionists at Bay, 1776–1854* (New York: Oxford University Press, 1990), 410–411.

33. Thomas Hart Benton, *Thirty Years' View, or, A History of the Working of the American Government for Thirty Years, from 1820 to 1850*, vol. 2 (New York: D. Appleton, 1856), 619–620.

34. Clay to the Editors of the National Intelligencer, April 17, 1844, in *Letters of Messrs. Clay, Benton, and Barrow on the Subject of the Annexation of Texas to the United States* (Pamphlet: n.p.), 1–5.

35. William S. Archer, quoted in Merk, *Slavery and the Annexation of Texas*, 80 (and see, generally, 77–82).

36. Fehrenbacher, *The Slaveholding Republic*, 124.

37. Peterson, *The Presidencies*, 255.

38. William J. Cooper Jr., *The South and the Politics of Slavery, 1826–1856* (Baton Rouge: Louisiana State University Press, 1978), 221.

39. Fehrenbacher, *The Slaveholding Republic*, 125; Campbell, *Gone to Texas*, 185–186.

40. Fehrenbacher, *The Slaveholding Republic*, 118, 126.

41. Karp, *This Vast Southern Empire*, 100.

42. Philip S. Foner, *A History of Cuba and Its Relations with the United States*, vol. 1, *1492–1845: From the Conquest of Cuba to La Escalera* (New York: International, 1962), 9.

43. Ofalia to Eaton, February 22, 1838, in *DCUS* 11:307–309; Eaton to Ofalia, in *DCUS* 11:310–313.

44. Karp, *This Vast Southern Empire*, 59.

45. Fehrenbacher, *The Slaveholding Republic*, 128.

46. Foner, *A History of Cuba* 1:10.

47. Eduardo Torres-Cuevas and Eusebio Reyes, *Esclavitud y Sociedad: Notas y documentos para la historia de la esclavitud negra en Cuba* (Havana: Editorial de Ciencias Sociales, 1986), 202 (author's translation).

48. Karp, *This Vast Southern Empire*, 66.

49. Webster to Robert B. Campbell, January 14, 1843, *DCUS* 11:26, 27, 28, 29 (emphasis in the original). See also Jerónimo Bécker, *Historia de las relaciones exteriores de España durante el siglo XIX*, vol. 2 (Madrid: Establecimiento Tipográfico de Jaimie Ratés, 1924), 56–57.

50. Robert L. Paquette, "The Everett–Del Monte Connection: A Study in the International Politics of Slavery," *Diplomatic History* 11, no. 1 (1987): 13.

51. Bécker, *Historia de las relaciones exteriores* 2:71 (author's translation).

52. James K. Polk, *The Diary of James K. Polk*, vol. 3, ed. Milo Milton Quaife (Chicago: A. C. McClurg, 1910), 446.

53. See, e.g., Fehrenbacher, *The Slaveholding Republic*, 128.

54. Buchanan to Robert B. Campbell, June 9, 1848, in *DCUS* 11:53.

55. Bécker, *Historia de las relaciones exteriores* 2:78 (author's translation).

56. Robert E. May, *Manifest Destiny's Underworld: Filibustering in Antebellum America* (Chapel Hill: University of North Carolina Press, 2002), 111.

57. George C. Herring, *From Colony to Superpower: U.S. Foreign Relations since 1776* (New York: Oxford University Press, 2008), 217.

58. Tom Chaffin, "'Sons of Washington': Narciso López, Filibustering, and U.S. Nationalism, 1848–1851," *Journal of the Early Republic* 15, no. 1 (1995): 79–108; May, *Manifest Destiny's Underworld*, 111.

59. Bécker, *Historia de las relaciones exteriores* 2:79 (author's translation). See also Elbert B. Smith, *The Presidencies of Zachary Taylor and Millard Fillmore* (Lawrence: University Press of Kansas, 1988), 86–89.

60. See Herminio Portell Vilá, *Narciso López y su época*, vol. 3 (Havana: Compañia Editora de Libros y Folletos O'Reilly, 1958), 37–38. For a more positive assessment of Fillmore's policy toward Cuba and the filibusters, see Lester D. Langley, "The Whigs and the Lopez Expeditions to Cuba, 1849–1851: A Chapter in Frustrating Diplomacy," *Revista de Historia de América* 71 (1971): 9–22.

61. See, e.g., H. Barrett Learned, "William Learned Marcy," in *American Secretaries of State and Their Diplomacy*, vol. 6, ed. Samuel Flagg Bemis (New York: Pageant, 1958), 84–85. On Spain's encouragement of a tripartite "abnegatory declaration," see Howden to Earl Granville, January 9, 1852, in *BFSP* 44:114. On the connection of the proposed agreement with filibustering, see especially May, *Manifest Destiny's Underworld*, 230. On the Whigs' "gradualist strategy" regarding expansion at this time, see Douglas Arthur Ley, "Expansionists All? Southern Senators and American Foreign Policy, 1841–1860" (PhD diss., University of Wisconsin–Madison, 1990), 219; and, especially, Matthew Mason, *Apostle of Union: A Political Biography of Edward Everett* (Chapel Hill: University of North Carolina Press, 2016), 189–192.

62. Government of Spain, Royal Decree [Real orden], September 16, 1851, quoted in Bécker, *Historia de las relaciones exteriores* 2:230 (author's translation).

63. Piero Gleijeses, "Clashing over Cuba: The United States, Spain, and Britain, 1853–1855," *Journal of Latin American Studies* 49, no. 2 (2016): 224; Herminio Portell Vilá, *Historía de Cuba en sus relaciones con los Estados Unidos y España*, vol. 2 (Havana: Biblioteca de Historia Filosophía y Sociología, 1939), 9 (author's translation).

64. Robert E. May, *The Southern Dream of a Caribbean Empire, 1854–1861* (Baton Rouge: Louisiana State University Press, 1973), 9.

65. Karp, *This Vast Southern Empire*, 188.

66. Perry to Pierce, January 10, 1853, in *DCUS* 9:685–686. On France's position regarding the transference of Cuba to another maritime power during Fillmore's administration, see Bécker, *Historia de las relaciones exteriores* 2:229.

67. Perry to Pierce, January 10, 1853, in *DCUS* 9:690 (emphasis in the original).

68. Gleijeses, "Clashing over Cuba," 224.

69. Learned, "William Learned Marcy," 187. On Marcy's selection for secretary of state, see Karp, *This Vast Southern Empire*, 189. On Marcy's policy preferences for Cuba, see Learned, "William Learned Marcy," 184–187.

70. On this point, see Karp, *This Vast Southern Empire*, 189.

71. Portell Vilá, *Historía de Cuba* 2:20 (author's translation).

72. Jennifer R. Green and Patrick M. Kirkwood, "Reframing the Antebellum Democratic Mainstream: Transatlantic Diplomacy and the Career of Pierre Soulé," *Civil War History* 61, no. 3 (2015): 218.

73. May, *The Southern Dream*, 41–42.

74. Karp, *This Vast Southern Empire*, 4.

75. Karp, *This Vast Southern Empire*, 3.

76. May, *The Southern Dream*, 10–11 (and see, generally, 10–12).

77. May, *The Southern Dream*, 11; Gleijeses, "Clashing over Cuba," 217.

78. Palmerston to Howden, July 18, 1851, quoted in Amos Aschbach Ettinger, *The Mission to Spain of Pierre Soulé, 1853–1855: A Study in the Cuban Diplomacy of the*

United States (New Haven, CT: Yale University Press, 1932), 43; Ettinger, *The Mission to Spain*, 4.

79. Karp, *This Vast Southern Empire*, 16.

80. Karp, *This Vast Southern Empire*, 185.

81. May, *The Southern Dream*, 22.

82. "Extract from the *National Intelligencer*, of November 25, 1852," in *BFSP* 44:212.

83. The speech is analyzed in depth in Ettinger, *The Mission to Spain*, 98–100.

84. Catherine Chancerel, *L'homme du Grand Fleuve* (Paris: CNRS Éditions, 2015), 320 (author's translation).

85. Portell Vilá, *Historia de Cuba* 2:272–273.

86. This discussion relies upon Portell Vilá, *Historia de Cuba* 2:274–275. See also Gleijeses, "Clashing over Cuba," 222.

87. Green and Kirkwood, "Reframing the Antebellum Democratic Mainstream," 212–213.

88. For background on the Africanization scare, see, e.g., C. Stanley Urban, "The Africanization of Cuba Scare, 1853–1855," *Hispanic American Historical Review* 37, no. 1 (1957): 30–32.

89. Russell to Howden, January 31, 1853, in *BFSP* 44:335.

90. Portell Vilá, *Historia de Cuba* 2:18 (author's translation).

91. Philip S. Foner, *A History of Cuba and Its Relations with the United States*, vol. 2, *1845–1895: From the Era of Annexation to the Beginning of the Second War for Independence* (New York: International, 1963), 76. See also Gleijeses, "Clashing over Cuba," 225.

92. Foner, *A History of Cuba* 2:77.

93. Urban, "The Africanization of Cuba Scare," 34.

94. "Latest Intelligence: England, France and Spain joined in the scheme to Africanize Cuba," *New York Daily Times*, October 25, 1853, 1.

95. Soulé to Marcy, December 23, 1853, in *DCUS* 11:732–733.

96. Soulé to Marcy, January 20, 1854, in *DCUS* 11:735–736.

97. "Important from Cuba," *New York Daily Times*, January 14, 1854, 2.

98. James Buchanan, "To Mr. Marcy (No. 14)," in *The Works of James Buchanan*, vol. 9, ed. John Bassett Moore (Philadelphia: J. B. Lippincott, 1909), 84.

99. Portell Vilá, *Historia de Cuba* 2:35 (author's translation).

100. See, e.g., Learned, William Learned Marcy," 187.

101. Marcy to Soulé, April 3, 1854, in *DCUS* 11:175, 176.

102. Marcy to Soulé, April 3, 1854, *DCUS* 11:176–177.

103. May, *The Southern Dream*, 54.

104. See May, *The Southern Dream*, 54; and Karp, *This Vast Southern Empire*, 193.

105. Marcy to Robertson, April 8, 1854, in *DCUS* 11:178.

106. May, *The Southern Dream*, 59.

107. Bécker, *Historia de las relaciones exteriores* 2:302 (author's translation).

108. Marqués de Viluma to the Minister of State (Luis José Sartorius), April 20, 1854, quoted in Bécker, *Historia de las relaciones exteriores* 2:302 (author's translation).

109. Alan Dowty, *The Limits of American Isolation: The United States and the Crimean War* (New York: New York University Press, 1971), 117.

110. Dowty, *The Limits of American Isolation*, 114.

111. Seibels to Marcy, December 13, 1854, quoted in Portell Vilá, *Historia de Cuba* 2:87 (author's translation).

112. Dowty, *The Limits of American Isolation*, 118.

113. Robertson to Marcy, June 27, 1854, in *DCUS* 11:797.

114. For a discussion of the *Black Warrior* Affair in connection with the Crimean War, see Dowty, *The Limits of American Isolation*, 113–118; and Gleijeses, "Clashing over Cuba," 228–229.

115. See Soulé to Marcy, July 15, 1854, in *DCUS* 11:798–799.

116. Foner, *A History of Cuba* 2:99.

117. Ettinger, *The Mission to Spain*, 342.

118. Karp, *This Vast Southern Empire*, 197. The literature on the Ostend Conference is extensive. For a full treatment, see Ettinger, *The Mission to Spain*, 339–412; see also John Ashworth, *Slavery, Capitalism, and Politics in the Antebellum Republic*, vol. 2, *The Coming of the Civil War, 1850–1861* (New York: Cambridge University Press, 2007), 395–398.

119. *Ostend Manifesto*, quoted in Ettinger, *The Mission to Spain*, 362, 363, 364.

120. See James Morton Callahan, *Cuba in International Relations: A Historical Study in American Diplomacy* (Baltimore: Johns Hopkins University Press, 1899), 298. See also May, *The Southern Dream*, 72; and Ashworth, *Slavery, Capitalism, and Politics*, 398.

121. Foner, *A History of Cuba* 2:103–104. May, *The Southern Dream*, 70.

122. See Portell Vilá, *Historía de Cuba* 2:89.

123. Gleijeses, "Clashing over Cuba," 229.

124. Portell Vilá, *Historía de Cuba* 2:96 (and see, generally, 96–98) (author's translation). On Pezuela and the arming of Cuban Blacks, see especially Gleijeses, "Clashing over Cuba," 226–227.

125. Gleijeses, "Clashing over Cuba," 235–236.

126. Callahan, *Cuba in International Relations*, 304.

127. Portell Vilá, *Historía de Cuba* 2:119 (author's translation).

128. Portell Vilá, *Historía de Cuba* 2:120 (author's translation).

129. *Congressional Globe*, Senate, 35th Congress, 2nd Session (1859), 905.

130. *Congressional Globe*, Senate, 35th Congress, 2nd Session (1859), 904.

131. *Congressional Globe*, Senate, 35th Congress, 2nd Session (1859), 907.

132. Substance of a statement made by Gabriel García Tassara to Lewis Cass, December 11, 1858, in *DCUS* 11:961.

133. Langley, "Slavery, Reform, and American Policy," 71.

6. "Its Peculiar Moral Force"

1. Howard Jones, *Abraham Lincoln and a New Birth of Freedom: The Union and Slavery in the Diplomacy of the Civil War* (Lincoln: University of Nebraska Press, 1999), 2. On the "nation-bound" historiography of the American Civil War, see especially Don H. Doyle, "Introduction: The Atlantic World and the Crisis of the 1860s," in *American Civil Wars: The United States, Latin America, Europe, and the Crisis of the 1860s*, ed. Don H. Doyle (Chapel Hill: University of North Carolina Press, 2017), 1.

2. R. J. M. Blackett, *Divided Hearts: Britain and the American Civil War* (Baton Rouge: Louisiana State University Press, 2001).

3. See Stève Sainlaude, *France and the American Civil War: A Diplomatic History*, trans. Jessica Edwards (Chapel Hill: University of North Carolina Press, 2019); Stève Sainlaude, *La gouvernment imperial et la guerre de Sécession (1861–1865): L'action diplomatique*

(Paris: L'Harmattan, 2011), and Stève Sainlaude, *La France et la Confédération sudiste (1861–1865): La question de la reconnaissance diplomatique pendant la guerre de Sécession* (Paris: L'Harmattan, 2011).

4. Wayne H. Bowen, *Spain and the American Civil War* (Columbia: University of Missouri Press, 2011).

5. Howard Jones, *Blue and Gray Diplomacy: A History of Union and Confederate Foreign Relations* (Chapel Hill: University of North Carolina Press, 2010).

6. See especially Don H. Doyle, *The Cause of All Nations: An International History of the American Civil War* (New York: Basic Books, 2015); and David T. Gleeson and Simon Lewis, eds., *The Civil War as Global Conflict: Transnational Meanings of the American Civil War* (Columbia: University of South Carolina Press, 2014).

7. Jay Sexton, *Debtor Diplomacy: Finance and American Foreign Relations in the Civil War Era 1837–1873* (Oxford: Clarendon, 2005).

8. See especially Michael Burlingame, *Abraham Lincoln: A Life*, vol. 2 (Baltimore: Johns Hopkins University Press, 2008). See also Joseph A. Fry, *Lincoln, Seward, and US Foreign Relations in the Civil War* (Lexington: University Press of Kentucky, 2019).

9. Allan Nevins, quoted in Jones, *Abraham Lincoln and a New Birth of Freedom*, 3.

10. Jones, *Blue and Gray Diplomacy*, 11.

11. Fry, *Lincoln, Seward, and US Foreign Relations*, 53. On Seward's early presumptuousness, see, e.g., Doyle, *The Cause*, 61–62. See also Burlingame, *Abraham Lincoln: A Life* 2:117–119.

12. Carl Schurz, quoted in Fry, *Lincoln, Seward, and US Foreign Relations*, 54.

13. Robert E. May, "Introduction," in *The Union, the Confederacy, and the Atlantic Rim*, rev. ed., ed. Robert E. May (Gainesville: University Press of Florida, 2013), 28.

14. Adams to Seward, January 17, 1862, in *Message of the President of the United States to the Two Houses of Congress at the Commencement of the Thirty-Seventh Congress, 1862*, vol. 1 (Washington, DC: G.P.O., 1862), 16.

15. Harriet Beecher Stowe, "A Reply," in *The Real War Will Never Get in the Books*, ed. Louis P. Masur (New York: Oxford University Press, 1993), 239.

16. Eric Foner, *The Fiery Trial: Abraham Lincoln and American Slavery* (New York: W. W. Norton, 2010), 132.

17. Don E. Fehrenbacher, *The Slaveholding Republic: An Account of the United States Government's Relations to Slavery* (New York: Oxford University Press, 2001), 133.

18. Foner, *The Fiery Trial*, 144.

19. Matthew Karp, *This Vast Southern Empire: Slaveholders at the Helm of American Foreign Policy* (Cambridge, MA: Harvard University Press, 2018), 5.

20. Kinley J. Brauer, "The Slavery Problem in the Diplomacy of the American Civil War," *Pacific Historical Review* 46, no. 3 (1977): 447.

21. Fry, *Lincoln, Seward, and US Foreign Relations*, 53.

22. Jones, *Blue and Gray Diplomacy*, 28–29.

23. Blackett, *Divided Hearts*, 75.

24. Jones, *Blue and Gray Diplomacy*, 36. On this point, see also Martin Crawford, *The Anglo-American Crisis of the Mid-Nineteenth Century: The Times and America, 1850–1862* (Athens: University of Georgia Press, 1987), 126.

25. Charles S. Campbell, *From Revolution to Rapprochement: The United States and Great Britain, 1783–1900* (New York: John Wiley and Sons, 1974), 96.

26. Fry, *Lincoln, Seward, and US Foreign Relations*, 54.

27. Jones, *Abraham Lincoln and a New Birth of Freedom*, 15.

28. Fry, *Lincoln, Seward, and US Foreign Relations*, 54.

29. Serge Gavronsky, *The French Liberal Opposition and the American Civil War* (New York: Humanities Press, 1968), 88–89.

30. George M. Blackburn, *French Newspaper Opinion on the American Civil War* (Westport, CT: Greenwood, 1997), 30.

31. Paul Pecquet du Bellet, *The Diplomacy of the Confederate Cabinet of Richmond and Its Agents Abroad: Being Memorandum Notes Taken in Paris during the Rebellion of the Southern States from 1861–1865*, ed. William Stanley Hoole (Tuscaloosa, AL: Confederate Publishing, 1963), 39–40. On efforts to found a newspaper supportive of the Confederacy, see, e.g., Sainlaude, *France and the American Civil War*, 81.

32. Jones, *Blue and Gray Diplomacy*, 21.

33. Sainlaude, *France and the American Civil War*, xiii, 100.

34. Gavronsky, *The French Liberal Opposition*, 42.

35. Gavronsky, *The French Liberal Opposition*, 88.

36. On Davis's inapt diplomatic appointments, see, e.g., Jones, *Blue and Gray Diplomacy*, 84–86.

37. Jones, *Blue and Gray Diplomacy*, 12, 13.

38. Sainlaude, *France and the American Civil War*, 141.

39. Jones, *Blue and Gray Diplomacy*, 12.

40. Jones, *Blue and Gray Diplomacy*, 323.

41. Doyle, *Cause of All Nations*, 39. See also Crawford, *The Anglo-American Crisis*, 126–127.

42. Eli N. Evans, *Judah P. Benjamin: The Jewish Confederate* (New York: Free Press, 1988), 185.

43. Michael Burlingame, *Abraham Lincoln: A Life*, vol. 1 (Baltimore: Johns Hopkins University Press, 2008), 701.

44. Foner, *The Fiery Trial*, 157–158.

45. Donald Jordan and Edwin J. Pratt, *Europe and the American Civil War* (Boston: Houghton Mifflin, 1931), 130.

46. Jones, *Abraham Lincoln and a New Birth of Freedom*, 36–37.

47. Fry, *Lincoln, Seward, and US Foreign Relations*, 48.

48. Sainlaude, *La France et la Confédération sudiste*, 109.

49. Sainlaude, *France and the American Civil War*, 107.

50. Sainlaude, *France and the American Civil War*, 107, 108.

51. Sainlaude, *La France et la Confédération sudiste*, 191 (author's translation). On Franco-Confederate relations and Mexico, see Sainlaude, *France and the American Civil War*, 110–125.

52. Sainlaude, *La France et la Confédération sudiste*, 195 (author's translation).

53. R. M. T. Hunter, quoted in Bowen, *Spain and the American Civil War*, 78.

54. Doyle, *Cause of All Nations*, 113.

55. Bowen, *Spain and the American Civil War*, 63.

56. Bowen, *Spain and the American Civil War*, 140.

57. Duncan Andrew Campbell, *English Public Opinion and the American Civil War* (Woodbridge, UK: Royal Historical Society / Boydell, 2003), 28–29; D. P. Crook, *The*

North, the South, and the Powers, 1861–1865 (New York: John Wiley and Sons, 1974), 35. See also Jones, *Blue and Gray Diplomacy*, 22.

58. Blackett, *Divided Hearts*, 168.

59. Jay Sexton, "Sexton on Campbell, 'English Public Opinion and the American Civil War'" (review), January 2005, https://networks.h-net.org/node/4113/reviews/4639/sexton-campbell-english-public-opinion-and-american-civil-war.

60. David Brown, *Palmerston: A Biography* (New Haven, CT: Yale University Press, 2010), 451 (emphasis in the original).

61. Campbell, *English Public Opinion*, 10.

62. Doyle, *The Cause of All Nations*, 61–62.

63. Fry, *Lincoln, Seward, and US Foreign Relations*, 41.

64. On this point, see, e.g., Dean B. Mahin, *One War at a Time: The International Dimensions of the American Civil War* (Washington, DC: Brassey's, 1999), 7–8.

65. Jones, *Blue and Gray Diplomacy*, 24.

66. Jones, *Blue and Gray Diplomacy*, 24; Mahin, *One War at a Time*, 8; Campbell, *English Public Opinion*, 31. On Seward's strategy as brinkmanship, see Crook, *The North, the South, and the Powers*, 63.

67. Crook, *The North, the South, and the Powers*, 63.

68. This summary of the *Trent* Affair follows the brief treatment in Howard Jones, "The *Trent* Affair," in *Encyclopedia of U.S. Foreign Relations*, vol. 4, ed. Bruce W. Jentleson, Thomas G. Paterson, and Nicholas X. Rizopoulos (New York: Oxford University Press, 1997), 206–207. For an extended discussion, see Howard Jones, *Union in Peril: The Crisis over British Intervention in the Civil War* (Lincoln: University of Nebraska Press, 1997); and Fry, *Lincoln, Seward, and US Foreign Relations*, 66–77.

69. Fry, *Lincoln, Seward, and US Foreign Relations*, 75.

70. Doyle, *The Cause of All Nations*, 81.

71. Jordan and Pratt, *Europe and the American Civil War*, 43.

72. Blackett *Divided Hearts*, 61, 21, 18.

73. Jones, *Abraham Lincoln and a New Birth of Freedom*, 39.

74. Carl Schurz, quoted in Burlingame, *Abraham Lincoln: A Life* 2:333.

75. Burlingame, *Abraham Lincoln: A Life* 2:351.

76. "Thunderer," *Times* (London), April 16, 1862, quoted in Burlingame, *Abraham Lincoln: A Life* 2:346.

77. For a useful, if overly literary, treatment of Clay's conversion to abolitionism, see H. Edward Richardson, *Cassius Marcellus Clay: Firebrand of Freedom* (Lexington: University Press of Kentucky, 1976), 21–24.

78. Richardson, *Cassius Marcellus Clay*, 91; R. F. Ivanov, *Diplomatiia Avraama Linkol'na* (Moscow: Mezhdunarodnie Otnosheniia, 1987), 167–168 (author's translation); John Motley, quoted in Walter Stahr, *Seward: Lincoln's Indispensable Man* (New York: Simon & Schuster, 2012), 346.

79. Seward to Adams, October 18, 1862, in *Message of the President* 1:212.

80. Howard Jones, "History and Mythology: The Crisis over British Intervention in the Civil War," in May, ed., *The Union, the Confederacy, and the Atlantic Rim*, 57.

81. Jones, *Blue and Gray Diplomacy*, 234, 235.

82. James M. McPherson, *Crossroads of Freedom: Antietam* (New York: Oxford University Press, 2002), 143.

83. See, e.g., Jones, *Blue and Gray Diplomacy*, 49; and Jones, *Abraham Lincoln and a New Birth of Freedom*, 48.

84. Joseph P. Reidy, "Armed Slaves and the Struggle for Republican Liberty in the U.S. Civil War," in *Arming Slaves: From Classical Times to the Modern Age*, ed. Christopher Leslie Brown and Philip D. Morgan (New Haven, CT: Yale University Press, 2006), 274.

85. J. A. Hobson, *Richard Cobden: The International Man* (London: T. Fisher Unwin, 1918), 377.

86. Fry, *Lincoln, Seward, and US Foreign Relations*, 107.

87. Quoted in Jones, *Abraham Lincoln and a New Birth of Freedom*, 116.

88. Quoted in Campbell, *English Public Opinion*, 131.

89. Fry, *Lincoln, Seward, and US Foreign Relations*, 107.

90. Lincoln to Speed, August 24, 1855, in Abraham Lincoln, *Speeches and Writings: 1832–1858*, ed. Don E. Fehrenbacher (New York: Literary Classics of the United States, 1989), 363.

91. *Sankt-Peterburgskie Vedomosti*, January 12, 1863.

92. *Sankt-Peterburgskie Vedomosti*, January 12, 1863.

93. See Jones, *Abraham Lincoln and a New Birth of Freedom*, 69.

94. *Sankt-Peterburgskie Vedomosti*, January 12, 1863.

95. *Sankt-Peterburgskie Vedomosti*, January 12, 1863.

96. *Sankt-Peterburgskie Vedomosti*, April 6, 1863, 1.

97. For a brief but insightful contrast of the liberation the American slaves and the Russian serfs, see Peter Kolchin, *Unfree Labor: American Slavery and Russian Serfdom* (Cambridge, MA: Belknap, 1987), 373–375. On *Sovremennik* and the liberation of the serfs, see Roxanne Easley, *The Emancipation of the Serfs in Russia: The Peace Arbitrators and Civil Society* (New York: Routledge, 2009), 159.

98. *Sovremennik* 44, no. 2 (1863): 333.

99. *Sovremennik* 44, no. 2 (1863): 336.

100. *Sovremennik* 44, no. 2 (1863): 338.

101. *Sovremennik* 44, no. 2 (1863): 340.

102. *Sovremennik* 44, no. 2 (1863): 341.

103. *Sovremennik* 44, no. 2 (1863): 343.

104. *Sovremennik* 44, no. 2 (1863): 347.

105. *Sovremennik* 44, no. 2 (1863): 348.

106. Édouard de Stoeckl to Alexander Gorchakov, February 10, 1863, Stoeckl Correspondence, Records of the Ministerstva Inostrannykh del, 1783–1868, Manuscript Division, Library of Congress, Washington, DC.

107. For a brief treatment of this subject, see Ivanov, *Diplomatiia Avraama Linkol'na*, 204–205.

108. *Sovremennik* 44, no. 2 (1863): 349.

109. See Howard Jones, "Wrapping the World in Fire: The Interventionist Crisis in the Civil War," in Doyle, ed., *American Civil Wars*, 51.

110. See Michael J. Douma, "The Lincoln Administration's Negotiations to Colonize African Americans in Dutch Suriname," *Civil War History* 61, no. 2 (2015): 111–137; Robert E. May, *Slavery, Race, and Conquest in the Tropics: Lincoln, Douglas, and the Future of Latin America* (New York: Cambridge University Press, 2013), esp. 268; and Phillip W. Magness and Sebastian N. Page, *Colonization after Emancipation: Lincoln and the Movement for Black Resettlement* (Columbia: University of Missouri Press, 2011).

111. See especially Allen C. Guelzo, review of Magness and Page, *Colonization after Emancipation*, *Journal of the Abraham Lincoln Association* 34, no. 1 (2013): 78–87.

112. For an extended treatment of Lincoln and the Panama scheme, see Paul J. Scheips, "Lincoln and the Chiriqi Colonization Project," *Journal of Negro History* 37, no. 4 (1952): 418–453; and May, *Slavery, Race, and Conquest*, esp. 255–267.

113. Magness and Page, *Colonization after Emancipation*, 4–5.

114. Burlingame, *Abraham Lincoln: A Life* 2:396.

115. May, *Slavery, Race, and Conquest*, 270.

116. May, *Slavery, Race, and Conquest*, 10.

117. Lyons to Russell, December 26, 1862, in *The American Civil War through British Eyes: Dispatches from British Diplomats*, vol. 2, *April 1862–February 1863*, ed. James J. Barnes and Patience P. Barnes (Kent, OH: Kent State University Press, 2005), 277–278. On Seward's distaste for colonization, see Magness and Page, *Colonization after Emancipation*, 15–16; and May, *Slavery, Race, and Conquest*, 261. See also Paul D. Escott, *Lincoln's Dilemma: Blair, Sumner, and the Struggle over Racism and Equality in the Civil War Era* (Charlottesville: University of Virginia Press, 2014), 190.

118. Sumner to John Bright, October 28, 1862, in Charles Sumner, *The Selected Letters of Charles Sumner*, ed. Beverly Wilson Palmer (Boston: Northeastern University Press, 1990), 128.

119. Seward to Lyons in Barnes and Barnes, ed., *The American Civil War*, 278–279.

120. Lyons to Russell in Barnes and Barnes, ed., *The American Civil War*, 280.

121. Magness and Page, *Colonization after Emancipation*, 21–22.

122. See J. P. Siwpersad, *De Nederlandse regering en de afschaffing van de Surinaamse slavernij, 1833–1863* (Groningen, Netherlands: Bouma's Boekhuis, 1979), 268.

123. Karwan Fatah-Black, *Eigendomsstrijd: De geschiedenis van slavernij en emancipatie in Suriname* (Amsterdam: Ambo / Anthos, 2018), 163–164.

124. Douma, "The Lincoln Administration's Negotiations," 118.

125. G. H. Uhlenbeck to Sombreff, June 25, 1862, in Michael Douma, "Archival Sources Relating to the U.S.-Dutch Negotiations to Colonize Freed African Americans in Suriname, 1860–1866" (unpublished manuscript). Douma has shared his transcriptions and translations of these documents with me, and I gratefully acknowledge his generosity. Any changes from his translations, and thus any errors, are my own. For the published documents, see Michael J. Douma, *The Colonization of Freed African Americans in Suriname: Archival Sources Relating to the U.S.-Dutch Negotiations, 1860–1866* (Leiden: Leiden University Press, 2019).

126. Sombreff to Roest van Limburg, July 1, 1862, and Roest van Limburg to Seward, July 19, 1862, in Douma, "Archival Sources" (manuscript).

127. Seward to Roest van Limburg, July 22, 1862, in Douma, "Archival Sources" (manuscript). See also Robert Franklin Durden, *James Shepherd Pike: Republicanism and the American Negro, 1850–1882* (Durham, NC: Duke University Press, 1957), 87.

128. Roest Van Limburg to Caleb Smith, September 19, 1862, and Roest van Limburg to Sombreff, September 25, 1862, in Douma, "Archival Sources" (manuscript).

129. Pike to Sombreff, October 31, 1862, in Douma, "Archival Sources" (manuscript).

130. Van Limburg to Sombreff, June 22, 1863, in Douma, "Archival Sources" (manuscript).

131. Seward to Pike, February 15, 1864, in Douma, "Archival Sources" (manuscript).

132. Durden, *James Shepherd Pike*, 92.

133. Magness and Page, 34, 37.

134. Durden, *James Shepherd Pike*, 93.

135. Douma, "The Lincoln Administration's Negotiations," 135.

136. Guelzo, review of Magness and Page, 87.

Epilogue

1. On Adams's complicated relationship with slavery, see Charles N. Edel, *Nation Builder: John Quincy Adams and the Grand Strategy of the Republic* (Cambridge, MA: Harvard University Press, 2014), 155–159.

2. Don E. Fehrenbacher, *The Slaveholding Republic: An Account of the United States Government's Relations to Slavery* (New York: Oxford University Press, 2001), 133.

3. George C. Herring, *From Colony to Superpower: U.S. Foreign Relations since 1776* (New York: Oxford University Press, 2008), 264–265, 271.

4. On this point, see Daniel Immerwahr, *How to Hide an Empire: A Short History of the Greater United States* (New York: Picador, 2019), 11–12; and Walter LaFeber, *The New Cambridge History of American Foreign Relations*, vol. 2, *The American Search for Opportunity, 1865–1913* (New York: Cambridge University Press, 2013), 48. For an analysis of the role of definitions of race in the shaping of American foreign relations, see especially Michael H. Hunt, *Ideology and U.S. Foreign Policy* (New Haven, CT: Yale University Press, 1987), 46–91.

5. Hunt, *Ideology and U.S. Foreign Policy*, 48 (and see, generally, 46–91).

6. Hunt, *Ideology and U.S. Foreign Policy*, 91.

7. See, e.g., Hunt, *Ideology and U.S. Foreign Policy*, 91.

8. Woodrow Wilson, quoted in John Milton Cooper Jr., *Woodrow Wilson: A Biography* (New York: Vintage Books, 2009), 25.

9. Margaret MacMillan, *Paris 1919: Six Months That Changed the World* (New York: Random House, 2002), 317.

10. Japanese delegation to Versailles, quoted in MacMillan, *Paris 1919*, 317–318.

11. Lloyd Ambrosius, *Woodrow Wilson and American Internationalism* (Cambridge: Cambridge University Press, 2017), 111.

12. MacMillan, *Paris 1919*, 320.

13. Immerwahr, *How to Hide an Empire*, 120.

14. William R. Nestor, *Power across the Pacific: A Diplomatic History of American Relations with Japan* (New York: New York University Press, 1996), 92.

15. See, e.g., MacMillan, *Paris 1919*, 321.

16. MacMillan, *Paris 1919*, 319.

Bibliographic Essay

The sum of general studies addressing slavery and American foreign relations is meager. Fortunately, the quality of what does exist is excellent, and provides guidance for further work. Any study of the topic begins with Don E. Fehrenbacher, *The Slaveholding Republic: An Account of the United States Government's Relations to Slavery* (New York: Oxford University Press, 2001); and Matthew Karp, *This Vast Southern Empire: Slaveholders at the Helm of American Foreign Policy* (Cambridge, MA: Harvard University Press, 2018).

Studies that address slavery and foreign relations in the Early Republic Period are more numerous. For an overall view of US foreign relations during the period, see William Earl Weeks, *The New Cambridge History of American Foreign Relations*, vol. 1, *Dimensions of the Early American Empire, 1754–1865* (New York: Cambridge University Press, 2013); and George C. Herring, *From Colony to Superpower: U.S. Foreign Relations since 1776* (New York: Oxford University Press, 2008). Matthew Mason, *Slavery and Politics in the Early American Republic* (Chapel Hill: University of North Carolina Press, 2006), provides an insightful analysis of its subject. Arthur Scherr, *John Adams, Slavery, and Race: Ideas, Politics, and Diplomacy in an Age of Crisis* (Santa Barbara, CA: Praeger, 2018), is a thorough study of the topic.

On US policy toward Haiti during the slave revolution, see Arthur Scherr, *Thomas Jefferson's Haitian Policy: Myths and Realities* (Lanham, MD: Lexington Books, 2011); Tim Matthewson, *A Proslavery Foreign Policy: Haitian-American Relations during the Early Republic* (Westport, CT: Praeger, 2003); relevant sections of Gerald Horn, *Confronting Black Jacobins: The United States, the Haitian Revolution, and the Origins of the Dominican Republic* (New York: Monthly Review Press, 2015); Philippe Girard, *Toussaint Louverture: A Revolutionary Life* (New York: Basic Books, 2016); and Thomas O. Ott, *The Haitian Revolution, 1789–1804* (Knoxville: University of Tennessee Press, 1973). Especially useful are Gordon S. Brown, *Toussaint's Clause: The Founding Fathers and the Haitian Revolution* (Jackson: University Press of Mississippi, 2005); and Ronald Angelo Johnson, *Diplomacy in Black and White: John Adams, Toussaint Louverture, and Their Atlantic World Alliance* (Athens: University of Georgia Press, 2014). See also Edward B.

Rugemer, "Slave Rebels and Abolitionists: The Black Atlantic and the Coming of the Civil War," *Journal of the Civil War Era* 2, no. 2 (2012): 179–202.

Harold E. Bergquist Jr., "Henry Middleton and the Arbitrament of the Anglo-American Slave Controversy by Tsar Alexander I," *South Carolina Historical Magazine* 82, no. 1 (1981): 20–31, provides a useful overview of the settlement of the issues of slaves carried away by the British. On American expansion during this period, see Frank Lawrence Owsley Jr. and Gene A. Smith, *Filibusters and Expansionists: Jeffersonian Manifest Destiny, 1800–1821* (Tuscaloosa: University of Alabama Press, 1997).

The literature on the Atlantic slave trade is extensive. See especially Herbert S. Klein, *The Atlantic Slave Trade* (Cambridge: Cambridge University Press, 2010); and Warren S. Howard, *American Slavers and the Federal Law, 1837–1862* (Berkeley: University of California Press, 1963). On the trade to Brazil, particularly useful is Gerald Horne, *The Deepest South: The United States, Brazil, and the African Slave Trade* (New York: New York University Press, 2007).

On early colonization efforts, see David F. Ericson, *Slavery in the American Republic: Developing the Federal Government, 1791–1861* (Lawrence: University Press of Kansas, 2011); and P. J. Staudenraus, *The African Colonization Movement, 1816–1865* (New York: Columbia University Press, 1961). The starting point for study of the American Colonization Society is Eric Burin, *Slavery and the Peculiar Solution: A History of the American Colonization Society* (Gainesville: University Press of Florida, 2005). For a significant state effort at colonization in Africa, see Penelope Campbell, *Maryland in Africa: The Maryland State Colonization Society, 1831–1857* (Urbana: University of Illinois Press, 1971). For treatments of the topic of colonization, Beverly C. Tomek and Matthew J. Hetrick, eds., *New Directions in the Study of American Recolonization* (Gainesville: University Press of Florida, 2017) is essential reading.

Larry Eugene Rivers, *Rebels and Runaways: Slave Resistance in Nineteenth-Century Florida* (Urbana: University of Illinois Press, 2013), is an excellent introduction to its topic. See also Matthew J. Clavin, *The Battle of Negro Fort: The Rise and Fall of a Fugitive Slave Community* (New York: New York University Press, 2019); and Irvin D. S. Winsboro and Joe Knetsch, "Florida Slaves, the 'Saltwater Railroad' to the Bahamas, and Anglo-American Diplomacy," *Journal of Southern History* 79, no. 1 (2013): 51–78.

The Negro Seamen Acts have been addressed most thoroughly in Michael Schoeppner, "Peculiar Quarantines: The Seamen Acts and Regulatory Authority in the Antebellum South," *Law and History Review* 31, no. 3 (2013): 559–586. On the South Carolina Association, see Alan F. January, "The South Carolina Association: An Agency for Race Control in Antebellum Charleston," *South Carolina Historical Magazine* 78, no. 3 (1977): 191–201.

The general topic of American expansion has produced a significant secondary literature. Helpful overviews are Richard H. Immerman, *Empire for Liberty: A History of American Imperialism from Benjamin Franklin to Paul Wolfowitz* (Princeton, NJ: Princeton University Press, 2010); William Earl Weeks, *Building the Continental Empire: American Expansion from the Revolution to the Civil War* (Chicago: Ivan R. Dee, 1997); Walter Nugent, *Habits of Empire: A History of American Expansion* (New York: Alfred A. Knopf, 2008); and Thomas R. Hietala, *Manifest Design: Anxious Aggrandizement in Late Jacksonian America* (Ithaca, NY: Cornell University Press, 1985). On Texas, see Randolph B. Campbell, *An Empire for Slavery: The Peculiar Institution in Texas, 1821–1865* (Baton Rouge: Louisiana State University Press, 1989); and Frederick Merk, *Slavery and the Annexation of Texas* (New York: Alfred A. Knopf, 1972). For treatments of US aims toward Latin America, see Robert E. May, *Manifest Destiny's Underworld: Filibustering in Antebellum America* (Chapel Hill: University of North Carolina Press, 2002); Tom Chaffin, "'Sons of Washington': Narciso López, Filibustering, and U.S. Nationalism, 1848–1851," *Journal of the Early Republic* 15, no. 1 (1995): 79–108; and Robert E. May, *The Southern Dream of a Caribbean Empire, 1854–1861* (Baton Rouge: Louisiana State University Press, 1973). Also useful for context is Piero Gleijeses, "Clashing over Cuba: The United States, Spain, and Britain, 1853–1855," *Journal of Latin American Studies* 49, no. 2 (2016): 215–241.

Relevant sections of biographies and studies of individuals can be useful guides for further research. In addition to those listed herein, see Francis D. Cogliano, *Emperor of Liberty: Thomas Jefferson's Foreign Policy* (New Haven, CT: Yale University Press, 2014); Lawrence S. Kaplan, *Alexander Hamilton: Ambivalent Anglophile* (Wilmington, DE: Scholarly Resources, 2002); Charles N. Edel, *Nation Builder: John Quincy Adams and the Grand Strategy of the Republic* (Cambridge, MA: Harvard University Press, 2014); James E. Lewis Jr., *John Quincy Adams: Policymaker for the Union* (Lanham, MD: Rowman and Littlefield, 2001); and William Earl Weeks, *John Quincy Adams and American Global Empire* (Lexington: University Press of Kentucky, 2002). Still useful for any study of Adams is Samuel Flagg Bemis, *John Quincy Adams and the Foundations of American Foreign Policy* (New York: Alfred A. Knopf, 1965). See also John Niven, *John Calhoun and the Price of Union: A Biography* (Baton Rouge: Louisiana State University Press, 1988); Christopher J. Leahy, *President without a Party: The Life of John Tyler* (Baton Rouge: Louisiana State University Press, 2020); and Matthew Mason, *Apostle of Union: A Political Biography of Edward Everett* (Chapel Hill: University of North Carolina Press, 2016).

On Abraham Lincoln and the Civil War era, the literature is daunting. Studies that deal with slavery and foreign relations in this period include Joseph A. Fry, *Lincoln, Seward, and U.S. Foreign Relations in the Civil War Era*

(Lexington: University Press of Kentucky, 2019); Howard Jones, *Blue and Gray Diplomacy: A History of Union and Confederate Foreign Relations* (Chapel Hill: University of North Carolina Press, 2010); Howard Jones, *Abraham Lincoln and a New Birth of Freedom: The Union and Slavery in the Diplomacy of the Civil War* (Lincoln: University of Nebraska Press, 1999); Howard Jones, *Union in Peril: The Crisis over British Intervention in the Civil War* (Lincoln: University of Nebraska Press, 1997); and Howard Jones, "History and Mythology: The Crisis over British Intervention in the Civil War," in *The Union, the Confederacy, and the Atlantic Rim*, rev. ed., ed. Robert E. May (Gainesville: University Press of Florida, 2013). Biographies of Lincoln generally contain little on foreign relations. For coverage of these issues, consult Michael Burlingame, *Abraham Lincoln: A Life*, vol. 2 (Baltimore: Johns Hopkins University Press, 2008).

For specific topics on the Civil War, see Stève Sainlaude, *France and the American Civil War: A Diplomatic History*, trans. Jessica Edwards (Chapel Hill: University of North Carolina Press, 2019); Lynn Marshall Case and Warren F. Spencer, *The United States and France: Civil War Diplomacy* (Philadelphia: University of Pennsylvania Press, 1970); Wayne H. Bowen, *Spain and the American Civil War* (Columbia: University of Missouri Press, 2011); and R. J. M Blackett, *Divided Hearts: Britain and the American Civil* War (Baton Rouge: Louisiana State University Press, 2001). The question of Lincoln and colonization has received significant treatment. On this topic, see especially Michael J. Douma, "The Lincoln Administration's Negotiations to Colonize African Americans in Dutch Suriname," *Civil War History* 61, no. 2 (2015): 111–137. Indispensable for the study of the Suriname colonization project is Michael J. Douma, *The Colonization of Freed African Americans in Suriname* (Leiden: Leiden University Press, 2019). On Lincoln and colonization in Latin America, see Robert E. May, *Slavery, Race, and Conquest in the Tropics: Lincoln, Douglas, and the Future of Latin America* (New York: Cambridge University Press, 2013); and Phillip W. Magness and Sebastian N. Page, *Colonization after Emancipation: Lincoln and the Movement for Black Resettlement* (Columbia: University of Missouri Press, 2011).

For studies that place the Civil War in a broader international context, see Robert E. May, ed., *The Union, the Confederacy, and the Atlantic Rim*, rev. ed. (Gainesville: University Press of Florida, 2013); Don H. Doyle, *The Cause of All Nations: An International History of the American Civil War* (New York: Basic Books, 2015); Don H. Doyle, ed., *American Civil Wars: The United States, Latin America, Europe, and the Crisis of the 1860s* (Chapel Hill: University of North Carolina Press, 2017); and David T. Gleeson and Simon Lewis, eds., *The Civil War as Global Conflict: Transnational Meanings of the American Civil War* (Columbia: University of South Carolina Press, 2014).

INDEX

Aberdeen, Lord, 93, 94, 95, 112, 124–28
abolition of slavery: Atlantic slave trade
  suppression and, 63, 64, 104–5, 107;
  Britain, antislavery movement, 66,
  124–26, 128, 129–31, 155, 165; colonization of freed slaves abroad and, 102;
  Dutch antislavery movement, 176;
  emancipation policy and Emancipation
  Proclamation, 61, 154, 166–74; ending
  direct effects of slavery on foreign
  relations, 182; initial downplaying of,
  in Civil War, 155, 156; Russian serfs,
  movement to liberate, 172, 216n97.
  See also moral arguments against slavery
ACS (American Colonization Society),
  80–82, 84–88, 97, 98, 101, 102
Adams, Charles Francis, 154–55, 156, 164,
  167
Adams, John, and Haitian revolution,
  43–53
Adams, John Quincy: on Atlantic slave trade,
  68–78, 102–3, 110; on "carrying off" of
  slaves by British in War of 1812, 18–19,
  21–26, 28, 29, 181; on colonization of freed
  slaves, 81–83; Congress of Panama and,
  1–3, 5; on destruction of Negro Fort and
  American acquisition of Florida, 31–32;
  evolution of views on slavery, 181, 218n1;
  foreign relations objectives of, 1, 5; Haitian
  revolution and, 47–48; Negro Seamen Acts
  and, 91
Adams-Onís (Transcontinental) Treaty of
  1819, 31, 193n88
Africa, Black American colonization of. *See*
  colonization of freed slaves abroad
Africa Squadron, 101, 113–14, 117–18
Africanization scare in Cuba, 138, 143–50
Alexander I (tsar), 9, 24–28
Alexander II (tsar), 169
American Colonization Society (ACS),
  80–82, 84–88, 97, 98, 101, 102

American Revolution, 2, 6, 9–10, 17, 32,
  34–35. *See also* Paris, Treaty of
Amiens, Treaty of (1802), 55
La Amistad (vessel), 93, 94
Amity, Commerce, and Navigation, Treaty
  of (Jay's Treaty, 1794), 13–17, 41–42, 43
Amphictyonic Congress of 1826 (Congress
  of Panama), 1–3, 5
Andrus, Joseph R., 84, 85
Anglo-American Convention of 1818, 24
Antietam, battle of, 167
antislavery movement. *See* abolition of
  slavery
Archer, William S., 132
Argyll, duke of, 156
Ashburton, Lord, 95, 96, 112–14
Ashmun, Jehudi, 87
Atlantic Monthly, 155
Atlantic slave trade, 62–96; Africa Squadron
  and, 101, 113–14, 117–18; Brazil and, 113,
  114–16; Britain, relations with, 63, 65–75,
  89–96, 102–20; British motivations for
  abolition of, 103–4, 111–12; colonization of
  freed slaves abroad and, 78–89; congressional legislation against, 64–65, 67–68, 72,
  80–81; congressional resolution regarding
  suppression of, 75–78; Constitution on, 64;
  convention of 1824 on, 76–78, 104; Cuba
  and, 106–8, 116–18, 144; domestic politics
  and, 77; escaped slaves in British territories
  and *Creole* Affair, 93–96; faulty international
  enforcement of ban on, 65–75; France and,
  66, 67, 104, 105, 110, 111–12; House
  Committee on suppression of, 73–74, 80;
  impressment in War of 1812, legacy of, 67,
  69–70, 111, 119; joint cruising, 71–72,
  112–14, 118; Lincoln's concession to search,
  65–66, 96, 97, 118–20, 166; Lyons-Seward
  Treaty (1862) as death knell of, 119–20;
  Middle Passage (Maafa), 62; Negro Seaman
  Acts, 89–92; opposition to / abolition of

CPSIA information can be obtained
at www.ICGtesting.com
Printed in the USA
LVHW101828060622
720597LV00014B/520/J

9 781501 761058